Shakespeare, William, 1564–1616.
    Tragedies ɪɪ: Romeo and Juliet, Othello, King Lear.
With biographical illus. and pictures of the setting of the
plays, together with introductions by John Masefield. New
York, Dodd, Mead ₍1967, °1966₎

    xxii, 336 p. illus. 22 cm. (Great illustrated classics)

    "Texts for these plays are from the Complete works of William
Shakespeare, edited by W. J. Craig."

    ɪ. Masefield, John, 1878–   ed. ɪɪ. Title.

PR2763.M3   822.33   66–28860

GREAT ILLUSTRATED CLASSICS

To the Reader.

This Figure, that thou here feeft put,
  It was for gentle Shakefpeare cut;
Wherein the Grauer had a ftrife
  with Nature, to out-doo the life:
O, could he but haue drawne his wit
  As well in fraffe, as he hath hit
His face; the Print would then furpaffe
  all, that was euer writ in braffe.
But, fince he cannot, Reader, looke
  Not on his Picture, but his Booke.

                         B. I.

Martin Droeshout's portrait of Shakespeare appears on the title page of the first folio of "Mr. William Shakespeare's Comedies, Histories, & Tragedies; Published according to the True Original Copies" and printed in London in 1623. Ben Jonson's verse "To the Reader" was printed on the facing page.

TRAGEDIES II

Romeo and Juliet, Othello,
King Lear

BY WILLIAM SHAKESPEARE

With biographical illustrations and pictures
of the setting of the plays, together
with introductions by
John Masefield

NEW YORK · DODD, MEAD & COMPANY

The texts for these plays are from the *Complete Works of William Shakespeare,* edited by W. J. Craig, M.A., and are used with permission of the Oxford University Press.

LIBRARY OF CONGRESS CATALOG CARD NUMBER: 66-28860
PRINTED IN THE UNITED STATES OF AMERICA

121482

CONTENTS

CONTENTS

ILLUSTRATIONS

THE PLAYS, AN INTRODUCTION

A GOOD many plays had been known in England before the time
of Shakespeare. Many versions of the *Mummers' Play* were then
played every year, and these, like some of the northern sword-
dances, seem to be relics of old or of very ancient drama, performed with song and music, with strange, effective ritual
costume, essential combat, personal dexterity, and suggestions of
sacrifice and festival. In the Cumnor *Mummers' Play,* the end-
ings of the sword-dances, and perhaps the great cake and the
wine-jubbe at Bampton, the festal moment is still suggested.
Some at least of these plays are very ancient, and are still played
here.

During the Middle Ages, various Guilds and Companies performed scenes, or cycles of scenes, from Scripture, or from the
Lives of the Saints held to be patrons of their mysteries, on certain days of the year. Probably few, if any, of these survived
Queen Mary. In any case, they had been in great measure sup-
planted by Moralities, or plays of ghostly counsel tending towards righteous living. These were performed in costume and
disguise, with the use of verse and song, and with exciting combat. In the *Mummers' Play,* the combat is between St. George
and the Turkish Knight, or some variant and perversion of the
original theme, that is supposed by some to be the Life and
Death of the Corn. In the Moralities, the combat is between a
human soul, or quality of the human soul, with the Devil, a
particular Vice, or definite Temptation.

These Moralities seem to have been so much liked, that they
became the profession of small groups who roamed the country

performing them at fairs and markets, in the open street, in the yards of inns, or in the halls of lords who gave them leave. The groups of men were small; each man could and would play four or five parts in a play; boys with unbroken voices played women. The cleverer groups added to the plays of homily, dance, music, social satire and cheerful comedy.

It was soon decided that these bands of men roaming from place to place with no fixed abode should everywhere obtain licence to perform. When Shakespeare was a little boy, it was ordained that each player should obtain from Court, or from some great lord, a warrant that he was the servant of the Court or Lord. Companies of players, musicians, acrobats and jugglers, used to performing together, applied thus for warrant of the entire body. The early companies thus became known as the Queen's men, Lord ——'s men, or the Admiral's men. Such warrants were, seemingly, gladly given, for plays were much liked; the Court and lords gave frequent performances in palaces and great houses, and were glad to have companies at hand by which these might be played.

In London, a City with old privileges and new prejudices, the players were both popular and disliked. Though the Court liked and encouraged players, wished to have them at command, and frequently employed them, the City, standing upon old privilege, discouraged performances within the City limits, yet feared to oppose the Court directly. With the new prejudice of growing trade and all the darkness of an intolerant religion, the City government urged that plays drew men from honest work, fostered idleness, encouraged lewdness, spread infection and were, besides, hateful to all true believers. Plays were so much loved, and the Court influence was so strong, that they could not prohibit plays wholly: a good many were still given in inn-yards and in private houses, but the players found it safer and saner to build the two first London theatres outside the City government in what was then the fairly open country of Shoreditch.

One of these theatres, *The Theatre*, was built of wood by James Burbage, a carpenter (once a player), whose son Richard became famous as an actor. It is supposed that Shakespeare began his theatrical career at *The Theatre* as one of Lord Strange's men. This company of Lord Strange's men, after various changes, combined with the famous company of the Lord Chamberlain, George Carey, the second Lord Hunsdon. Shakespeare remained with it throughout his career, playing at *The Theatre*, *The Curtain*, *The Rose*, *The Globe*, and no doubt other theatres and in many halls and palaces until he left the stage.

The Elizabethan theatres, whatever their shape, square, oblong, round or several-sided, were built in the main of wood on stone or brick foundations. They stood perhaps as much as forty feet high, in three storeys, tiers or galleries of seats round three sides of the stage.

The design was that of the inn-yard in which so many early plays had been performed, with the actors in the yard, or on an open wagon in the yard, and the spectators either in the inn-galleries or standing in the yard round the players.

The stage and the top-storey of seats were roofed-over with tiles or thatch. The space or yard between the stage and the galleries was not roofed: it contained no seats, but it held many spectators who stood.

The three storeys of seats were divided by partitions into what we should now call boxes. These were known as "Gentlemen's rooms" and "Two-penny rooms." The standing-room round the stage could be had for one penny. Those in the standing-room could press close up to the front and to two sides of the stage. They saw the players in the round; not, as we see them in the modern theatre, like people framed in a picture, shut from us by many bright lights.

The stage or acting area was big, considering the size of the theatre. It was a strong raised platform projecting from the wall at the back of it right out into the house. It stood (one would suppose) four or five feet high, so that there might be room below it for actors whose entrances and exits were to be through trap-doors.

It may well be that some stages had a very slight ramp or slope downwards from the back towards the front to make certain movements a little clearer to the audience. Possibly, some stages were divided by a step into fore-stage and back-stage, with a curtain that could wholly shut away the back-stage while an inner scene was set upon it. Much genius was in the theatres: it is probable that many good devices were tried and used.

At the back of the stage was a wall of which very great theatrical use was made. This wall was, as one would suppose, designed like the outer wall of a house, with one, two or three doors, and possibly windows also, all opening, in case of need, upon the stage. Genius was in the theatre: it would have been easy to change the appearance of these doors, to make them Royal, Roman, or Medieval, as the play demanded, or to curtain them over, if the play needed tents, or simply to close the opening with a tapestry.

One or two of these doors led to the players' tiring-room or rooms; but in some of the theatres one of these openings must have been wide enough to display on occasion a ramped inner-room behind it. In certain plays the double doors or curtains were opened, and the ramped inner-room displayed, so that the audience could see, in case of need, some expected death-bed or other show.

Above the stage floor of this back wall was the second floor, also of very great importance. Across the front of this second floor ran a balcony or gallery. The second floor had a door, or doors, and windows opening upon this balcony. It is likely that on occasion a door here, too, could be thrown open to display, a ramped inner chamber. If not needed in the play, this gallery could be let to spectators.

This balcony or gallery could be reached from the stage by stairs, possibly from both sides of the stage, in sight of the audience, possibly from within the tiring-rooms hidden from the audience, in whatever method was convenient to the players. In the great play of *Macbeth,* I think that the stairs were on the stage, central and visible, but possibly temporary, like a ship's gangway, and that two doors, both visible to the audience, opened on to the gallery.

It is shameful that even now we have no permanent Elizabethan stage in which these features, and their wonderful practical uses, can be studied at will throughout the year. Good plays need nothing more than the French writer's minimum, "a plank, two actors and a passion." The Elizabethan theatre provided planks wherever the players in their passion could wish to go, high above, or below, their hearers, or so close to them that they could take them into their confidence, and gather strength from their sympathy.

In one way, the Elizabethan theatre was ill-equipped. It was unlit. Performances were in the afternoons in daylight, and were doubtless made impossible on many days by extremities of weather.

Performances were forbidden whenever thirty persons or more had died of the plague in the week within the City limits. In some summers this closed the theatres for a season at a time.

It seems likely that most of the plays were played through with not more than two or three very short pauses in the action. With a turbulent crowd standing round the stage, impatient, and prone to speak its mind, delay was dangerous. Our impression is that the playing and speaking were both much swifter than is usual today. The closeness of the audience and the rush of the imagined action both made for speed. Acting, as needed in the plays that fashion had suddenly made necessary, was as new to England as the plays: it was young, lively, and had genius, even supreme genius, to direct and advise it. We need not doubt that the acting had all the merits and demerits of the plays: there must have been splendour even if there were crudity.

As women were not then allowed to act in public, the parts of women were played by boys. This made much more easy the playwright's frequent device of a heroine who, in the action, pretends to be a boy. The boys no doubt acted well; they so often do; and the audience delighted then, as now, in the double skill that acted an assumed sex and an imagined character.

Unfortunately, the clever boy could only play as a woman until his voice broke; then, if he played at all, he had to begin afresh with new methods, though with much stage experience and skill.

Little or no scenery was used or needed in these plays: it was so much rubbish in the way; the play was the thing. Now and then there may have been some decoration of banners on the outward wall, or a change in the appearance of the door, by tapestry or otherwise.

Few properties were used or needed. It may interest a reader to read through a play, noting down on paper the properties that will be needed in any performance. It will soon be startlingly clear that these are very few: a settle or chair of state; something to hide behind (often the settle can be used for this); a bank of flowers, a bed for someone to die upon (again the settle); something to kill with; something to drink from; something that will look like money.

The settle or bank of flowers may well have been upon the stage throughout the performances. Death-beds, or tables of prepared feast, could be drawn out by trained stagehands from within the inner-room at the back of the stage; and removed when done with.

One property very frequently used in the historical plays is an image of a newly cut-off human head. This the audience demanded, and eyed critically; they were used to such sights, and the imitation had to be good. There must have been several heads all ready for display in the Globe's property room.

Though the scenery and properties were simple and few, the plays were well dressed: the costumes, cloaks, armour, banners, jewels, hats and crests were frequently costly and of great splendour. The action was made lovely to look upon: the eye was delighted. Frequently a play was interrupted by a dumb-show, a ballet of masked dancers, a costumed masque, a procession with singing, torches, and the scattering of flowers.

At the end of the performance of a play, there was often a light brief entertainment called a jig, with dance, song and comedy neatly mixed to play the audience away. In what were called the private houses elaborate music and singing were frequent before and during the performances.

Throughout Shakespeare's theatrical life, the action of a play was often interrupted by a battle; so often that the question arises, how were stage-battles then fought? As they were plainly much liked by the audiences, they must have been exciting and interesting, which they are not, as a rule, in modern stage-practice.

Some of the most inventive brains in England were then in the theatres. These men devised the battles and the means by which they were to be performed. They had at their disposal (probably) a considerable number of men who could be hired for crowd- or battle-scenes, the professional hired men, sometimes called supers. Most of these were well used to the carriage and exercise of sword and buckler; all were active, and eager to make their battles better than the battles at the rival house. All players well understood how to raise excitement by noises, the rolling of cannonballs down slopes of wood, iron or canvas, the discharge of "chambers," or small cases of gunpowder, from the quick-firing guns of the time, the varied beats and calls of drums and trumpets, the cheers and war-cries of men and the clashing of swords and bucklers. They also very well understood that simulated conflict can be made most exciting and interesting if skill be used; and that if one or two men on the stage fight skilfully the audience will watch and cheer as others, on the stage, encourage them.

Many men, at some time, have seen in the East sword-and-buckler, or short-spear-and-buckler, contests, so well imitated by players that they have marvelled and held their breaths.

Doubtless such skill often marked the battles in the Curtain, the Rose and the Globe, when York, Gloucester, Caesar or Macbeth put his fortune to the test, after two hours of suspense, and destiny swung this way and that before a thousand watchers, each cheering on his man.

Theatrical life then had in it some elements of battle: the companies were in rivalry. The houses competed; the poets of each house were spurred on and stimulated by what their rivals wrote, either to imitate or to do better. A successful invention in one house would be used or improved upon by the rival. This competition, in a time knowing nothing of copyright, led to much taking that would now be counted theft, to quarrels of bitterness, and to duels.

The theatres were profitable, in spite of the City's hostility. When Shakespeare began theatrical life, it is thought that there were only two theatres. When he died, about twenty-five or twenty-six years later, there were six, in or just outside the limits of the City. Such a fervour for a mingling of lovely arts and skills has not been known here since.

Some have wondered, and enquired, where and how Shakespeare came to know poetry and poets. We do not know.

He plainly knew the best lyrical and narrative poetry of his time before he knew the theatre; but being in the theatre he was in a home of poetry and in the presence of poets. Most plays then were in verse: to this day, three centuries since that day ceased, actors speak of their parts as their "lines." The poet who wrote the lines was in the house, probably acting in the company with two or three other poets; their talk was all of poetry; the talk of the company was all of poetical invention; the interest of the company was in success in a poetical rivalry of passionate fervour. In another theatre, in the next ward, or in a neighbouring inn, a rival poet might at any moment draw their public from them by invention newer and stranger, by an instinct touching the Fortune of the moment, or some happy fore-sight of what would be Fortune on the morrow. It behoved all in the company to watch what was being done in every company elsewhere; for in poetry the moods change swiftly in passionate antithesis, and the beauty in one theatre challenged the reason in a second or the mockery of a third.

In the theatre world, even in the meanest rank, this extraordinary Youth of sensitiveness and sudden sympathy was in a world of poetry such as earth had not known; and if for the moment he was in one faction of the cause, it was the leading faction and he was to keep it so.

Poetry at that time was being written by many gifted men in many ways, all of them exquisite and attractive to a youth so sensitive. Reading was still a new delight to the world. Poets had not yet lost the excitement of being able to digress. When poems had been

> read . . . or ellës sung

their hearers had kept poets to the point. Now that poems were read from books, the poets could stray into all manner of musings, descriptions, the hiding of meanings, tricks of rhetoric, artifice of surprise, allusion known only to the elect, quotation delightful to the few, and take their readers with them. Like themselves, the readers were in revolt from the Middle Ages; the Renaissance was upon them; the natural manner was despised: it wanted art.

As in Italy and France, the Revival of Learning had made known something of the power and civility of ancient Rome, and rather less of the beauty and wisdom of Greece. In the ecstasy of the new knowledge, many enthusiasts were trying the ancient forms. All this excitement and experiment of discovery and rediscovery was in the City about this young man; and sweet and startling it no doubt was to him. These things, these methods, were tried and re-tried in the theatres: the young men heard, saw, and took part in them; interested in them all, for all were ways of mind, with some power of revealing the imagined and touching the heart, and all, being new, seemed bright, and each, however fanciful, was a part of the art to be mastered.

London was then a squalid crowded vigorous city within her ancient boundaries. There was a small overflow into the suburbs, to Southwark, along Holborn, up Fleet Street and the Strand, and out over Moorfields. The places named in Ben Jonson's *A Tale of a Tub,* Kentish Town, Pancras, Maribone, etc., long-since engulfed by the town, were then remote villages in the country. It has been reckoned that the city population grew steadily and rapidly during Shakespeare's life, in spite of plague and pestilence. When he died, it may have contained a quarter of a million inhabitants. Some have thought that the population of England, then, was less than five millions.

Though the city was not great, the hearts and minds of the

people were in fervour and ferment; and, if, after Shakespeare's death, gloomy horror quenched the ferment, it could not quench the beauty wrought.

Much of the City that Shakespeare knew was burned in the Fire of London, 1666, but various old prints show us its appearance from the south, as a fine, narrow strip of city, full of churches, with the Tower to the East, St. Paul's to the West, and the river full of boats and small shipping, crossing by Old London Bridge. The prints of course show nothing of the dirt, the darkness and the overcrowding that marked every city of the time. It was a capital city, the heart and brain of the Kingdom, a port of trade, the centre of government, and certainly a propounding- and testing-place for all ways of thought and skills of men.

In the little London of that time, the gates of which were decked with the heads of rebels (there are nineteen, in Visscher's engraving, on London Bridge alone) many kinds of poetry were being tried with many varieties of power and artifice. Ballads, songs, tales, allegories, far-fetched conceits, translations from the classical and other tongues, were in print or passed about by voice and in manuscript. In the theatre, the wooden declamation of unrhymed wooden lines, after changes and experiments with rhyme, in couplet or quatrain, with passages possibly accompanied with music, had suddenly been lifted into personal outburst by the cry of Marlowe:

> Is it not brave to be a King, Techelles,
> Usumcusane and Theridamas?
> Is it not passing brave to be a King,
> And ride in triumph through Persepolis?

Players and playgoers had decided that it was brave to be a King, even if he talked nonsense and did wickedness. They were all for that indulgence of the will, though all still held, with Kyd, that wickedness brought a judgment upon itself, and that one of the wickednesses was too great personal success, that in some way upset a balance that Life wished to be kept.

Kyd had been the master playwright, with plays of the punishment of wickedness, at great cost, after long sorrow. Marlowe gave declamation a lyrical force, and all felt the excitement of the change.

Among some of the older Elizabethan scholars and English poets, there may be traced a feeling, based upon the very slightest foundation, that Marlowe was in some way a helper of the young Shakespeare, a shower of the way to him, possibly a friend.

They were of the same age, but Marlowe was mature, the King of his art, the leader of the young, while Shakespeare was a beginner, groping still.

Young men eager in the arts readily become acquainted. In that little London it may have been easier than it is today.

It is clear that if they met at all it must have been under conditions that forbade any jealousy or rivalry. It is almost certain that they met and that they worked together, more than once, with other poets, in providing piece-meal historical plays in verse while such things pleased.

When and how they met cannot be known, but it is certain that Shakespeare, already an exquisite poet knowing nothing about the stage, did enter the world of the theatre. It is certain that soon after he entered that world he was deeply moved by Marlowe's verse: he imitated every good point in it. Soon after Marlowe's death, he alludes to him, as I think, in *Love's Labour's Lost;* later, he quotes him (tenderly) in *As You Like It;* still later, with gentleness, he mocks at his extravagances, in *King Henry IV, Part II,* and elsewhere.

Let us assume that they met in the frequent relation of the master receiving incense and the disciple receiving recognition, a noble relation, luckily constant in the world, by which all the arts are maintained.

With what work did the young Shakespeare begin his practice of writing for the theatre?

Who knows? Who can tell?

Is it not likely that he tried some themes beyond his power at the time, that yet showed to the poets near him an aptitude and grace unusual however immature?

Is it not likely that the young player was allowed, or encouraged, to try his hand at some suggested scene, something that would give a rest to a player, or add to the variety of the act?

After the wild success of *Tamburlaine the Great*, the First Part, that burned like a fire all the waxwork in the art, was there not presently some hint of a small change here and there?

Did not someone suggest the scene of the Virgins, and did not Shakespeare write it? Could this be one of his first contributions to the theatre?

Leaving suggestions and suppositions, the reader knows that Shakespeare's fellow-actors, Heminges and Condell, who knew the truth, ascribed certain plays to him, and printed them as his, in what is called the first folio, of 1623. With all of these plays Shakespeare certainly had much to do.

CHRONOLOGY

Shakespeare's biographical dates are based upon existing official records. The dates of his plays can only be approximate.

1564, April 26. Christening of Shakespeare at Stratford parish church.

1582, November 27. License for Marriage of Shakespeare to Anne Hathaway.

1583, May 26. Christening of Susanna Shakespeare.

1585, February 2. Christening of Hamnet and Judith Shakespeare.

1590–91. *Henry VI.*

1592. *Richard III, Titus Andronicus.*

1593–94. *Venus and Adonis, Comedy of Errors, Two Gentlemen of Verona, Taming of the Shrew, Love's Labour's Lost, Sonnets, The Rape of Lucrece.*

1595. *Romeo and Juliet, Richard II.*

1596. August 11. Burial of Hamnet Shakespeare.
A Midsummer Night's Dream, King John.

1597. *Merchant of Venice, Part 1 Henry IV.*

1598. *Part 2 Henry IV, Merry Wives.*

1599. Opening of Globe Theatre. *Henry V, Much Ado.*

1600. *As You Like It, Twelfth Night.*

1601. September 8. Burial of the poet's father, John Shakespeare.
Julius Caesar(?), Hamlet.

1602. *Troilus and Cressida(?).*

1603. *All's Well, Measure for Measure.*

1604. *Othello.*

1605. *Timon of Athens.*

1606. *King Lear, Macbeth.*

1607, June 5. Marriage of Shakespeare's daughter Susanna to John

Hall in Stratford. *Anthony and Cleopatra, Coriolanus.*

1608. February 21. Christening of Shakespeare's granddaughter, Elizabeth Hall. The only grandchild born in the poet's lifetime.

1608, September 9. Burial of the poet's mother, Mary Shakespeare. *Pericles.*

1609, May 20. Registration of *Sonnets. Cymbeline.*

1610. Probable migration of Shakespeare to Stratford. *The Winter's Tale.*

1611. *The Tempest.*

1612. *Henry VIII.*

1613, June 29. The Globe burned down during a performance of *Henry VIII. Two Noble Kinsmen(?).*

1616, April 23. Death of Shakespeare.

April 25. Burial of 'Will. Shakspere, gent.'

Romeo and Juliet

INTRODUCTION

Written, it is thought, in some form, very early, and, possibly, being a successful piece, changed here and there for revivals, in later years.

Source of the Plot. The story existed in many forms, mostly Italian. Shakespeare took it from Arthur Broke's metrical version (*Romeus and Juliet*), and possibly consulted the prose version in William Painter's *Palace of Pleasure.* The tale had been dramatised and performed before Arthur Broke published his poem in 1562. The play (if it existed a generation later) may have helped Shakespeare. It is now lost.

The Fable. The houses of Montague and Capulet are at feud in Verona.

Romeo, of the house of Montague, falls in love with Juliet, of the house of Capulet. She returns his love. A friar marries them.

In a street brawl, which Romeo does his best to stop, Mercutio, Romeo's friend, is killed by Tybalt, Juliet's cousin. Carried away by passion, Romeo kills Tybalt. He is banished from Verona.

The Capulets plan to marry Juliet to the Count Paris.

Juliet, in great distress, consults the Friar who married her to Romeo. He gives her a potion to create an apparent death in her, to the end that she may be buried in the family vault, taken thence and restored to life by himself, and then conveyed to Romeo. He writes to Romeo, telling him of the plan; but the letter miscarries. Juliet takes the potion, and is laid in the tomb as dead.

3

The Count Paris comes by night to the tomb, to mourn her there. Romeo, who has heard only that his love is dead, also comes to the tomb. The two lovers fight, and Romeo kills Paris. He then takes a poison and dies at Juliet's side.

The Friar enters to restore Juliet to life. Juliet awakens to find her lover dead. The Friar, being alarmed, leaves the tomb. Juliet stabs herself with Romeo's dagger and dies.

The feud of the Montagues and Capulets is brought to an end. The leaders of the two houses are reconciled over the bodies of the lovers.

Various signs show that most of the play is very early work: there is much use of rhyme: a good deal of prose full of quibbles and mistakings of the word; and much reference to a dark lady, much such a lady as that described in the Sonnets, and called here Rosaline, as in *The Comedy of Errors*. She, too, has a high forehead, a white face, black eyes and brows and much effect upon hearts. It is possible that in some early draft of this play, she may have appeared as a character: in the version known to us, she is only talked of, as a love of Romeo's who is at once forgotten when Juliet appears. She is talked of more than is usual in dramatic practice: and Shakespeare's personal reason for this is not known. It would have been easier and simpler for him to introduce her, even for a moment, as a character. Possibly, the necessary boy could not be had; perhaps his voice broke before rehearsal and the part had to be omitted.

The masterly opening scene must be later than much of the play. In later scenes, touches of wisdom and of savagery read like additions from a maturer Shakespeare: but the play is young man's work and about youth. It has been loved all over the world for three and a half centuries: little can be said about it now that will not seem tame to the enthusiasm it has aroused. Blake expressed dislike of those who said "irritating things in the midst of tears and joy."

We must wonder for what young players Shakespeare wrote Mercutio and Juliet: he had two in his mind, no doubt: a special two. Romeo would have been comparatively easy to cast: but what boy played the Nurse; consider the effect of a boy playing the Nurse.

We must also wonder how, in the early performances, they played the fourth scene in Act I. It is a night scene, outside the Capulets' house: the young men of the Montagues plan to attend the Capulets' feast as masquers, to enter the house disguised, dance, and come away. If discovered, they will be set upon, man-handled, perhaps killed. While the party is on the stage outside the house, arranging their costumes, masks, torches and lanterns, in deadly peril, even there, Mercutio makes his long speech about Queen Mab and her bringing of dreams. Ah, that we could hear the Mercutio for whose special talent and delight that fantasy was written. Why did Shakespeare give such a speech to such a character at that moment? How was the speech taken and the scene played? It is a fantasy of tiny things told at full length by a character not yet fully revealed to the audience, who has the theatre to himself for a full two and a half minutes. At first, one would suppose that it is not designed to display the character of Mercutio; for that bright sprig of mockery and wild-fire seems such a very different person in the coming scenes. It is clear that the unknown player made a success of it; for Shakespeare was then a beginner and the management did not cut the speech. That management, no doubt, like the audience, knew a good deal about the broils and factions of city houses and cliques. Understanding well the peril which those young men were so gaily preparing on the stage, the audience must have found that fairy fantasy the very height of careless audacity in the speaker, and those few minutes of delay in peril an almost unbearable suspense.

Long afterwards, in a scene much more famous, Shakespeare was to use this device again.

A play lives by suspense and surprise during a conflict. This play, in its beginning, shows a conflict between two great houses and the possibility that love between two young members of the families might end the feud. But for the impatience of hot blood this end might have been reached; all falls otherwise. A sudden, passionate love drives out from Romeo a sentimental love for another, and changes the modest Juliet to a scheming liar: it results, almost at once, in five violent deaths and much broken-heartedness: all this, from impatiences springing from the first fever. As is frequent in the theatre world, little accidents become of deep importance. In this play of mad hurry, the delays are as fatal as the impatience: the Friar's letter to Romeo is delayed: the Friar is a few moments too late in arriving at the tomb: Juliet wakes from her trance too late. The two houses are reconciled when both have lost all who might have made the peace beautiful and enduring.

Another feud than that of the houses is touched on: the feud between youth and age, from the point of view of youth. Shakespeare was later to show it from the point of view of age.

Plague must have been ever-present in England in the years of Shakespeare's life. It was very fatal in London in the early fifteen-nineties. Some knowledge of what happened in plague-time is shown in the tale of the delay of the Friar's letter.

The verse is mainly that of Shakespeare's first personal manner. The prologue is a sonnet; the chorus is a second sonnet; both very clear in their theatrical service. The Friar utters some lines of grave simple charm; the loveliest outcry of the play is surely Romeo's:

> Death, that hath suck'd the honey of thy breath,
> Hath had no power yet upon thy beauty:
> Thou are not conquer'd; beauty's ensign yet
> Is crimson in thy lips and in thy cheeks,
> And death's pale flag is not advanced there.

DRAMATIS PERSONÆ

ESCALUS, Prince of Verona
PARIS, a young Nobleman, Kinsman to the Prince
MONTAGUE,
CAPULET, } Heads of two Houses at variance with each other
UNCLE to CAPULET
ROMEO, son to Montague
MERCUTIO, Kinsman to the Prince,
BENVOLIO, Nephew to Montague, } Friends to Romeo
TYBALT, Nephew to Lady Capulet
FRIAR LAURENCE, a Franciscan
FRIAR JOHN, of the same Order
BALTHASAR, Servant to Romeo
SAMPSON,
GREGORY, } Servants to Capulet
PETER, Servant to Juliet's Nurse
ABRAHAM, Servant to Montague
AN APOTHECARY
THREE MUSICIANS
PAGE to MERCUTIO; PAGE to PARIS; another PAGE; an OFFICER
LADY MONTAGUE, Wife to Montague
LADY CAPULET, Wife to Capulet
JULIET, Daughter to Capulet
NURSE to JULIET
CITIZENS of Verona; male and female Kinsfolk to both Houses;
    MASQUERS, GUARDS, WATCHMEN and ATTENDANTS
CHORUS

SCENE. *Verona: Once (in the Fifth Act), at Mantua*

7

Prologue

Enter CHORUS.

CHORUS. *Two households, both alike in dignity,*
   In fair Verona, where we lay our scene,
From ancient grudge break to new mutiny,
   Where civil blood makes civil hands unclean.
From forth the fatal loins of these two foes
   A pair of star-cross'd lovers take their life;
Whose misadventur'd piteous overthrows
   Do with their death bury their parents' strife.
The fearful passage of their death-mark'd love,
   And the continuance of their parents' rage,
Which, but their children's end, nought could remove,
   Is now the two hours' traffick of our stage;
The which if you with patient ears attend,
What here shall miss, our toil shall strive to mend.   *[Exit.*

Bryarly Lee as Juliet and Stephen Joyce as Romeo in the New York Shakespeare Festival production that played all five boroughs of the city in the summer of 1954.

Act 1

Scene I. Verona. A Public Place

Enter SAMPSON *and* GREGORY, *armed with swords and bucklers.*

SAMPSON. Gregory, o' my word, we'll not carry coals.

GREGORY. No, for then we should be colliers.

SAMPSON. I mean, an we be in choler, we'll draw.

GREGORY. Ay, while you live, draw your neck out o' the collar.

SAMPSON. I strike quickly, being moved.

GREGORY. But thou art not quickly moved to strike.

SAMPSON. A dog of the house of Montague moves me.

GREGORY. To move is to stir, and to be valiant is to stand; therefore, if thou art moved, thou runnest away.

SAMPSON. A dog of that house shall move me to stand: I will take the wall of any man or maid of Montague's.

GREGORY. That shows thee a weak slave; for the weakest goes to the wall.

SAMPSON. 'Tis true; and therefore women, being the weaker vessels, are ever thrust to the wall: therefore I will push Montague's men from the wall, and thrust his maids to the wall.

GREGORY. The quarrel is between our masters and us their men.

SAMPSON. 'Tis all one, I will show myself a tyrant: when I have fought with the men, I will be cruel with the maids; I will cut off their heads.

GREGORY. The heads of the maids?

SAMPSON. Ay, the heads of the maids, or their maidenheads; take it in what sense thou wilt.

9

GREGORY. They must take it in sense that feel it.

SAMPSON. Me they shall feel while I am able to stand; and 'tis known I am a pretty piece of flesh.

GREGORY. 'Tis well thou art no fish; if thou hadst, thou hadst been poor John. Draw thy tool; here comes two of the house of the Montagues.

Enter ABRAHAM *and* BALTHASAR.

SAMPSON. My naked weapon is out; quarrel, I will back thee.

GREGORY. How! turn thy back and run?

SAMPSON. Fear me not.

GREGORY. No, marry; I fear thee!

SAMPSON. Let us take the law of our sides; let them begin.

GREGORY. I will frown as I pass by, and let them take it as they list.

SAMPSON. Nay, as they dare. I will bite my thumb at them; which is a disgrace to them, if they bear it.

ABRAHAM. Do you bite your thumb at us, sir?

SAMPSON. I do bite my thumb, sir.

ABRAHAM. Do you bite your thumb at us, sir?

SAMPSON. [*Aside to* GREGORY.] Is the law of our side if I say ay?

GREGORY. [*Aside to* SAMPSON.] No.

SAMPSON. No, sir, I do not bite my thumb at you, sir; but I bite my thumb, sir.

GREGORY. Do you quarrel, sir?

ABRAHAM. Quarrel, sir! no, sir.

SAMPSON. If you do, sir, I am for you: I serve as good a man as you.

ABRAHAM. No better.

SAMPSON. Well, sir.

GREGORY. [*Aside to* SAMPSON.] Say, 'better;' here comes one of my master's kinsmen.

SAMPSON. Yes, better, sir.

ABRAHAM. You lie.

SAMPSON. Draw, if you be men. Gregory, remember thy swashing blow.   [*They fight.*

Enter BENVOLIO.

BENVOLIO. Part, fools!
Put up your swords; you know not what you do.
                                        [*Beats down their swords.*
Enter TYBALT.

TYBALT. What! art thou drawn among these heartless hinds?
Turn thee, Benvolio, look upon thy death.
BENVOLIO. I do but keep the peace: put up thy sword,
Or manage it to part these men with me.
TYBALT. What! drawn, and talk of peace? I hate the word,
As I hate hell, all Montagues, and thee.
Have at thee, coward!   [*They fight.*

*Enter several persons of both houses, who join the fray;
then enter* CITIZENS, *with clubs and partisans.*

CITIZENS. Clubs, bills, and partisans! strike! beat them down!
Down with the Capulets! down with the Montagues!

Enter CAPULET *in his gown, and* LADY CAPULET.

CAPULET. What noise is this? Give me my long sword, ho!
LADY CAPULET. A crutch, a crutch! Why call you for a sword?
CAPULET. My sword, I say! Old Montague is come,
And flourishes his blade in spite of me.

Enter MONTAGUE *and* LADY MONTAGUE.

MONTAGUE. Thou villain Capulet! Hold me not; let me go.
LADY MONTAGUE. Thou shalt not stir one foot to seek a foe.

Enter PRINCE *with his Train.*

PRINCE. Rebellious subjects, enemies to peace,
Profaners of this neighbour-stained steel,—
Will they not hear? What ho! you men, you beasts,
That quench the fire of your pernicious rage
With purple fountains issuing from your veins,
On pain of torture, from those bloody hands
Throw your mis-temper'd weapons to the ground,

And hear the sentence of your moved prince.
Three civil brawls, bred of an airy word,
By thee, old Capulet, and Montague,
Have thrice disturb'd the quiet of our streets,
And made Verona's ancient citizens
Cast by their grave beseeming ornaments,
To wield old partisans, in hands as old,
Canker'd with peace, to part your canker'd hate.
If ever you disturb our streets again
Your lives shall pay the forfeit of the peace.
For this time, all the rest depart away:
You, Capulet, shall go along with me;
And, Montague, come you this afternoon
To know our further pleasure in this case,
To old Free-town, our common judgment-place.
Once more, on pain of death, all men depart.
　　　　[*Exeunt all but* MONTAGUE, LADY MONTAGUE, *and* BENVOLIO.
　　MONTAGUE. Who set this ancient quarrel new abroach?
Speak, nephew, were you by when it began?
　　BENVOLIO. Here were the servants of your adversary
And your close fighting ere I did approach:
I drew to part them; in the instant came
The fiery Tybalt, with his sword prepar'd,
Which, as he breath'd defiance to my ears,
He swung about his head, and cut the winds,
Who, nothing hurt withal hiss'd him in scorn.
While we were interchanging thrusts and blows,
Came more and more, and fought on part and part,
Till the prince came, who parted either part.
　　LADY MONTAGUE. O! where is Romeo? saw you him to-day?
Right glad I am he was not at this fray.
　　BENVOLIO. Madam, an hour before the worshipp'd sun
Peer'd forth the golden window of the east,
A troubled mind drave me to walk abroad;
Where, underneath the grove of sycamore
That westward rooteth from the city's side,
So early walking did I see your son:

Towards him I made; but he was ware of me,
And stole into the covert of the wood:
I, measuring his affections by my own,
That most are busied when they're most alone,
Pursu'd my humour not pursuing his,
And gladly shunn'd who gladly fled from me.

MONTAGUE. Many a morning hath he there been seen,
With tears augmenting the fresh morning's dew,
Adding to clouds more clouds with his deep sighs:
But all so soon as the all-cheering sun
Should in the furthest east begin to draw
The shady curtains from Aurora's bed,
Away from light steals home my heavy son,
And private in his chambers pens himself,
Shuts up his windows, locks fair daylight out,
And makes himself an artificial night.
Black and portentous must this humour prove
Unless good counsel may the cause remove.

BENVOLIO. My noble uncle, do you know the cause?
MONTAGUE. I neither know it nor can learn of him.
BENVOLIO. Have you importun'd him by any means?
MONTAGUE. Both by myself and many other friends:
But he, his own affections' counsellor,
Is to himself, I will not say how true,
But to himself so secret and so close,
So far from sounding and discovery,
As is the bud bit with an envious worm,
Ere he can spread his sweet leaves to the air,
Or dedicate his beauty to the sun.
Could we but learn from whence his sorrows grow,
We would as willingly give cure as know.

BENVOLIO. See where he comes: so please you, step aside;
I'll know his grievance, or be much denied.
MONTAGUE. I would thou wert so happy by thy stay,
To hear true shrift. Come, madam, let's away.

[*Exeunt* MONTAGUE *and* LADY.

Enter ROMEO.

BENVOLIO. Good morrow, cousin.

ROMEO.   Is the day so young?

BENVOLIO. But now struck nine.

ROMEO.   Ay me! sad hours seem long.
Was that my father that went hence so fast?

BENVOLIO. It was. What sadness lengthens Romeo's hours?

ROMEO. Not having that, which having, makes them short.

BENVOLIO. In love?

ROMEO. Out—

BENVOLIO. Of love?

ROMEO. Out of her favour, where I am in love.

BENVOLIO. Alas! that love, so gentle in his view,
Should be so tyrannous and rough in proof.

ROMEO. Alas! that love, whose view is muffled still,
Should, without eyes, see pathways to his will.
Where shall we dine? O me! What fray was here?
Yet tell me not, for I have heard it all.
Here's much to do with hate, but more with love:
Why then, O brawling love! O loving hate!
O any thing! of nothing first create.
O heavy lightness! serious vanity!
Mis-shapen chaos of well-seeming forms!
Feather of lead, bright smoke, cold fire, sick health!
Still-waking sleep, that is not what it is!
This love feel I, that feel no love in this.
Dost thou not laugh?

BENVOLIO.   No, coz, I rather weep.

ROMEO. Good heart, at what?

BENVOLIO. At thy good heart's oppression.

ROMEO. Why, such is love's transgression.
Griefs of mine own lie heavy in my breast,
Which thou wilt progagate to have it press'd
With more of thine: this love that thou hast shown
Doth add more grief to too much of mine own.
Love is a smoke rais'd with the fume of sighs;
Being purg'd, a fire sparkling in lovers' eyes;
Being vex'd, a sea nourish'd with lovers' tears:

What is it else? a madness most discreet,
A choking gall, and a preserving sweet.
Farewell, my coz.   [*Going.*
    BENVOLIO.   Soft, I will go along;
An if you leave me so, you do me wrong.
    ROMEO. Tut! I have lost myself; I am not here;
This is not Romeo, he's some other where.
    BENVOLIO. Tell me in sadness, who is that you love.
    ROMEO. What! shall I groan and tell thee?
    BENVOLIO.   Groan! why, no;
But sadly tell me who.
    ROMEO. Bid a sick man in madness make his will;
Ah! word ill urg'd to one that is so ill.
In sadness, cousin, I do love a woman.
    BENVOLIO. I aim'd so near when I suppos'd you lov'd.
    ROMEO. A right good mark-man! And she's fair I love.
    BENVOLIO. A right fair mark, fair coz, is soonest hit.
    ROMEO. Well, in that hit you miss: she'll not be hit
With Cupid's arrow; she hath Dian's wit;
And, in strong proof of chastity well arm'd,
From love's weak childish bow she lives unharm'd.
She will not stay the siege of loving terms,
Nor bide the encounter of assailing eyes,
Nor ope her lap to saint-seducing gold:
O! she is rich in beauty; only poor
That, when she dies, with beauty dies her store.
    BENVOLIO. Then she hath sworn that she will still live chaste?
    ROMEO. She hath, and in that sparing makes huge waste;
For beauty, starv'd with her severity,
Cuts beauty off from all posterity.
She is too fair, too wise, wisely too fair,
To merit bliss by making me despair:
She hath forsworn to love, and in that vow
Do I live dead that live to tell it now.
    BENVOLIO. Be rul'd by me; forget to think of her.
    ROMEO. O! teach me how I should forget to think.
    BENVOLIO. By giving liberty unto thine eyes:

Examine other beauties.

ROMEO.   'Tis the way
To call hers exquisite, in question more.
These happy masks that kiss fair ladies' brows
Being black put us in mind they hide the fair;
He, that is strucken blind cannot forget
The precious treasure of his eyesight lost:
Show me a mistress that is passing fair,
What doth her beauty serve but as a note
Where I may read who pass'd that passing fair?
Farewell: thou canst not teach me to forget.

BENVOLIO. I'll pay that doctrine, or else die in debt.

[*Exeunt.*

Scene II.   The Same. A Street

Enter CAPULET, PARIS, *and* SERVANT.

CAPULET. But Montague is bound as well as I,
In penalty alike; and 'tis not hard, I think,
For men so old as we to keep the peace.

PARIS. Of honourable reckoning are you both;
And pity 'tis you liv'd at odds so long.
But now, my lord, what say you to my suit?

CAPULET. But saying o'er what I have said before:
My child is yet a stranger in the world,
She hath not seen the change of fourteen years;
Let two more summers wither in their pride
Ere we may think her ripe to be a bride.

PARIS. Younger than she are happy mothers made.

CAPULET. And too soon marr'd are those so early made.
Earth hath swallow'd all my hopes but she,
She is the hopeful lady of my earth:
But woo her, gentle Paris, get her heart,
My will to her consent is but a part;
An she agree, within her scope of choice
Lies my consent and fair according voice.

This night I hold an old accustom'd feast,
Whereto I have invited many a guest
Such as I love; and you, among the store,
One more, most welcome, makes my number more.
At my poor house look to behold this night
Earth-treading stars that make dark heaven light:
Such comfort as do lusty young men feel
When well-apparel'd April on the heel
Of limping winter treads, even such delight
Among fresh female buds shall you this night
Inherit at my house; hear all, all see,
And like her most whose merit most shall be:
Which on more view, of many mine being one
May stand in number, though in reckoning none.
Come, go with me. [*To* SERVANT, *giving him a paper.*] Go, sirrah,
    trudge about
Through fair Verona; find those persons out
Whose names are written there, and to them say,
My house and welcome on their pleasure stay.

> [*Exeunt* CAPULET *and* PARIS.

SERVANT. Find them out whose names are written here! It is
written that the shoemaker should meddle with his yard, and
the tailor with his last, the fisher with his pencil, and the painter
with his nets; but I am sent to find those persons, whose names
are here writ, and can never find what names the writing person
hath here writ. I must to the learned. In good time.

Enter BENVOLIO *and* ROMEO.

BENVOLIO. Tut! man, one fire burns out another's burning,
One pain is lessen'd by another's anguish;
Turn giddy, and be holp by backward turning;
    One desperate grief cures with another's languish:
Take thou some new infection to thy eye,
And the rank poison of the old will die.
ROMEO. Your plantain leaf is excellent for that.
BENVOLIO. For what, I pray thee?
ROMEO.   For your broken shin.

BENVOLIO. Why, Romeo, art thou mad?

ROMEO. Not mad, but bound more than a madman is;
Shut up in prison, kept without my food,
Whipp'd and tormented, and—Good den, good fellow.

SERVANT. God gi' good den. I pray, sir, can you read?

ROMEO. Ay, mine own fortune in my misery.

SERVANT. Perhaps you have learn'd it without book: but, I
pray, can you read any thing you see?

ROMEO. Ay, if I know the letters and the language.

SERVANT. Ye say honestly; rest you merry!   [Offering to go.

ROMEO. Stay, fellow; I can read.

*Signior Martino and his wife and daughters; County Anselme
and his beauteus sisters; the lady widow of Vitruvio; Signior
Placentio, and his lovely nieces; Mercutio and his brother Valen-
tine; mine uncle Capulet, his wife and daughters; my fair niece
Rosaline; Livia; Signior Valentio and his cousin Tybalt; Lucio
and the lively Helena.*
A fair assembly: whither should they come?

SERVANT. Up.

ROMEO. Whither?

SERVANT. To supper; to our house.

ROMEO. Whose house?

SERVANT. My master's.

ROMEO. Indeed, I should have asked you that before.

SERVANT. Now I'll tell you without asking. My master is the
great rich Capulet; and if you be not of the house of Montagues,
I pray, come and crush a cup of wine. Rest you merry!   [Exit.

BENVOLIO. At this same ancient feast of Capulet's,
Sups the fair Rosaline, whom thou so lov'st,
With all the admired beauties of Verona:
Go thither; and, with unattainted eye
Compare her face with some that I shall show,
And I will make thee think thy swan a crow.

ROMEO. When the devout religion of mine eye
Maintains such falsehood, then turn tears to fires!
And these, who often drown'd could never die,
Transparent heretics, be burnt for liars!

This 1778 etching shows a contemporary Juliet, Act 4, Scene III: "Romeo I come! This I do drink to thee."

This etching from 1785 shows Juliet in Act 5, Scene III: "Yea noise? then I'll be brief. O happy dagger!"

One fairer than my love! the all-seeing sun
Ne'er saw her match since first the world begun.
   BENVOLIO. Tut! you saw her fair, none else being by,
Herself pois'd with herself in either eye;
But in that crystal scales let there be weigh'd
Your lady's love against some other maid
That I will show you shining at this feast,
And she shall scant show well that now shows best.
   ROMEO. I'll go along, no such sight to be shown,
But to rejoice in spendour of mine own.   *[Exeunt.*

Scene III. The Same. A Room in Capulet's House

Enter LADY CAPULET *and* NURSE.

   LADY CAPULET. Nurse, where's my daughter? call her forth to
  me.
   NURSE. Now, by my maidenhead, at twelve year old,—
I bade her come. What, lamb! what, lady-bird!
God forbid! where's this girl? what, Juliet!

Enter JULIET.

   JULIET. How now! who calls?
   NURSE. Your mother.
   JULIET.   Madam, I am here.
What is your will?
   LADY CAPULET. This is the matter. Nurse, give leave awhile.
We must talk in secret: nurse, come back again;
I have remember'd me, thou's hear our counsel.
Thou know'st my daughter's of a pretty age.
   NURSE. Faith, I can tell her age unto an hour.
   LADY CAPULET. She's not fourteen.
   NURSE.   I'll lay fourteen of my teeth—
And yet to my teen be it spoken I have but four—
She is not fourteen. How long is it now
To Lammas-tide?
   LADY CAPULET. A fortnight and odd days.

NURSE. Even or odd, of all days in the year,
Come Lammas-eve at night shall be fourteen.
Susan and she—God rest all Christian souls!—
Were of an age. Well, Susan is with God;
She was too good for me. But, as I said,
On Lammas-eve at night shall she be fourteen;
That shall she, marry; I remember it well.
'Tis since the earthquake now eleven years;
And she was wean'd, I never shall forget it,
Of all the days of the year, upon that day;
For I had then laid wormwood to my dug,
Sitting in the sun under the dove-house wall;
My lord and you were then at Mantua.
Nay, I do bear a brain:—but, as I said,
When it did taste the wormwood on the nipple
Of my dug and felt it bitter, pretty fool!
To see it tetchy and fall out with the dug.
'Shake,' quoth the dove-house: 'twas no need, I trow,
To bid me trudge:
And since that time it is eleven years;
For then she could stand high lone; nay, by the rood,
She could have run and waddled all about;
For even the day before she broke her brow:
And then my husband—God be with his soul!
A' was a merry man—took up the child:
'Yea,' quoth he, 'dost thou fall upon thy face?
Thou wilt fall backward when thou hast more wit;
Wilt thou not, Jule?' and, by my halidom,
The pretty wretch left crying, and said 'Ay.'
To see now how a jest shall come about!
I warrant, an I should live a thousand years,
I never should forget it: 'Wilt thou not, Jule?' quoth he;
And, pretty fool, it stinted and said 'Ay.'
  LADY CAPULET. Enough of this; I pray thee, hold thy peace.
  NURSE. Yes, madam. Yet I cannot choose but laugh,
To think it should leave crying, and say 'Ay.'
And yet, I warrant, it had upon its brow

A bump as big as a young cockerel's stone;
A parlous knock; and it cried bitterly:
'Yea,' quoth my husband, 'fall'st upon thy face?
Thou wilt fall backward when thou com'st to age;
Wilt thou not, Jule?' it stinted and said 'Ay.'

JULIET. And stint thou too, I pray thee, nurse, say I.

NURSE. Peace, I have done. God mark thee to his grace!
Thou wast the prettiest babe that e'er I nursed:
An I might live to see thee married once,
I have my wish.

LADY CAPULET. Marry, that 'marry' is the very theme
I came to talk of. Tell me, daughter Juliet,
How stands your disposition to be married?

JULIET. It is an honour that I dream not of.

NURSE. An honour! were not I thine only nurse,
I would say thou hadst suck'd wisdom from thy teat.

LADY CAPULET. Well, think of marriage now: younger than
    you,
Here in Verona, ladies of esteem,
Are made already mothers: by my count,
I was your mother much upon these years
That you are now a maid. Thus then in brief,
The valiant Paris seeks you for his love.

NURSE. A man, young lady! lady, such a man
As all the world—why, he's a man of wax.

LADY CAPULET. Verona's summer hath not such a flower.

NURSE. Nay, he's a flower: in faith, a very flower.

LADY CAPULET. What say you? can you love the gentleman?
This night you shall behold him at our feast;
Read o'er the volume of young Paris' face
And find delight writ there with beauty's pen;
Examine every married lineament,
And see how one another lends content;
And what obscur'd in this fair volume lies
Find written in the margent of his eyes.
This precious book of love, this unbound lover,
To beautify him, only lacks a cover:

The fish lives in the sea, and 'tis much pride
For fair without the fair within to hide:
That book in many eyes doth share the glory,
That in gold clasps locks in the golden story:
So shall you share all that he doth possess,
By having him making yourself no less.

    NURSE. No less! nay, bigger; women grow by men.
    LADY CAPULET. Speak briefly, can you like of Paris' love?
    JULIET. I'll look to like, if looking liking move;
But no more deep will I endart mine eye
Than your consent gives strength to make it fly.

    Enter a SERVANT.

    SERVANT. Madam, the guests are come, supper served up, you
called, my young lady asked for, the nurse cursed in the pantry,
and everything in extremity. I must hence to wait; I beseech
you, follow straight.
    LADY CAPULET. We follow thee. Juliet, the county stays.
    NURSE. Go, girl, seek happy nights to happy days.   [*Exeunt.*

Scene IV. *The Same. A Street*

    Enter ROMEO, MERCUTIO, BENVOLIO, *with five or six Maskers,*
    Torch-Bearers, and Others.

    ROMEO. What! shall this speech be spoke for our excuse,
Or shall we on without apology?
    BENVOLIO. The date is out of such prolixity:
We'll have no Cupid hood-wink'd with a scarf,
Bearing a Tartar's painted bow of lath,
Scaring the ladies like a crow-keeper;
Nor no without-book prologue, faintly spoke
After the prompter, for our entrance:
But, let them measure us by what they will,
We'll measure them a measure, and be gone.
    ROMEO. Give me a torch: I am not for this ambling;
Being but heavy, I will bear the light.

MERCUTIO. Nay, gentle Romeo, we must have you dance.

ROMEO. Not I, believe me: you have dancing shoes
With nimble soles; I have a soul of lead
So stakes me to the ground I cannot move.

MERCUTIO. You are a lover; borrow Cupid's wings,
And soar with them above a common bound.

ROMEO. I am too sore enpierced with his shaft
To soar with his light feathers; and so bound
I cannot bound a pitch above dull woe:
Under love's heavy burden do I sink.

MERCUTIO. And, to sink in it, should you burden love;
Too great oppression for a tender thing.

ROMEO. Is love a tender thing? it is too rough,
Too rude, too boisterous; and it pricks like thorn.

MERCUTIO. If love be rough with you, be rough with love;
Prick love for pricking, and you beat love down.
Give me a case to put my visage in: [*Putting on a mask.*
A visor for a visor! what care I,
What curious eye doth quote deformities?
Here are the beetle brows shall blush for me.

BENVOLIO. Come, knock and enter; and no sooner in,
But every man betake him to his legs.

ROMEO. A torch for me; let wantons, light of heart,
Tickle the senseless rushes with their heels,
For I am proverb'd with a grandsire phrase;
I'll be a candle-holder, and look on.
The game was ne'er so fair, and I am done.

MERCUTIO. Tut! dun's the mouse, the constable's own word:
If thou art Dun, we'll draw thee from the mire,
Of—save your reverence—love, wherein thou stick'st
Up to the ears. Come, we burn daylight, ho!

ROMEO. Nay, that's not so.

MERCUTIO.   I mean, sir, in delay
We waste our lights in vain, like lamps by day.
Take our good meaning, for our judgment sits
Five times in that ere once in our five wits.

ROMEO. And we mean well in going to this masque;
But 'tis no wit to go.
    MERCUTIO.   Why, may one ask?
    ROMEO. I dream'd a dream to-night.
    MERCUTIO.   And so did I.
    ROMEO. Well, what was yours?
    MERCUTIO.   That dreamers often lie.
    ROMEO. In bed asleep, while they do dream things true.
    MERCUTIO. O! then, I see, Queen Mab hath been with you.
    BENVOLIO. Queen Mab! What's she?
    MERCUTIO. She is the fairies' midwife, and she comes
In shape no bigger than an agate-stone
On the fore-finger of an alderman,
Drawn with a team of little atomies
Athwart men's noses as they lie asleep:
Her waggon-spokes made of long spinners' legs;
The cover, of the wings of grasshoppers;
The traces, of the smallest spider's web;
The collars, of the moonshine's watery beams;
Her whip, of cricket's bone; the lash, of film;
Her waggoner, a small grey-coated gnat,
Not half so big as a round little worm
Prick'd from the lazy finger of a maid;
Her chariot is an empty hazel-nut,
Made by the joiner squirrel or old grub,
Time out o' mind the fairies' coach-makers.
And in this state she gallops night by night
Through lovers' brains, and then they dream of love;
O'er courtiers' knees, that dream on curtsies straight;
O'er lawyers' fingers, who straight dream on fees;
O'er ladies' lips, who straight on kisses dream;
Which oft the angry Mab with blisters plagues,
Because their breaths with sweetmeats tainted are.
Sometimes she gallops o'er a courtier's nose,
And then dreams he of smelling out a suit;
And sometimes comes she with a tithe-pig's tail,
Tickling a parson's nose as a' lies asleep,

Then dreams he of another benefice;
Sometimes she driveth o'er a soldier's neck,
And then dreams he of cutting foreign throats,
Of breaches, ambuscadoes, Spanish blades,
Of healths five fathom deep; and then anon
Drums in his ear, at which he starts and wakes;
And, being thus frighted, swears a prayer or two,
And sleeps again. This is that very Mab
That plats the manes of horses in the night;
And bakes the elf-locks in foul sluttish hairs,
Which once untangled much misfortune bodes;
This is the hag, when maids lie on their backs,
That presses them and learns them first to bear,
Making them women of good carriage:
This is she—
   ROMEO.   Peace, peace! Mercutio, peace!
Thou talk'st of nothing.
   MERCUTIO.   True, I talk of dreams,
Which are the children of an idle brain,
Begot of nothing but vain fantasy;
Which is as thin of substance as the air,
And more inconstant than the wind, who woos
Even now the frozen bosom of the north,
And, being anger'd, puffs away from thence,
Turning his face to the dew-dropping south.
   BENVOLIO. This wind you talk of blows us from ourselves;
Supper is done, and we shall come too late.
   ROMEO. I fear too early; for my mind misgives
Some consequence yet hanging in the stars
Shall bitterly begin his fearful date
With this night's revels, and expire the term
Of a despised life clos'd in my breast
By some vile forfeit of untimely death.
But he, that hath the steerage of my course,
Direct my sail! On, lusty gentlemen.
   BENVOLIO. Strike, drum.   *[Exeunt.*

Scene V. The Same. A Hall in Capulet's House

MUSICIANS *waiting. Enter* SERVINGMEN.

FIRST SERVANT. Where's Potpan, that he helps not to take away? he shift a trencher! he scrape a trencher!

SECOND SERVANT. When good manners shall lie all in one or two men's hands, and they unwashed too, 'tis a foul thing.

FIRST SERVANT. Away with the joint-tools, remove the court-cupboard, look to the plate. Good thou, save me a piece of marchpane; and, as thou lovest me, let the porter let in Susan Grindstone and Nell. Anthony! and Potpan!

SECOND SERVANT. Ay, boy; ready.

FIRST SERVANT. You are looked for and called for, asked for and sought for in the great chamber.

THIRD SERVANT. We cannot be here and there too.

SECOND SERVANT. Cheerly, boys; be brisk awhile, and the longer liver take all. [*They retire behind.*

Enter CAPULET *and* JULIET *and Others of his house, meeting the Guests and Maskers.*

CAPULET. Welcome, gentlemen! ladies that have their toes
Unplagu'd with corns will walk a bout with you.
Ah ha! my mistresses, which of you all
Will now deny to dance? she that makes dainty, she,
I'll swear, hath corns; am I come near ye now?
Welcome, gentlemen! I have seen the day
That I have worn a visor, and could tell
A whispering tale in a fair lady's ear
Such as would please; 'tis gone, 'tis gone, 'tis gone.
You are welcome, gentlemen! Come, musicians, play.
A hall! a hall! give room, and foot it, girls.
[*Music plays, and they dance.*
More light, ye knaves! and turn the tables up,
And quench the fire, the room has grown too hot.
Ah! sirrah, this unlook'd-for sport comes well.
Nay, sit, nay, sit, good cousin Capulet,

For you and I are past our dancing days;
How long is 't now since last yourself and I
Were in a mask?

    SECOND CAPULET. By'r Lady, thirty years.

    CAPULET. What, man! 'tis not so much, 'tis not so much:
'Tis since the nuptial of Lucentio,
Come Pentecost as quickly as it will,
Some five and twenty years; and then we mask'd.

    SECOND CAPULET. 'Tis more, 'tis more; his son is elder, sir.
His son is thirty.

    CAPULET.   Will you tell me that?
His son was but a ward two years ago.

    ROMEO. What lady is that which doth enrich the hand
Of yonder knights?

    SERVANT. I know not, sir.

    ROMEO. O! she doth teach the torches to burn bright.
It seems she hangs upon the cheek of night
Like a rich jewel in an Ethiop's ear;
Beauty too rich for us, for earth too dear!
So shows a snowy dove trooping with crows,
As yonder lady o'er her fellows shows.
The measure done, I'll watch her place of stand,
And, touching hers, makes blessed my rude hand.
Did my heart love till now? forswear it, sight!
For I ne'er saw true beauty till this night.

    TYBALT. This, by his voice, should be a Montague.
Fetch me my rapier, boy. What! dares the slave
Come hither, cover'd with an antick face,
To fleer and scorn at our solemnity?
Now, by the stock and honour of my kin,
To strike him dead I hold it not a sin.

    CAPULET. Why, how now, kinsman! wherefore storm you so?

    TYBALT. Uncle, this is a Montague, our foe;
A villain that is hither come in spite,
To scorn at our solemnity this night.

    CAPULET. Young Romeo, is it?

    TYBALT.   'Tis he, that villain Romeo.

CAPULET. Content thee, gentle coz, let him alone:
He bears him like a portly gentleman;
And, to say truth, Verona brags of him
To be a virtuous and well-govern'd youth.
I would not for the wealth of all this town
Here in my house do him disparagement;
Therefore be patient, take no note of him:
It is my will; the which if thou respect,
Show a fair presence and put off these frowns,
An ill-beseeming semblance for a feast.

TYBALT. It fits, when such a villain is a guest:
I'll not endure him.

CAPULET.   He shall be endur'd:
What! goodman boy; I say, he shall, go to;
Am I the master here, or you? go to.
You'll not endure him! God shall mend my soul!
You'll make a mutiny amongst my guests!
You will set cock-a-hoop! you'll be the man!

TYBALT. Why, uncle, 'tis a shame.

CAPULET.   Go to, go to;
You are a saucy boy—is't so indeed?—
This trick may chance to scathe you.—I know what:
You must contrary me! marry, 'tis time.
Well said, my hearts! You are a princox; go:
Be quiet, or—More light, more light!—For shame!
I'll make you quiet. What! cheerly, my hearts!

TYBALT. Patience perforce with wilful choler meeting
Makes my flesh tremble in their different greeting.
I will withdraw; but this intrusion shall
Now seeming sweet convert to bitter gall.   [*Exit.*

ROMEO. [*To* JULIET.] If I profane with my unworthiest hand
   This holy shrine, the gentle sin is this;
My lips, two blushing pilgrims, ready stand
   To smooth that rough touch with a tender kiss.

JULIET. Good pilgrim, you do wrong your hand too much,
   Which mannerly devotion shows in this;
For saints have hands that pilgrims' hands do touch,

And palm to palm in holy palmers' kiss.

ROMEO. Have not saints lips, and holy palmers too?

JULIET. Ay, pilgrim, lips that they must use in prayer.

ROMEO. O! then, dear saint, let lips do what hands do;
They pray, grant thou, lest faith turn to despair.

JULIET. Saints do not move, though grant for prayers' sake.

ROMEO. Then move not, while my prayers' effect I take.
Thus from my lips, by thine, my sin is purg'd.   [*Kissing her.*

JULIET. Then have my lips the sin that they have took.

ROMEO. Sin from my lips? O trespass sweetly urg'd!
Give me my sin again.

JULIET.   You kiss by the book.

NURSE. Madam, your mother craves a word with you.

ROMEO. What is her mother?

NURSE.   Marry, bachelor,
Her mother is the lady of the house,
And a good lady, and a wise, and virtuous:
I nurs'd her daughter, that you talk'd withal;
I tell you he that can lay hold of her
Shall have the chinks.

ROMEO.   Is she a Capulet?
O dear account! my life is my foe's debt.

BENVOLIO. Away, be gone; the sport is at the best.

ROMEO. Ay, so I fear; the more is my unrest.

CAPULET. Nay, gentlemen, prepare not to be gone;
We have a trifling foolish banquet towards.
Is it e'en so? Why then, I thank you all;
I thank you, honest gentlemen; good-night.
More torches here! Come on then, let's to bed.
Ah! sirrah, by my fay, it waxes late;
I'll to my rest.   [*Exeunt all except* JULIET *and* NURSE.

JULIET. Come hither, nurse. What is yond gentleman?

NURSE. The son and heir of old Tiberio.

JULIET. What's he that now is going out of door?

NURSE. Marry, that, I think, be young Petruchio.

JULIET. What's he, that follows there, that would not dance?

NURSE. I know not.

JULIET. Go, ask his name.—If he be married,
My grave is like to be my wedding bed.

NURSE. His name is Romeo, and a Montague;
The only son of your great enemy.

JULIET. My only love sprung from my only hate!
Too early seen unknown, and known too late!
Prodigious birth of love it is to me,
That I must love a loathed enemy.

NURSE. What's this, what's this?

JULIET.   A rime I learn'd even now
Of one I danc'd withal.   [One calls within, 'JULIET!'

NURSE.   Anon, anon!—
Come, let's away; the strangers are all gone.   [Exeunt.

Prologue

Enter CHORUS.

CHORUS. *Now old desire doth in his death-bed lie,*
  And young affection gapes to be his heir;
That fair for which love groan'd for and would die,
  With tender Juliet match'd, is now not fair.
Now Romeo is belov'd and loves again,
  Alike bewitched by the charm of looks,
But to his foe suppos'd he must complain,
  And she steal love's sweet bait from fearful hooks:
Being held a foe, he may not have access
  To breathe such vows as lovers us'd to swear;
And she as much in love, her means much less
  To meet her new-beloved any where:
But passion lends them power, time means, to meet,
Tempering extremity with extreme sweet.   [Exit.

31

Act 2

Scene I. Verona. A Lane by the Wall of Capulet's Orchard

Enter ROMEO.

ROMEO. Can I go forward when my heart is here?
Turn back, dull earth, and find thy centre out.
              [He climbs the wall, and leaps down within it.

Enter BENVOLIO *and* MERCUTIO.

BENVOLIO. Romeo! my cousin Romeo!
MERCUTIO.   He is wise;
And, on my life, hath stol'n him home to bed.
BENVOLIO. He ran this way, and leap'd this orchard wall:
Call, good Mercutio.
MERCUTIO.   Nay, I'll conjure too.
Romeo! humours! madman! passion! lover!
Appear thou in the likeness of a sigh:
Speak but one rime and I am satisfied;
Cry but 'Ay me!' couple but 'love' and 'dove;'
Speak to my gossip Venus one fair word.
One nickname for her purblind son and heir,
Young Adam Cupid, he that shot so trim
When King Cophetua lov'd the beggar-maid.
He heareth not, he stirreth not, he moveth not;
The ape is dead, and I must conjure him.
I conjure thee by Rosaline's bright eyes,
By her high forehead, and her scarlet lip,
By her fine foot, straight leg, and quivering thigh,

And the demesnes that there adjacent lie,
That in thy likeness thou appear to us.

BENVOLIO. An if he hear thee, thou wilt anger him.

MERCUTIO. This cannot anger him: 'twould anger him
To raise a spirit in his mistress' circle
Of some strange nature, letting it there stand
Till she had laid it, and conjur'd it down;
That were some spite: my invocation
Is fair and honest, and in his mistress' name
I conjure only but to raise up him.

BENVOLIO. Come, he hath hid himself among these trees,
To be consorted with the humorous night:
Blind is his love and best befits the dark.

MERCUTIO. If love be blind, love cannot hit the mark.
Now will he sit under a medlar tree,
And wish his mistress were that kind of fruit
As maids call medlars, when they laugh alone.
O Romeo! that she were, O! that she were
An open *et cætera*, thou a poperin pear.
Romeo, good night: I'll to my truckle-bed;
This field-bed is too cold for me to sleep:
Come, shall we go?

BENVOLIO.   Go, then; for 'tis in vain
To seek him here that means not to be found.   [*Exeunt.*

Scene II. *The Same. Capulet's Orchard*

Enter ROMEO.

ROMEO. He jests at scars, that never felt a wound.
          [JULIET *appears above at a window.*
But, soft! what light through yonder window breaks?
It is the east, and Juliet is the sun!
Arise, fair sun, and kill the envious moon,
Who is already sick and pale with grief,
That thou her maid art far more fair than she:
Be not her maid, since she is envious;
Her vestal livery is but sick and green,

And none but fools do wear it; cast it off.
It is my lady; O! it is my love:
O! that she knew she were.
She speaks, yet she says nothing: what of that?
Her eye discourses; I will answer it.
I am too bold, 'tis not to me she speaks:
Two of the fairest stars in all the heaven,
Having some business, do entreat her eyes
To twinkle in their spheres till they return.
What if her eyes were there, they in her head?
The brightness of her cheek would shame those stars
As daylight doth a lamp; her eyes in heaven
Would through the airy region stream so bright
That birds would sing and think it were not night.
See! how she leans her cheek upon her hand:
O! that I were a glove upon that hand,
That I might touch that cheek.

  JULIET.   **Ay me!**
  ROMEO.   **She speaks:**
O! speak again, bright angel; for thou art
As glorious to this night, being o'er my head,
As a winged messenger of heaven
Unto the white-upturned wond'ring eyes
Of mortals, that fall back to gaze on him
When he bestrides the lazy-pacing clouds,
And sails upon the bosom of the air.

  JULIET. O Romeo, Romeo! wherefore art thou Romeo?
Deny thy father, and refuse thy name;
Or, if thou wilt not, be but sworn my love,
And I'll no longer be a Capulet.

  ROMEO. [*Aside.*] Shall I hear more, or shall I speak at this?
  JULIET. 'Tis but thy name that is my enemy;
Thou art thyself though, not a Montague.
What's Montague? it is nor hand, nor foot,
Nor arm, nor face, nor any other part
Belonging to a man. O! be some other name:
What's in a name? that which we call a rose

Two turn-of-the-century Juliets. Mrs. Patrick Campbell (*left*) as she appeared in London in 1895, and Miss Maude Adams (*right*) as she appeared in New York City in 1899. Both actresses were tremendously successful.

By any other name would smell as sweet;
So Romeo would, were he not Romeo call'd,
Retain that dear perfection which he owes
Without that title. Romeo, doff thy name;
And for that name, which is no part of thee,
Take all myself.

ROMEO. I take thee at thy word.
Call me but love, and I'll be new baptiz'd;
Henceforth I never will be Romeo.

JULIET. What man art thou, that, thus bescreen'd in night,
So stumblest on my counsel?

ROMEO. By a name
I know not how to tell thee who I am:
My name, dear saint, is hateful to myself,
Because it is an enemy to thee:
Had I it written, I would tear the word.

JULIET. My ears have not yet drunk a hundred words
Of that tongue's uttering, yet I know the sound:
Art thou not Romeo, and a Montague?

ROMEO. Neither, fair maid, if either thee dislike.

JULIET. How cam'st thou hither, tell me, and wherefore?
The orchard walls are high and hard to climb,
And the place death, considering who thou art,
If any of my kinsmen find thee here.

ROMEO. With love's light wings did I o'er-perch these walls;
For stony limits cannot hold love out,
And what love can do that dares love attempt;
Therefore thy kinsmen are no stop to me.

JULIET. If they do see thee they will murder thee.

ROMEO. Alack! there lies more peril in thine eye
Than twenty of their swords: look thou but sweet,
And I am proof against their enmity.

JULIET. I would not for the world they saw thee here.

ROMEO. I have night's cloak to hide me from their eyes;
And but thou love me, let them find me here;
My life were better ended by their hate,
Than death prorogued, wanting of thy love.

JULIET. By whose direction found'st thou out this place?

ROMEO. By Love, that first did prompt me to inquire;
He lent me counsel, and I lent him eyes.
I am no pilot; yet, wert thou as far
As that vast shore wash'd with the furthest sea,
I would adventure for such merchandise.

JULIET. Thou know'st the mask of night is on my face,
Else would a maiden blush bepaint my cheek
For that which thou hast heard me speak to-night.
Fain would I dwell in form, fain, fain deny
What I have spoke: but farewell compliment!
Dost thou love me? I know thou wilt say 'Ay;'
And I will take thy word; yet, if thou swear'st,
Thou mayst prove false; at lovers' perjuries,
They say, Jove laughs. O gentle Romeo!
If thou dost love, pronounce it faithfully:
Or if thou think'st I am too quickly won,
I'll frown and be perverse and say thee nay,
So thou wilt woo; but else, not for the world.
In truth, fair Montague, I am too fond,
And therefore thou mayst think my haviour light:
But trust me, gentleman I'll prove more true
Than those that have more cunning to be strange.
I should have been more strange, I must confess,
But that thou over-heard'st, ere I was 'ware,
My true love's passion: therefore pardon me,
And not impute this yielding to light love,
Which the dark night hath so discovered.

ROMEO. Lady, by yonder blessed moon I swear
That tips with silver all these fruit-tree tops,—

JULIET. O! swear not by the moon, the inconstant moon,
That monthly changes in her circled orb,
Lest that thy love prove likewise variable.

ROMEO. What shall I swear by?

JULIET.   Do not swear at all;
Or, if thou wilt, swear by thy gracious self,
Which is the god of my idolatry.

And I'll believe thee.

ROMEO.   If my heart's dear love—

JULIET. Well, do not swear. Although I joy in thee,
I have no joy of this contract to-night:
It is too rash, too unadvis'd, too sudden;
Too like the lightning, which doth cease to be
Ere one can say it lightens. Sweet, good-night!
This bud of love, by summer's ripening breath,
May prove a beauteous flower when next we meet.
Good-night, good-night! as sweet repose and rest
Come to thy heart as that within my breast!

ROMEO. O! wilt thou leave me so unsatisfied?

JULIET. What satisfaction canst thou have to-night?

ROMEO. The exchange of thy love's faithful vow for mine.

JULIET. I gave thee mine before thou didst request it;
And yet I would it were to give again.

ROMEO. Wouldst thou withdraw it? for what purpose, love?

JULIET. But to be frank, and give it thee again.
And yet I wish but for the thing I have:
My bounty is as boundless as the sea,
My love as deep; the more I give to thee,
The more I have, for both are infinite.   [NURSE *calls within.*
I hear some noise within; dear love, adieu!
Anon, good nurse! Sweet Montague, be true.
Stay but a little, I will come again.   [*Exit above.*

ROMEO. O blessed, blessed night! I am afeard,
Being in night, all this is but a dream,
Too flattering-sweet to be substantial.

   Re-enter JULIET, *above.*

JULIET. Three words, dear Romeo, and good-night indeed.
If that thy bent of love be honourable,
Thy purpose marriage, send me word to-morrow,
By one that I'll procure to come to thee,
Where, and what time, thou wilt perform the rite;
And all my fortunes at thy foot I'll lay,
And follow thee my lord throughout the world.

NURSE. [*Within.*] Madam!

JULIET. I come, anon.—But if thou mean'st not well,
I do beseech thee,—

NURSE. [*Within.*] Madam!

JULIET.   By and by; I come:—
To cease thy suit, and leave me to my grief:
To-morrow will I send.

ROMEO.   So thrive my soul,—

JULIET. A thousand times good-night!   [*Exit above.*

ROMEO. A thousand times the worse, to want thy light.
Love goes toward love, as schoolboys from their books;
But love from love, toward school with heavy looks.   [*Retiring.*

Re-enter JULIET, *above.*

JULIET. Hist! Romeo, hist! O! for a falconer's voice,
To lure this tassel-gentle back again.
Bondage is hoarse, and may not speak aloud,
Else would I tear the cave where Echo lies,
And make her airy tongue more hoarse than mine,
With repetition of my Romeo's name.

ROMEO. It is my soul that calls upon my name:
How silver-sweet sound lovers' tongues by night,
Like softest music to attending ears!

JULIET. Romeo!

ROMEO.   My dear!

JULIET.   At what o'clock to-morrow
Shall I send to thee?

ROMEO.   At the hour of nine.

JULIET. I will not fail; 'tis twenty years till then.
I have forgot why I did call thee back.

ROMEO. Let me stand here till thou remember it.

JULIET. I shall forget, to have thee still stand there,
Remembering how I love thy company.

ROMEO. And I'll still stay, to have thee still forget,
Forgetting any other home but this.

JULIET. 'Tis almost morning; I would have thee gone;
And yet no further than a wanton's bird,

Who lets it hop a little from her hand,
Like a poor prisoner in his twisted gyves,
And with a silk thread plucks it back again,
So loving-jealous of his liberty.

ROMEO. I would I were thy bird.

JULIET.   Sweet, so would I:
Yet I should kill thee with much cherishing.
Good-night, good-night! parting is such sweet sorrow
That I shall say good-night till it be morrow.   [*Exit.*

ROMEO. Sleep dwell upon thine eyes, peace in thy breast!
Would I were sleep and peace, so sweet to rest!
Hence will I to my ghostly father's cell,
His help to crave, and my dear hap to tell.   [*Exit.*

Scene III. *The Same. Friar Laurence's Cell*

Enter FRIAR LAURENCE, *with a basket.*

FRIAR LAURENCE. The grey-ey'd morn smiles on the frowning
    night,
Chequering the eastern clouds with streaks of light,
And flecked darkness like a drunkard reels
From forth day's path and Titan's fiery wheels:
Now, ere the sun advance his burning eye
The day to cheer and night's dank dew to dry,
I must up-fill this osier cage of ours
With baleful weeds and precious-juiced flowers.
The earth that's nature's mother is her tomb;
What is her burying grave that is her womb,
And from her womb children of divers kind
We sucking on her natural bosom find,
Many for many virtues excellent,
None but for some, and yet all different.
O! mickle is the powerful grace that lies
In herbs, plants, stones, and their true qualities:
For nought so vile that on the earth doth live
But to the earth some special good doth give,

Nor aught so good but strain'd from that fair use
Revolts from true birth, stumbling on abuse:
Virtue itself turns vice, being misapplied,
And vice sometime's by action dignified.
Within the infant rind of this weak flower
Poison hath residence and medicine power:
For this, being smelt, with that part cheers each part;
Being tasted, slays all senses with the heart.
Two such opposed foes encamp them still
In man as well as herbs, grace and rude will;
And where the worser is predominant,
Full soon the canker death eats up that plant.

    Enter ROMEO.

    ROMEO. Good morrow, father!
    FRIAR LAURENCE.   *Benedicite!*
What early tongue so sweet saluteth me?
Young son, it argues a distemper'd head
So soon to bid good morrow to thy bed:
Care keeps his watch in every old man's eye,
And where care lodges, sleep will never lie;
But where unbruised youth with unstuff'd brain
Doth couch his limbs, there golden sleep doth reign:
Therefore thy earliness doth me assure
Thou art up-rous'd by some distemperature;
Or if not so, then here I hit it right,
Our Romeo hath not been in bed to-night.
    ROMEO.   That last is true; the sweeter rest was mine.
    FRIAR LAURENCE. God pardon sin! wast thou with Rosaline?
    ROMEO.   With Rosaline, my ghostly father? no;
I have forgot that name, and that name's woe.
    FRIAR LAURENCE. That's my good son: but where hast thou
      been, then?
    ROMEO. I'll tell thee, ere thou ask it me again.
I have been feasting with mine enemy,
Where on a sudden one hath wounded me,
That's by me wounded: both our remedies

Within thy help and holy physic lies:
I bear no hatred, blessed man; for, lo!
My intercession likewise steads my foe.

    FRIAR LAURENCE. Be plain, good son, and homely in thy drift;
Riddling confession finds but riddling shrift.

    ROMEO. Then plainly know my heart's dear love is set
On the fair daughter of rich Capulet:
As mine on hers, so hers is set on mine;
And all combin'd, save what thou must combine
By holy marriage: when and where and how
We met we woo'd and made exchange of vow,
I'll tell thee as we pass; but this I pray,
That thou consent to marry us to-day.

    FRIAR LAURENCE. Holy Saint Francis! what a change is here;
Is Rosaline, whom thou didst love so dear,
So soon forsaken? young men's love then lies
Not truly in their hearts, but in their eyes.
Jesu Maria! what a deal of brine
Hath wash'd thy sallow cheeks for Rosaline;
How much salt water thrown away in waste,
To season love, that of it doth not taste!
The sun not yet thy sighs from heaven clears,
Thy old groans ring yet in my ancient ears;
Lo! here upon thy cheek the stain doth sit
Of an old tear that is not wash'd off yet.
If e'er thou wast thyself and these woes thine,
Thou and these woes were all for Rosaline:
And art thou chang'd? pronounce this sentence then:
Women may fall, when there's no strength in men.

    ROMEO. Thou chidd'st me oft for loving Rosaline.

    FRIAR LAURENCE. For doting, not for loving, pupil mine.

    ROMEO. And bad'st me bury love.

    FRIAR LAURENCE.   Not in a grave,
To lay one in, another out to have.

    ROMEO. I pray thee, chide not; she, whom I love now
Doth grace for grace and love for love allow;
The other did not so.

FRIAR LAURENCE.   O! she knew well
Thy love did read by rote and could not spell.
But come, young waverer, come, go with me,
In one respect I'll thy assistant be;
For this alliance may so happy prove,
To turn your households' rancour to pure love.
ROMEO.   O! let us hence; I stand on sudden haste.
FRIAR LAURENCE.   Wisely and slow; they stumble that run fast.
[Exeunt.

Scene IV. The Same. A Street

Enter BENVOLIO *and* MERCUTIO.

MERCUTIO.   Where the devil should this Romeo be?
Came he not home to-night?
BENVOLIO.   Not to his father's; I spoke with his man.
MERCUTIO.   Why that same pale hard-hearted wench, that Rosaline,
Torments him so, that he will sure run mad.
BENVOLIO.   Tybalt, the kinsman of old Capulet,
Hath sent a letter to his father's house.
MERCUTIO.   A challenge, on my life.
BENVOLIO.   Romeo will answer it.
MERCUTIO.   Any man that can write may answer a letter.
BENVOLIO.   Nay, he will answer the letter's master, how he
dares, being dared.
MERCUTIO.   Alas! poor Romeo, he is already dead; stabbed
with a white wench's black eye; shot through the ear with a
love-song; the very pin of his heart cleft with the blind bow-boy's
butt-shaft; and is he a man to encounter Tybalt?
BENVOLIO.   Why, what is Tybalt?
MERCUTIO.   More than prince of cats, I can tell you. O! he is
the courageous captain of compliments. He fights as you sing
prick-song, keeps time, distance, and proportion; rests me his
minim rest, one, two, and the third in your bosom; the very
butcher of a silk button, a duellist, a duellist; a gentleman of

A cast of *Romeo and Juliet* on an ornate Victorian stage. The setting is in sharp contrast to the simplicity of an Elizabethan stage. The photograph was taken in 1899.

the very first house, of the first and second cause. Ah! the immortal passado! the punto reverso! the hay!

BENVOLIO. The what?

MERCUTIO. The pox of such antick, lisping, affecting fantasticoes, these new tuners of accents!—'By Jesu, a very good blade! —a very tall man! a very good whore.'—Why, is not this a lamentable thing, grandsire, that we should be thus afflicted with these strange flies, these fashion-mongers, these *pardonnez-mois*, who stand so much on the new form that they cannot sit at ease on the old bench? O, their *bons*, their *bons!*

Enter ROMEO.

BENVOLIO. Here comes Romeo, here comes Romeo.

MERCUTIO. Without his roe, like a dried herring. O flesh, flesh, how art thou fishified; Now is he for the numbers that Petrarch flowed in: Laura to his lady was but a kitchen-wench; marry, she had a better love to be-rime her; Dido a dowdy; Cleopatra a gipsy; Helen and Hero hildings and harlots; Thisbe, a grey eye or so, but not to the purpose. Signior Romeo, *bon jour!* there's a French salutation to your French slop. You gave us the counterfeit fairly last night.

ROMEO. Good morrow to you both. What counterfeit did I give you?

MERCUTIO. The slip, sir, the slip; can you not conceive?

ROMEO. Pardon, good Mercutio, my business was great; and in such a case as mine a man may strain courtesy.

MERCUTIO. That's as much as to say, such a case as yours constrains a man to bow in the hams.

ROMEO. Meaning—to curtsy.

MERCUTIO. Thou hast most kindly hit it.

ROMEO. A most courteous exposition.

MERCUTIO. Nay, I am the very pink of courtesy.

ROMEO. Pink for flower.

MERCUTIO. Right.

ROMEO. Why, then, is my pump well flowered.

MERCUTIO. Well said; follow me this jest now till thou hast

worn out the pump, that, when the single sole of it is worn, the jest may remain after the wearing sole singular.

ROMEO. O single-soled jest! solely singular for the singleness.

MERCUTIO. Come between us, good Benvolio; my wit faints.

ROMEO. Switch and spurs, switch and spurs; or I'll cry a match.

MERCUTIO. Nay, if thy wits run the wild-goose chase, I have done, for thou hast more of the wild-goose in one of thy wits than, I am sure, I have in my whole five. Was I with you there for the goose?

ROMEO. Thou wast never with me for anything when thou wast not here for the goose.

MERCUTIO. I will bite thee by the ear for that jest.

ROMEO. Nay, good goose, bite not.

MERCUTIO. Thy wit is a very bitter sweeting; it is a most sharp sauce.

ROMEO. And is it not then well served in to a sweet goose?

MERCUTIO. O! here's a wit of cheveril, that stretches from an inch narrow to an ell broad.

ROMEO. I stretch it out for that word 'broad;' which added to the goose, proves thee far and wide a broad goose.

MERCUTIO. Why, is not this better now than groaning for love? now art thou sociable, now art thou Romeo; now art thou what thou art, by art as well as by nature: for this drivelling love is like a great natural, that runs lolling up and down to hide his bauble in hole.

BENVOLIO. Stop there, stop there.

MERCUTIO. Thou desirest me to stop in my tale against the hair.

BENVOLIO. Thou wouldst else have made thy tale large.

MERCUTIO. O! thou art deceived; I would have made it short; for I was come to the whole depth of my tale, and meant indeed to occupy the argument no longer.

ROMEO. Here's goodly gear!

Enter NURSE *and* PETER.

MERCUTIO. A sail, a sail!

BENVOLIO. Two, two; a shirt and a smock.

NURSE. Peter!

PETER. Anon!

NURSE. My fan, Peter.

MERCUTIO. Good Peter, to hide her face; for her fan's the fairer face.

NURSE. God ye good morrow, gentlemen.

MERCUTIO. God ye good den, fair gentlewoman.

NURSE. Is it good den?

MERCUTIO. 'Tis no less, I tell you; for the bawdy hand of the dial is now upon the prick of noon.

NURSE. Out upon you! what a man are you!

ROMEO. One, gentlewoman, that God hath made for himself to mar.

NURSE. By my troth, it is well said; 'for himself to mar,' quoth a'?—Gentlemen, can any of you tell me where I may find the young Romeo?

ROMEO. I can tell you; but young Romeo will be older when you have found him than he was when you sought him: I am the youngest of that name, for fault of a worse.

NURSE. You say well.

MERCUTIO. Yea! is the worst well? very well took, i' faith; wisely, wisely.

NURSE. If you be he, sir, I desire some confidence with you.

BENVOLIO. She will indite him to some supper.

MERCUTIO. A bawd, a bawd, a bawd! So ho!

ROMEO. What has thou found?

MERCUTIO. No hare, sir; unless a hare, sir, in a lenten pie, that is something stale and hoar ere it be spent.   [*Sings.*

> An old hare hoar, and an old hare hoar,
>   Is very good meat in Lent:
> But a hare that is hoar, is too much for a score,
>   When it hoars ere it be spent.

Romeo, will you come to your father's? we'll to dinner thither.

ROMEO. I will follow you.

MERCUTIO. Farewell, ancient lady; farewell,

Lady, lady, lady.

[*Exeunt* MERCUTIO *and* BENVOLIO.

NURSE. Marry, farewell! I pray you, sir, what saucy merchant was this, that was so full of his ropery?

ROMEO. A gentleman, nurse, that loves to hear himself talk, and will speak more in a minute than he will stand to in a month.

NURSE. An a' speak anything against me, I'll take him down, an a' were lustier than he is, and twenty such Jacks; and if I cannot, I'll find those that shall. Scurvy knave! I am none of his flirt-gills; I am none of his skeins-mates. [*To* PETER.] And thou must stand by too, and suffer every knave to use me at his pleasure!

PETER. I saw no man use you at his pleasure; if I had, my weapon should quickly have been out, I warrant you. I dare draw as soon as another man, if I see occasion in a good quarrel, and the law on my side.

NURSE. Now, afore God, I am so vexed, that every part about me quivers. Scurvy knave! Pray you, sir, a word; and as I told you, my young lady bade me inquire you out; what she bid me say I will keep to myself; but first let me tell ye, if ye should lead her into a fool's paradise, as they say, it were a very gross kind of behaviour, as they say: for the gentlewoman is young; and, therefore, if you should deal double with her, truly it were an ill thing to be offered to any gentlewoman, and very weak dealing.

ROMEO. Nurse, commend me to thy lady and mistress. I protest unto thee,—

NURSE. Good heart! and, i' faith, I will tell her as much. Lord, Lord! she will be a joyful woman.

ROMEO. What wilt thou tell her, nurse? thou dost not mark me.

NURSE. I will tell her, sir, that you do protest; which, as I take it, is a gentlemanlike offer.

ROMEO. Bid her devise

Some means to come to shrift this afternoon;
And there she shall at Friar Laurence's cell,
Be shriv'd and married. Here is for thy pains.
   NURSE. No, truly, sir; not a penny.
   ROMEO. Go to; I say, you shall.
   NURSE. This afternoon, sir? well, she shall be there.
   ROMEO. And stay, good nurse; behind the abbey wall:
Within this hour my man shall be with thee,
And bring thee cords made like a tackled stair;
Which to the high top-gallant of my joy
Must be my convoy in the secret night.
Farewell! Be trusty, and I'll quit thy pains.
Farewell! Commend me to thy mistress.
   NURSE. Now God in heaven bless thee! Hark you, sir.
   ROMEO. What sayst thou, my dear nurse?
   NURSE. Is your man secret? Did you ne'er hear say,
Two may keep counsel, putting one away?
   ROMEO. I warrant thee my man's as true as steel.
   NURSE. Well, sir; my mistress is the sweetest lady—Lord, Lord!
—when 'twas a little prating thing,—O! there's a nobleman in
town, one Paris, that would fain lay knife aboard; but she, good
soul, had as lief see a toad, a very toad, as see him. I anger her
sometimes and tell her that Paris is the properer man; but, I'll
warrant you, when I say so, she looks as pale as any clout in the
versal world. Doth not rosemary and Romeo begin both with a
letter?
   ROMEO. Ay, nurse: what of that? both with an R.
   NURSE. Ah! mocker; that's the dog's name. R is for the—No; I
know it begins with some other letter: and she had the prettiest
sententious of it, of you and rosemary, that it would do you
good to hear it.
   ROMEO. Commend me to thy lady.
   NURSE. Ay, a thousand times.   [*Exit* ROMEO.
Peter!
   PETER. Anon!
   NURSE. Before, and apace.   [*Exeunt.*

Scene V. The Same. Capulet's Garden

Enter JULIET.

JULIET. The clock struck nine when I did send the nurse;
In half an hour she promis'd to return.
Perchance she cannot meet him: that's not so.
O! she is lame: love's heralds should be thoughts.
Which ten times faster glide than the sun's beams,
Driving back shadows over lowering hills:
Therefore do nimble-pinion'd doves draw Love,
And therefore hath the wind-swift Cupid wings.
Now is the sun upon the highmost hill
Of this day's journey, and from nine till twelve
Is three long hours, yet she is not come.
Had she affections, and warm youthful blood,
She'd be as swift in motion as a ball;
My words would bandy her to my sweet love,
And his to me:
But old folks, many feign as they were dead;
Unwieldy, slow, heavy and pale as lead.

Enter NURSE *and* PETER.

O God! she comes. O honey nurse! what news?
Hast thou met with him? Send thy man away.
    NURSE. Peter, stay at the gate.   [*Exit* PETER.
    JULIET. Now, good sweet nurse; O Lord! why look'st thou
      sad?
Though news be sad, yet tell them merrily;
If good, thou sham'st the music of sweet news
By playing it to me with so sour a face.
    NURSE. I am aweary, give me leave awhile:
Fie, how my bones ache! What a jaunce have I had!
    JULIET. I would thou hadst my bones, and I thy news.
Nay, come, I pray thee, speak; good, good nurse, speak.
    NURSE. Jesu! what haste? can you not stay awhile?
Do you not see that I am out of breath?

JULIET. How art thou out of breath when thou hast breath
To say to me that thou art out of breath?
The excuse that thou dost make in this delay
Is longer than the tale thou dost excuse.
Is thy news good, or bad? answer to that;
Say either, and I'll stay the circumstance:
Let me be satisfied, is't good or bad?

NURSE. Well, you have made a simple choice; you know not
how to choose a man: Romeo! no, not he; though his face be
better than any man's, yet his leg excels all men's; and for a
hand, and a foot, and a body, though they be not to be talked
on, yet they are past compare. He is not the flower of courtesy,
but I'll warrant him, as gentle as a lamb. Go thy ways, wench;
serve God. What! have you dined at home?

JULIET. No, no: but all this did I know before.
What says he of our marriage? what of that?

NURSE. Lord! how my head aches; what a head have I!
It beats as it would fall in twenty pieces.
My back o' t'other side; O! my back, my back!
Beshrew your heart for sending me about,
To catch my death with jauncing up and down.

JULIET. I' faith, I am sorry that thou art not well.
Sweet, sweet, sweet nurse, tell me, what says my love?

NURSE. Your love says, like an honest gentleman, and a courteous, and a kind, and a handsome, and, I warrant, a virtuous,—
Where is your mother?

JULIET. Where is my mother! why, she is within;
Where should she be? How oddly thou repliest:
'Your love says, like an honest gentleman,
Where is your mother?'

NURSE.   O! God's lady dear,
Are you so hot? Marry, come up, I trow;
Is this the poultice for my aching bones?
Henceforward do your messages yourself.

JULIET. Here's such a coil! come, what says Romeo?

NURSE. Have you got leave to go to shrift to-day?

JULIET. I have.

NURSE. Then hie you hence to Friar Laurence' cell,
There stays a husband to make you a wife:
Now comes the wanton blood up in your cheeks,
They'll be in scarlet straight at any news.
Hie you to church; I must another way,
To fetch a ladder, by the which your love
Must climb a bird's nest soon when it is dark;
I am the drudge and toil in your delight,
But you shall bear the burden soon at night.
Go; I'll to dinner: hie you to the cell.
JULIET. Hie to high fortune! Honest nurse, farewell.

[*Exeunt.*

Scene VI. *The Same. Friar Laurence's Cell*

Enter FRIAR LAURENCE *and* ROMEO.

FRIAR LAURENCE. So smile the heaven upon this holy act,
That after hours with sorrow chide us not!
ROMEO. Amen, amen! but come what sorrow can,
It cannot countervail the exchange of joy
That one short minute gives me in her sight:
Do thou but close our hands with holy words,
Then love-devouring death do what he dare;
It is enough I may but call her mine.
FRIAR LAURENCE. These violent delights have violent ends,
And in their triumph die, like fire and powder,
Which, as they kiss consume: the sweetest honey
Is loathsome in his own deliciousness
And in the taste confounds the appetite:
Therefore love moderately; long love doth so;
Too swift arrives as tardy as too slow.

Enter JULIET.

Here comes the lady: O! so light a foot
Will ne'er wear out the everlasting flint:
A lover may bestride the gossamer

That idles in the wanton summer air,
And yet not fall; so light is vanity.

JULIET. Good even to my ghostly confessor.

FRIAR LAURENCE. Romeo shall thank thee, daughter, for us
both.

JULIET. As much to him, else are his thanks too much.

ROMEO. Ah! Juliet, if the measure of thy joy
Be heap'd like mine, and that thy skill be more
To blazon it, then sweeten with thy breath
This neighbour air, and let rich music's tongue
Unfold the imagin'd happiness that both
Receive in either by this dear encounter.

JULIET. Conceit, more rich in matter than in words,
Brags of his substance, not of ornament:
They are but beggars that can count their worth;
But my true love is grown to such excess
I cannot sum up half my sum of wealth.

FRIAR LAURENCE. Come, come with me, and we will make
short work;
For, by your leaves, you shall not stay alone
Till holy church incorporate two in one. [*Exeunt.*

Act 3

Scene I. Verona. A Public Place

Enter MERCUTIO, BENVOLIO, PAGE, *and* SERVANTS.

BENVOLIO. I pray thee, good Mercutio, let's retire:
The day is hot, the Capulets abroad,
And, if we meet, we shall not 'scape a brawl;
For now, these hot days, is the mad blood stirring.

MERCUTIO. Thou art like one of those fellows that when he enters the confines of a tavern claps me his sword upon the table and says, 'God send me no need of thee!' and by the operation of the second cup draws him on the drawer, when, indeed, there is no need.

BENVOLIO. Am I like such a fellow?

MERCUTIO. Come, come, thou art as hot a Jack in thy mood as any in Italy; and as soon moved to be moody, and as soon moody to be moved.

BENVOLIO. And what to?

MERCUTIO. Nay, an there were two such, we should have none shortly, for one would kill the other. Thou! why, thou wilt quarrel with a man that hath a hair more or a hair less in his beard than thou hast. Thou wilt quarrel with a man for cracking nuts, having no other reason but because thou hast hazel eyes. What eye, but such an eye, would spy out such a quarrel? Thy head is as full of quarrels as an egg is full of meat, and yet thy head hath been beaten as addle as an egg for quarrelling. Thou hast quarrelled with a man for coughing in the street, because he hath wakened thy dog that hath lain asleep in the sun. Didst thou not fall out with a tailor for wearing his new doublet before Easter? with another, for tying his new shoes with old riband? and yet thou wilt tutor me from quarrelling!

BENVOLIO. An I were so apt to quarrel as thou art, any man should buy the fee-simple of my life for an hour and a quarter.

MERCUTIO. The fee-simple! O simple!

BENVOLIO. By my head, here come the Capulets.

MERCUTIO. By my heel, I care not.

Enter TYBALT, *and Others.*

TYBALT. Follow me close, for I will speak to them. Gentlemen, good den! a word with one of you.

MERCUTIO. And but one word with one of us? Couple it with something; make it a word and a blow.

TYBALT. You shall find me apt enough to that, sir, an you will give me occasion.

MERCUTIO. Could you not take some occasion without giving?

TYBALT. Mercutio, thou consort'st with Romeo,—

MERCUTIO. Consort! What! dost thou make us minstrels? an thou make minstrels of us, look to hear nothing but discords: here's my fiddle-stick; here's that shall make you dance. 'Zounds! consort!

BENVOLIO. We talk here in the public haunt of men:
Either withdraw unto some private place,
Or reason coldly of your grievances,
Or else depart; here all eyes gaze on us.

MERCUTIO. Men's eyes were made to look, and let them gaze;
I will not budge for no man's pleasure, I.

Enter ROMEO.

TYBALT. Well, peace be with you, sir. Here comes my man.

MERCUTIO. But I'll be hang'd, sir, if he wear your livery:
Marry, go before to field, he'll be your follower;
Your worship in that sense may call him 'man.'

TYBALT. Romeo, the hate I bear thee can afford
No better term than this,—thou art a villain.

ROMEO. Tybalt, the reason that I have to love thee
Doth much excuse the appertaining rage

To such a greeting; villain am I none,
Therefore farewell; I see thou know'st me not.
    TYBALT. Boy, this shall not excuse the injuries
That thou hast done me; therefore turn and draw.
    ROMEO. I do protest I never injur'd thee,
But love thee better than thou canst devise,
Till thou shalt know the reason of my love:
And so, good Capulet, which name I tender
As dearly as my own, be satisfied.
    MERCUTIO. O calm, dishonourable, vile submission!
Alla stoccata carries it away.   *[Draws.*
Tybalt, you rat-catcher, will you walk?
    TYBALT. What wouldst thou have with me?
    MERCUTIO. Good king of cats, nothing but one of your nine
lives, that I mean to make bold withal, and, as you shall use me
hereafter, dry-beat the rest of the eight. Will you pluck your
sword out of his pilcher by the ears? make haste, lest mine be
about your ears ere it be out.
    TYBALT. *[Drawing.]* I am for you.
    ROMEO. Gentle Mercutio, put thy rapier up.
    MERCUTIO. Come, sir, your passado.   *[They fight.*
    ROMEO. Draw, Benvolio; beat down their weapons.
Gentlemen, for shame, forbear this outrage!
Tybalt, Mercutio, the prince expressly hath
Forbidden bandying in Verona streets.
Hold, Tybalt! good Mercutio!
                  [Exeunt TYBALT *and his Partisans.*
    MERCUTIO.   I am hurt.
A plague o' both your houses! I am sped.
Is he gone, and hath nothing?
    BENVOLIO.   What! art thou hurt?
    MERCUTIO. Ay, ay, a scratch, a scratch; marry, 'tis enough.
Where is my page? Go, villain, fetch a surgeon.   *[Exit* PAGE.
    ROMEO. Courage, man; the hurt cannot be much.
    MERCUTIO. No, 'tis not so deep as a well, nor so wide as a
church door; but 'tis enough, 'twill serve: ask for me to-morrow,
and you shall find me a grave man. I am peppered, I warrant, for

this world. A plague o' both your houses! 'Zounds, a dog, a rat,
a mouse, a cat, to scratch a man to death! a braggart, a rogue, a
villain, that fights by the book of arithmetic! Why the devil came
you between us? I was hurt under your arm.

    ROMEO. I thought all for the best.

    MERCUTIO. Help me into some house, Benvolio,
Or I shall faint. A plague o' both your houses!
They have made worms' meat of me: I have it,
And soundly too:—your houses!

                 [*Exeunt* MERCUTIO *and* BENVOLIO.

    ROMEO. This gentleman, the prince's near ally,
My very friend, hath got his mortal hurt
In my behalf; my reputation stain'd
With Tybalt's slander, Tybalt, that an hour
Hath been my kinsman. O sweet Juliet!
Thy beauty hath made me effeminate,
And in my temper soften'd valour's steel!

    Re-enter BENVOLIO.

    BENVOLIO. O Romeo, Romeo! brave Mercutio's dead;
That gallant spirit hath aspir'd the clouds,
Which too untimely here did scorn the earth.

    ROMEO. This day's black fate on more days doth depend;
This but begins the woe others must end.

    Re-enter TYBALT.

    BENVOLIO. Here comes the furious Tybalt back again.

    ROMEO. Alive! in triumph! and Mercutio slain!
Away to heaven, respective lenity,
And fire-ey'd fury be my conduct now!
Now, Tybalt, take the villain back again
That late thou gav'st me; for Mercutio's soul
Is but a little way above our heads,
Staying for thine to keep him company:
Either thou, or I, or both, must go with him.

    TYBALT. Thou wretched boy, that didst consort him here,
Shalt with him hence.

ROMEO.   This shall determine that.

          [*They fight:* TYBALT *falls.*

BENVOLIO. Romeo, away! be gone!
The citizens are up, and Tybalt slain.
Stand not amaz'd: the prince will doom thee death
If thou art taken: hence! be gone! away!

    ROMEO. O! I am Fortune's fool.

    BENVOLIO.   Why doth thou stay?

          [*Exit* ROMEO.

Enter CITIZENS, *&c.*

    FIRST CITIZEN. Which way ran he that kill'd Mercutio?
Tybalt, that murderer, which way ran he?

    BENVOLIO. There lies that Tybalt.

    FIRST CITIZEN.   Up, sir, go with me.
I charge thee in the prince's name, obey.

Enter PRINCE, *attended:* MONTAGUE, CAPULET, *their Wives,
and Others.*

    PRINCE. Where are the vile beginners of this fray?

    BENVOLIO. O noble prince! I can discover all
The unlucky manage of this fatal brawl:
There lies the man, slain by young Romeo,
That slew thy kinsman, brave Mercutio.

    LADY CAPULET. Tybalt, my cousin! O my brother's child!
O prince! O cousin! husband! O! the blood is spill'd
Of my dear kinsman. Prince, as thou art true,
For blood of ours shed blood of Montague.
O cousin, cousin!

    PRINCE. Benvolio, who began this bloody fray?

    BEVOLIO. Tybalt, here slain, whom Romeo's hand did slay:
Romeo, that spoke him fair, bade him bethink
How nice the quarrel was, and urg'd withal
Your high displeasure: all this, uttered
With gentle breath, calm look, knees humbly bow'd,
Could not take truce with the unruly spleen
Of Tybalt deaf to peace, but that he tilts

With piercing steel at bold Mercutio's breast,
Who, all as hot, turns deadly point to point,
And, with a martial scorn, with one hand beats
Cold death aside, and with the other sends
It back to Tybalt, whose dexterity
Retorts it: Romeo he cries aloud,
'Hold, friends! friends, part!' and, swifter than his tongue
His agile arm beats down their fatal points,
And 'twixt them rushes; underneath whose arm
An envious thrust from Tybalt hit the life
Of stout Mercutio, and then Tybalt fled;
But by and by comes back to Romeo,
Who had but newly entertain'd revenge,
And to 't they go like lightning, for, ere I
Could draw to part them, was stout Tybalt slain,
And, as he fell, did Romeo turn and fly.
This is the truth, or let Benvolio die.

LADY CAPULET. He is a kinsman to the Montague;
Affection makes him false, he speaks not true:
Some twenty of them fought in this black strife
And all those twenty could but kill one life.
I beg for justice, which thou, prince, must give;
Romeo slew Tybalt, Romeo must not live.

PRINCE. Romeo slew him, he slew Mercutio;
Who now the price of his dear blood doth owe?

MONTAGUE. Not Romeo, prince, he was Mercutio's friend,
His fault concludes but what the law should end,
The life of Tybalt.

PRINCE.   And for that offence
Immediately we do exile him hence:
I have an interest in your hate's proceeding,
My blood for your rude brawls doth lie a-bleeding;
But I'll amerce you with so strong a fine
That you shall all repent the loss of mine.
I will be deaf to pleading and excuses;
Nor tears nor prayers shall purchase out abuses;
Therefore use none; let Romeo hence in haste,

Else, when he's found, that hour is his last.
Bear hence this body and attend our will:
Mercy but murders, pardoning those that kill.   [*Exeunt.*

Scene II. The Same. Capulet's Orchard

Enter JULIET.

JULIET. Gallop apace, you fiery-footed steeds,
Towards Phœbus' lodging; such a waggoner
As Phæthon would whip you to the west,
And bring in cloudy night immediately.
Spread thy close curtain, love-performing night!
That runaway's eyes may wink, and Romeo
Leap to these arms, untalk'd of and unseen!
Lovers can see to do their amorous rites
By their own beauties; or, if love be blind,
It best agrees with night. Come, civil night,
Thou sober-suited matron, all in black,
And learn me how to lose a winning match,
Play'd for a pair of stainless maidenhoods:
Hood my unmann'd blood, bating in my cheeks,
With thy black mantle; till strange love, grown bold,
Think true love acted simple modesty.
Come, night! come, Romeo! come, thou day in night!
For thou wilt lie upon the wings of night,
Whiter than new snow on a raven's back.
Come, gentle night; come, loving, black-brow'd night,
Give me my Romeo: and, when he shall die,
Take him and cut him out in little stars,
And he will make the face of heaven so fine
That all the world will be in love with night,
And pay no worship to the garish sun.
O! I have bought the mansion of a love,
But not possess'd it, and, though I am sold,
Not yet enjoy'd. So tedious is this day
As is the night before some festival

To an impatient child that hath new robes
And may not wear them. O! here comes my nurse,

Enter NURSE *with cords.*

And she brings news; and every tongue that speaks
But Romeo's name speaks heavenly eloquence.
Now nurse, what news? What hast thou there? the cords
That Romeo bade thee fetch?

 NURSE.   Ay, ay, the cords.

             [Throws them down.

 JULIET. Ah me! what news? why dost thou wring thy hands?

 NURSE. Ah well-a-day! he's dead, he's dead, he's dead!
We are undone, lady, we are undone!
Alack the day! he's gone, he's killed, he's dead!

 JULIET. Can heaven be so envious?

 NURSE.   Romeo can,
Though heaven cannot. O! Romeo, Romeo;
Who ever would have thought it? Romeo!

 JULIET. What devil art thou that dost torment me thus?
This torture should be roar'd in dismal hell.
Hath Romeo slain himself? say thou but 'I,'
And that bare vowel, 'I,' shall poison more
Than the death-darting eye of cockatrice:
I am not I, if there be such an 'I;'
Or those eyes shut that make thee answer 'I.'
If he be slain, say 'I;' or if not 'no:'
Brief sounds determine of my weal or woe.

 NURSE. I saw the wound, I saw it with mine eyes,
God save the mark! here on his manly breast:
A piteous corse, a bloody piteous corse;
Pale, pale as ashes, all bedaub'd in blood,
All in gore blood; I swounded at the sight.

 JULIET. O break, my heart!—poor bankrupt, break at once!
To prison, eyes, ne'er look on liberty!
Vile earth, to earth resign; end motion here;
And thou and Romeo press one heavy bier!

 NURSE. O Tybalt, Tybalt! the best friend I had;

O courteous Tybalt! honest gentleman!
That ever I should live to see thee dead!

JULIET. What storm is this that blows so contrary?
Is Romeo slaughter'd, and is Tybalt dead?
My dearest cousin, and my dearer lord?
Then, dreadful trumpet, sound the general doom!
For who is living if those two are gone?

NURSE. Tybalt is gone, and Romeo banished;
Romeo, that kill'd him, he is banished.

JULIET. O God! did Romeo's hand shed Tybalt's blood?

NURSE. It did, it did; alas the day! it did.

JULIET. O serpent heart, hid with a flowering face!
Did ever dragon keep so fair a cave?
Beautiful tyrant! fiend angelical!
Dove-feather'd raven! wolvish-ravening lamb!
Despised substance of divinest show!
Just opposite to what thou justly seem'st;
A damned saint, an honourable villain!
O, nature! what hadst thou to do in hell
When thou didst bower the spirit of a fiend
In mortal paradise of such sweet flesh?
Was ever book containing such vile matter
So fairly bound? O! that deceit should dwell
In such a gorgeous palace.

NURSE.   There's no trust,
No faith, no honesty in men; all naught,
All perjur'd, all dissemblers, all forsworn.
Ah! where's my man? give me some *aqua vitæ:*
These griefs, these woes, these sorrows make me old.
Shame come to Romeo!

JULIET.   Blister'd be thy tongue
For such a wish! he was not born to shame:
Upon his brow shame is asham'd to sit;
For 'tis a throne where honour may be crown'd
Sole monarch of the universal earth.
O! what a beast was I to chide at him.

NURSE. Will you speak well of him that kill'd your cousin?

JULIET. Shall I speak ill of him that is my husband?
Ah! poor my lord, what tongue shall smooth thy name,
When I, thy three-hours wife, have mangled it?
But, wherefore, villain, didst thou kill my cousin?
That villain cousin would have kill'd my husband:
Back, foolish tears, back to your native spring;
Your tributary drops belong to woe,
Which you, mistaking, offer up to joy.
My husband lives, that Tybalt would have slain;
And Tybalt's dead, that would have slain my husband:
All this is comfort; wherefore weep I then?
Some word there was, worser than Tybalt's death,
That murder'd me: I would forget it fain;
But O! it presses to my memory,
Like damned guilty deeds to sinners' minds.
'Tybalt is dead, and Romeo banished!'
That 'banished,' that one word 'banished,'
Hath slain ten thousand Tybalts. Tybalt's death
Was woe enough, if it had ended there:
Or, if sour woe delights in fellowship,
And needly will be rank'd with other griefs,
Why follow'd not, when she said 'Tybalt's dead,'
Thy father, or thy mother, nay, or both,
Which modern lamentation might have mov'd?
But with a rearward following Tybalt's death,
'Romeo is banished!' to speak that word
Is father, mother, Tybalt, Romeo, Juliet,
All slain, all dead: 'Romeo is banished!'
There is no end, no limit, measure, bound
In that word's death; no words can that woe sound.—
Where is my father and my mother, nurse?
NURSE. Weeping and wailing over Tybalt's corse:
Will you go to them? I will bring you thither.
JULIET. Wash they his wounds with tears: mine shall be spent,
When theirs are dry, for Romeo's banishment.
Take up those cords. Poor ropes, you are beguil'd,
Both you and I, for Romeo is exil'd:

He made you for a highway to my bed,
But I, a maid, die maiden-widowed.
Come, cords; come, nurse; I'll to my wedding bed;
And death, not Romeo, take my maidenhead!

    NURSE. Hie to your chamber; I'll find Romeo
To comfort you: I wot well where he is.
Hark ye, your Romeo will be here to-night:
I'll to him; he is hid at Laurence's cell.

    JULIET. O! find him; give this ring to my true knight,
And bid him come to take his last farewell.   [*Exeunt.*

Scene III.   The Same. Friar Laurence's Cell

Enter FRIAR LAURENCE.

    FRIAR LAURENCE. Romeo, come forth; come forth, thou fearful man:
Affliction is enamour'd of thy parts,
And thou art wedded to calamity.

Enter ROMEO.

    ROMEO. Father, what news? what is the prince's doom?
What sorrow craves acquaintance at my hand,
That I yet know not?

    FRIAR LAURENCE.   Too familiar
Is my dear son with such sour company:
I bring thee tidings of the prince's doom.

    ROMEO. What less than doomsday is the prince's doom?

    FRIAR LAURENCE. A gentler judgment vanish'd from his lips,
Not body's death, but body's banishment.

    ROMEO. Ha! banishment! be merciful, say 'death;'
For exile hath more terror in his look,
Much more than death: do not say 'banishment.'

    FRIAR LAURENCE. Hence from Verona art thou banished.
Be patient, for the world is broad and wide.

    ROMEO. There is no world without Verona walls,
But purgatory, torture, hell itself.

Hence banished is banish'd from the world,
And world's exile is death; then 'banished,'
Is death mis-term'd. Calling death 'banished,'
Thou cutt'st my head off with a golden axe,
And smil'st upon the stroke that murders me.
    FRIAR LAURENCE. O deadly sin! O rude unthankfulness!
Thy fault our law calls death; but the kind prince,
Taking thy part, hath rush'd aside the law,
And turn'd that black word death to banishment:
This is dear mercy, and thou seest it not.
    ROMEO. 'Tis torture, and not mercy: heaven is here,
Where Juliet lives; and every cat and dog
And little mouse, every unworthy thing,
Live here in heaven and may look on her;
But Romeo may not: more validity,
More honourable state, more courtship lives
In carrion flies than Romeo: they may seize
On the white wonder of dear Juliet's hand,
And steal immortal blessing from her lips,
Who, even in pure and vestal modesty,
Still blush, as thinking their own kisses sin;
Flies may do this, but I from this must fly:
They are free men, but I am banished.
And sayst thou yet that exile is not death?
Hadst thou no poison mix'd, no sharp-ground knife,
No sudden mean of death, though ne'er so mean,
But 'banished' to kill me? 'Banished!'
O friar! the damned use that word in hell;
Howlings attend it: how hast thou the heart,
Being a divine, a ghostly confessor,
A sin-absolver, and my friend profess'd,
To mangle me with that word 'banished?'
    FRIAR LAURENCE. Thou fond mad man, hear me but speak a
    word.
    ROMEO. O! thou wilt speak again of banishment.
    FRIAR LAURENCE. I'll give thee armour to keep off that word;
Adversity's sweet milk, philosophy,

To comfort thee, though thou art banished.

ROMEO. Yet 'banished!' Hang up philosophy!
Unless philosophy can make a Juliet,
Displant a town, reverse a prince's doom,
It helps not, it prevails not: talk no more.

FRIAR LAURENCE. O! then I see that madmen have no ears.

ROMEO. How should they, when that wise men have no eyes?

FRIAR LAURENCE. Let me dispute with thee of thy estate.

ROMEO. Thou canst not speak of that thou dost not feel:
Wert thou as young as I, Juliet thy love,
An hour but married, Tybalt murdered,
Doting like me, and like me banished,
Then mightst thou speak, then mightst thou tear thy hair,
And fall upon the ground, as I do now,
Taking the measure of an unmade grave. [*Knocking within.*

FRIAR LAURENCE. Arise; one knocks: good Romeo, hide thyself.

ROMEO. Not I; unless the breath of heart-sick groans,
Mist-like, infold me from the search of eyes. [*Knocking.*

FRIAR LAURENCE. Hark! how they knock. Who's there? Romeo arise;

Thou wilt be taken. Stay awhile; Stand up; [*Knocking.*
Run to my study. By and by! God's will!
What wilfulness is this! I come, I come! [*Knocking.*
Who knocks so hard? whence come you? what's your will?

NURSE. [*Within.*] Let me come in, and you shall know my errand:
I come from Lady Juliet.

FRIAR LAURENCE.   Welcome, then.

Enter NURSE.

NURSE. O holy friar! O! tell me, holy friar,
Where is my lady's lord? where's Romeo?

FRIAR LAURENCE. There on the ground, with his own tears made drunk.

NURSE. O! he is even in my mistress' case,
Just in her case!

FRIAR LAURENCE. O woeful sympathy!
Piteous predicament! Even so lies she,
Blubbering and weeping, weeping and blubbering.
Stand up, stand up; stand, an you be a man:
For Juliet's sake, for her sake, rise and stand;
Why should you fall into so deep an O?
  ROMEO. Nurse!
  NURSE. Ah, sir! ah, sir! Well, death's the end of all.
  ROMEO. Spak'st thou of Juliet? how is it with her?
Doth she not think of me an old murderer,
Now I have stain'd the childhood of our joy
With blood remov'd but little from her own?
Where is she? and how doth she? and what says
My conceal'd lady to our cancell'd love?
  NURSE. O! she says nothing, sir, but weeps and weeps;
And now falls on her bed; and then starts up,
And Tybalt calls, and then on Romeo cries,
And then down falls again.
  ROMEO.   As if that name,
Shot from the deadly level of a gun,
Did murder her; as that name's cursed hand
Murder'd her kinsman. O! tell me, friar, tell me,
In what vile part of this anatomy
Doth my name lodge? tell me, that I may sack
The hateful mansion.   [*Drawing his sword.*
  FRIAR LAURENCE.   Hold thy desperate hand:
Art thou a man? thy form cries out thou art:
Thy tears are womanish; thy wild acts denote
The unreasonable fury of a beast:
Unseemly woman in a seeming man;
Or ill-beseeming beast in seeming both!
Thou hast amaz'd me: by my holy order,
I thought thy disposition better temper'd.
Hast thou slain Tybalt? wilt thou slay thyself?
And slay thy lady that in thy life lives,
By doing damned hate upon thyself?
Why rail'st thou on thy birth, the heaven, and earth?

Since birth, and heaven, and earth, all three do meet
In thee at once, which thou at once wouldst lose.
Fie, fie! thou sham'st thy shape, thy love, thy wit,
Which, like a usurer, abound'st in all,
And usest none in that true use indeed
Which should bedeck thy shape, thy love, thy wit.
Thy noble shape is but a form of wax,
Digressing from the valour of a man
Thy dear love, sworn, but hollow perjury,
Killing that love which thou hast vow'd to cherish;
Thy wit, that ornament to shape and love,
Misshapen in the conduct of them both,
Like powder in a skilless soldier's flask,
To set a-fire by thine own ignorance,
And thou dismember'd with thine own defence.
What! rouse thee, man; thy Juliet is alive,
For whose dear sake thou wast but lately dead;
There art thou happy: Tybalt would kill thee,
But thou slew'st Tybalt; there art thou happy too:
The law that threaten'd death becomes thy friend,
And turns it to exile; there art thou happy:
A pack of blessing light upon thy back;
Happiness courts thee in her best array;
But, like a misbehav'd and sullen wench,
Thou pout'st upon thy fortune and thy love.
Take heed, take heed, for such die miserable.
Go, get thee to thy love, as was decreed,
Ascend her chamber, hence and comfort her;
But look thou stay not till the watch be set,
For then thou canst not pass to Mantua;
Where thou shalt live, till we can find a time
To blaze your marriage, reconcile your friends,
Beg pardon of the prince, and call thee back
With twenty hundred thousand times more joy
Than thou went'st forth in lamentation.
Go before, nurse: commend me to thy lady;
And bid her hasten all the house to bed,

Which heavy sorrow makes them apt unto:
Romeo is coming.
    NURSE. O Lord! I could have stay'd here all the night
To hear good counsel: O! what learning is.
My lord, I'll tell my lady you will come.
    ROMEO. Do so, and bid my sweet prepare to chide.
    NURSE. Here, sir, a ring she bid me give you, sir.
Hie you, make haste, for it grows very late.   [*Exit.*
    ROMEO. How well my comfort is reviv'd by this!
    FRIAR LAURENCE. Go hence; good-night; and here stands all
    your state:
Either be gone before the watch be set,
Or by the break of day disguis'd from hence:
Sojourn in Mantua; I'll find out your man,
And he shall signify from time to time
Every good hap to you that chances here.
Give me thy hand; 'tis late: farewell; good-night.
    ROMEO. But that a joy past joy calls out on me,
It were a grief so brief to part with thee:
Farewell.   [*Exeunt.*

Scene IV.   *The Same. A Room in Capulet's House*

Enter CAPULET, LADY CAPULET, *and* PARIS.

    CAPULET. Things have fall'n out, sir, so unluckily,
That we have had no time to move our daughter:
Look you, she lov'd her kinsman Tybalt dearly,
And so did I: well, we were born to die.
'Tis very late, she'll not come down to-night:
I promise you, but for your company,
I would have been a-bed an hour ago.
    PARIS. These times of woe afford no time to woo.
Madam, good-night: commend me to your daughter.
    LADY CAPULET. I will, and know her mind early to-morrow;
To-night she's mew'd up to her heaviness.
    CAPULET. Sir Paris, I will make a desperate tender

Of my child's love: I think she will be rul'd
In all respects by me; nay, more, I doubt it not.
Wife, go you to her ere you go to bed;
Acquaint her here of my son Paris' love;
And bid her, mark you me, on Wednesday next—
But, soft! what day is this?

PARIS.   Monday, my lord.

CAPULET. Monday! ha, ha! Well, Wednesday is too soon;
O' Thursday let it be: o' Thursday, tell her,
She shall be married to this noble earl.
Will you be ready? do you like this haste?
We'll keep no great ado; a friend or two;
For, hark you, Tybalt being slain so late,
It may be thought we held him carelessly,
Being our kinsman, if we revel much.
Therefore we'll have some half a dozen friends,
And there an end. But what say you to Thursday?

PARIS. My lord, I would that Thursday were to-morrow.

CAPULET. Well, get you gone: o' Thursday be it then.
Go you to Juliet ere you go to bed,
Prepare her, wife, against this wedding-day.
Farewell, my lord. Light to my chamber, ho!
Afore me! it is so very very late,
That we may call it early by and by.
Good-night.   [*Exeunt.*

Scene V. *The Same. Juliet's Chamber*

Enter ROMEO *and* JULIET.

JULIET. Wilt thou be gone? it is not yet near day:
It was the nightingale, and not the lark,
That pierc'd the fearful hollow of thine ear;
Nightly she sings on yon pomegranate tree:
Believe me, love, it was the nightingale.

ROMEO. It was the lark, the herald of the morn,
No nightingale: look, love, what envious streaks

Do lace the severing clouds in yonder east:
Night's candles are burnt out, and jocund day
Stands tiptoe on the misty mountain tops:
I must be gone and live, or stay and die.

JULIET. Yon light is not daylight, I know it, I:
It is some meteor that the sun exhales,
To be to thee this night a torch-bearer,
And light thee on thy way to Mantua:
Therefore stay yet; thou need'st not to be gone.

ROMEO. Let me be ta'en, let me be put to death;
I am content, so thou wilt have it so.
I'll say yon grey is not the morning's eye,
'Tis but the pale reflex of Cynthia's brow;
Nor that is not the lark, whose notes do beat
The vaulty heaven so high above our heads:
I have more care to stay than will to go:
Come, death, and welcome! Juliet wills it so.
How is't, my soul? let's talk; it is not day.

JULIET. It is, it is; hie hence, be gone, away!
It is the lark that sings so out of tune,
Straining harsh discords and unpleasing sharps.
Some say the lark makes sweet division;
This doth not so, for she divideth us:
Some say the lark and loathed toad change eyes;
O! now I would they had chang'd voices too,
Since arm from arm that voice doth us affray,
Hunting thee hence with hunts-up to the day.
O! now be gone; more light and light it grows.

ROMEO. More light and light; more dark and dark our woes.

Enter NURSE.

NURSE. Madam!

JULIET. Nurse!

NURSE. Your lady mother is coming to your chamber:
The day is broke; be wary, look about.   [*Exit.*

JULIET. Then, window, let day in, and let life out.

ROMEO. Farewell, farewell! one kiss, and I'll descend.

[*Descends.*

JULIET. Art thou gone so? my lord, my love, my friend!
I must hear from thee every day in the hour,
For in a minute there are many days:
O! by this count I shall be much in years
Ere I again behold my Romeo.

ROMEO. Farewell!
I will omit no opportunity
That may convey my greetings, love, to thee.

JULIET. O! think'st thou we shall ever meet again?

ROMEO. I doubt it not; and all these woes shall serve
For sweet discourses in our time to come.

JULIET. O God! I have an ill-divining soul:
Me thinks I see thee, now thou art so low,
As one dead in the bottom of a tomb:
Either my eyesight fails, or thou look'st pale.

ROMEO. And trust me, love, in my eye so do you:
Dry sorrow drinks our blood. Adieu! adieu!   [*Exit.*

JULIET. O fortune, fortune! all men call thee fickle:
If thou art fickle, what dost thou with him
That is renown'd for faith? Be fickle, fortune;
For then, I hope, thou wilt not keep him long,
But send him back.

LADY CAPULET. [*Within.*] Ho, daughter! are you up?

JULIET. Who is't that calls? is it my lady mother?
Is she not down so late, or up so early?
What unaccustom'd cause procures her hither?

Enter LADY CAPULET.

LADY CAPULET. Why, how now, Juliet!

JULIET.   Madam, I am not well.

LADY CAPULET. Evermore weeping for your cousin's death?
What! wilt thou wash him from his grave with tears?
And if thou couldst, thou couldst not make him live;
Therefore, have done: some grief shows much of love;
But much of grief shows still some want of wit.

JULIET. Yet let me weep for such a feeling loss.

LADY CAPULET. So shall you feel the loss, but not the friend
Which you weep for.

JULIET.　　　　　　　Feeling so the loss,
I cannot choose but ever weep the friend.

LADY CAPULET. Well, girl, thou weep'st not so much for his
　death,
As that the villain lives which slaughter'd him.

JULIET. What villain, madam?

LADY CAPULET.　　　　　That same villain, Romeo.

JULIET. [*Aside.*] Villain and he be many miles asunder.
God pardon him! I do, with all my heart;
And yet no man like he doth grieve my heart.

LADY CAPULET. That is because the traitor murderer lives.

JULIET. Ay, madam, from the reach of these my hands.
Would none but I might venge my cousin's death!

LADY CAPULET. We will have vengeance for it, fear thou not:
Then weep no more. I'll send to one in Mantua,
Where that same banish'd runagate doth live,
Shall give him such an unaccustom'd dram
That he shall soon keep Tybalt company:
And then, I hope, thou wilt be satisfied.

JULIET. Indeed, I never shall be satisfied
With Romeo, till I behold him—dead—
Is my poor heart so for a kinsman vex'd:
Madam, if you could find out but a man
To bear a poison, I would temper it,
That Romeo should, upon receipt thereof,
Soon sleep in quiet. O! how my heart abhors
To hear him nam'd, and cannot come to him,
To wreak the love I bore my cousin Tybalt
Upon his body that hath slaughter'd him.

LADY CAPULET. Find thou the means, and I'll find such a man.
But now I'll tell thee joyful tidings, girl.

JULIET. And joy comes well in such a needy time:
What are they, I beseech your ladyship?

LADY CAPULET. Well, well, thou hast a careful father, child;

One who, to put thee from thy heaviness,
Hath sorted out a sudden day of joy
That thou expect'st not, nor I look'd not for.
  JULIET. Madam, in happy time, what day is that?
  LADY CAPULET. Marry, my child, early next Thursday morn
The gallant, young, and noble gentleman,
The County Paris, at Saint Peter's church,
Shall happily make thee there a joyful bride.
  JULIET. Now, by Saint Peter's church, and Peter too,
He shall not make me there a joyful bride.
I wonder at this haste; that I must wed
Ere he that should be husband comes to woo.
I pray you, tell my lord and father, madam,
I will not marry yet; and, when I do, I swear,
It shall be Romeo, whom you know I hate,
Rather than Paris. These are news indeed!
  LADY CAPULET. Here comes your father; tell him so yourself,
And see how he will take it at your hands.

   Enter CAPULET *and* NURSE.

  CAPULET. When the sun sets, the air doth drizzle dew;
But the sunset of my brother's son
It rains downright.
How now! a conduit, girl? What! still in tears?
Evermore showering? In one little body
Thou counterfeit'st a bark, a sea, a wind;
For still thy eyes, which I may call the sea,
Do ebb and flow with tears; the bark thy body is,
Sailing in this salt flood; the winds, thy sighs;
Who, raging with thy tears, and they with them,
Without a sudden calm, will overset
Thy tempest-tossed body. How now, wife!
Have you deliver'd to her our decree?
  LADY CAPULET. Ay, sir; but she will none, she gives you
   thanks.
I would the fool were married to her grave!
  CAPULET. Soft! take me with you, take me with you, wife.

How! will she none? doth she not give us thanks?
Is she not proud? doth she not count her bless'd,
Unworthy as she is, that we have wrought
So worthy a gentleman to be her bridegroom?
 JULIET. Not proud, you have; but thankful, that you have:
Proud can I never be of what I hate;
But thankful even for hate, that is meant love.
 CAPULET. How now! how now, chop-logic! What is this?
'Proud,' and 'I thank you,' and 'I thank you not;'
And yet 'not proud;' mistress minion, you,
Thank me no thankings, nor proud me no prouds,
But fettle your fine joints 'gainst Thursday next,
To go with Paris to Saint Peter's church,
Or I will drag thee on a hurdle thither.
Out, you green-sickness carrion! out, you baggage!
You tallow face!
 LADY CAPULET. Fie, fie! what, are you mad?
 JULIET. Good father, I beseech you on my knees,
Hear me with patience but to speak a word.
 CAPULET. Hang thee, young baggage! disobedient wretch!
I tell thee what, get thee to church o' Thursday,
Or never after look me in the face.
Speak not, reply not, do not answer me;
My fingers itch.—Wife, we scarce thought us bless'd
That God had lent us but this only child;
But now I see this one is one too much,
And that we have a curse in having her.
Out on her, hilding!
 NURSE.   God in heaven bless her!
You are to blame, my lord, to rate her so.
 CAPULET. And why, my lady wisdom? hold your tongue,
Good prudence; smatter with your gossips, go.
 NURSE. I speak no treason.
 CAPULET.   O! God ye good den.
 NURSE. May not one speak?
 CAPULET.   Peace, you mumbling fool,
Utter your gravity o'er a gossip's bowl;

For here we need it not.

    LADY CAPULET.   You are too hot.

    CAPULET. God's bread! it makes me mad.

Day, night, hour, tide, time, work, play,
Alone, in company, still my care hath been
To have her match'd; and having now provided
A gentleman of noble parentage,
Of fair demesnes, youthful, and nobly train'd,
Stuff'd, as they say, with honourable parts,
Proportion'd as one's thought would wish a man;
And then to have a wretched puling fool,
A whining mammet, in her fortune's tender,
To answer 'I'll not wed,' 'I cannot love,'
'I am too young,' 'I pray you, pardon me;'
But, an you will not wed, I'll pardon you:
Graze where you will, you shall not house with me:
Look to't, think on't, I do not use to jest.
Thursday is near; lay hand on heart, advise.
An you be mine, I'll give you to my friend;
An you be not, hang, beg, starve, die in the streets,
For, by my soul, I'll ne'er acknowledge thee,
Nor what is mine shall never do thee good.
Trust to't, bethink you; I'll not be forsworn.   [*Exit.*

    JULIET. Is there no pity sitting in the clouds,
That sees into the bottom of my grief?
O! sweet my mother, cast me not away:
Delay this marriage for a month, a week;
Or, if you do not, make the bridal bed
In that dim monument where Tybalt lies.

    LADY CAPULET. Talk not to me, for I'll not speak a word.
Do as thou wilt, for I have done with thee.   [*Exit.*

    JULIET. O God! O nurse! how shall this be prevented?
My husband is on earth, my faith in heaven;
How shall that faith return again to earth,
Unless that husband send it me from heaven
By leaving earth? comfort me, counsel me.
Alack, alack! that heaven should practise stratagems

Susan Shentall as Juliet from The Rank Organisation presentation *Romeo and Juliet*, filmed in Verona, Italy. The film won a premier award at the Venice Film Festival.

Upon so soft a subject as myself!
What sayst thou? hast thou not a word of joy?
Some comfort, nurse?

    NURSE.   Faith, here it is. Romeo
Is banished; and all the world to nothing
That he dares ne'er come back to challenge you;
Or, if he do, it needs must be by stealth.
Then, since the case so stands as now it doth,
I think it best you married with the county.
O! he's a lovely gentleman;
Romeo's a dishclout to him: an eagle, madam,
Hath not so green, so quick, so fair an eye
As Paris hath. Beshrew my very heart,
I think you are happy in this second match,
For it excells your first: or if it did not,
Your first is dead; or 'twere as good he were,
As living here and you no use of him.

    JULIET. Speakest thou from thy heart?

    NURSE.   And from my soul too;
Or else beshrew them both.

    JULIET.   Amen!

    NURSE.   What!

    JULIET. Well, thou hast comforted me marvellous much.
Go in; and tell my lady I am gone,
Having displeas'd my father, to Laurence' cell,
To make confession and to be absolv'd.

    NURSE. Marry, I will; and this is wisely done.   [*Exit.*

    JULIET. Ancient damnation! O most wicked fiend!
Is it more sin to wish me thus forsworn,
Or to dispraise my lord with that same tongue
Which she hath prais'd him with above compare
So many thousand times? Go, counsellor;
Thou and my bosom henceforth shall be twain.
I'll to the friar, to know his remedy:
If all else fail, myself have power to die.   [*Exit.*

Act 4

Scene I. Verona. Friar Laurence's Cell

Enter FRIAR LAURENCE *and* PARIS.

FRIAR LAURENCE. On Thursday, sir? the time is very short.

PARIS. My father Capulet will have it so;
And I am nothing slow to slack his haste.

FRIAR LAURENCE. You say you do not know the lady's mind:
Uneven is the course, I like it not.

PARIS. Immoderately she weeps for Tybalt's death,
And therefore have I little talk'd of love;
For Venus smiles not in a house of tears.
Now, sir, her father counts it dangerous
That she doth give her sorrow so much sway,
And in his wisdom hastes our marriage
To stop the inundation of her tears;
Which, too much minded by herself alone,
May be put from her by society.
Now do you know the reason of this haste.

FRIAR LAURENCE. [*Aside.*] I would I knew not why it should
      be slow'd.
Look, sir, here comes the lady towards my cell.

Enter JULIET.

PARIS. Happily met, my lady and my wife!

JULIET. That may be, sir, when I may be a wife.

PARIS. That may be must be, love, on Thursday next.

JULIET. What must be shall be.

FRIAR LAURENCE.   That's a certain text.

76

PARIS. Come you to make confession to this father?

JULIET. To answer that, I should confess to you.

PARIS. Do not deny to him that you love me.

JULIET. I will confess to you that I love him.

PARIS. So will ye, I am sure, that you love me.

JULIET. If I do so, it will be of more price,
Being spoke behind your back, than to your face.

PARIS. Poor soul, thy face is much abus'd with tears.

JULIET. The tears have got small victory by that;
For it was bad enough before their spite.

PARIS. Thou wrong'st it, more than tears, with that report.

JULIET. That is no slander, sir, which is a truth;
And what I spake, I spake it to my face.

PARIS. Thy face is mine, and thou hast slander'd it.

JULIET. It may be so, for it is not mine own.
Are you at leisure, holy father, now;
Or shall I come to you at evening mass?

FRIAR LAURENCE. My leisure serves me, pensive daughter,
now:
My lord, we must entreat the time alone.

PARIS. God shield, I should disturb devotion!
Juliet, on Thursday early will I rouse you:
Till then, adieu; and keep this holy kiss.   [Exit.

JULIET. O! shut the door! and when thou hast done so,
Come weep with me; past hope, past cure, past help!

FRIAR LAURENCE. Ah! Juliet, I already know thy grief;
It strains me past the compass of my wits:
I hear thou must, and nothing may prorogue it,
On Thursday next be married to this county.

JULIET. Tell me not, friar, that thou hear'st of this,
Unless thou tell me how I may prevent it:
If, in thy wisdom, thou canst give no help,
Do thou but call my resolution wise,
And with this knife I'll help it presently.
God join'd my heart and Romeo's, thou our hands;
And ere this hand, by thee to Romeo seal'd,
Shall be the label to another deed,

Or my true heart with treacherous revolt
Turn to another, this shall slay them both.
Therefore, out of thy long-experienc'd time,
Give me some present counsel; or behold,
'Twixt my extremes and me this bloody knife
Shall play the umpire, arbitrating that
Which the commission of thy years and art
Could to no issue of true honour bring.
Be not so long to speak; I long to die,
If what thou speak'st speak not of remedy.

    FRIAR LAURENCE. Hold, daughter; I do spy a kind of hope,
Which craves as desperate an execution
As that is desperate which we would prevent.
If, rather than to marry County Paris,
Thou hast the strength of will to slay thyself,
Then is it likely thou wilt undertake
A thing like death to chide away this shame.
That cop'st with death himself to 'scape from it;
And, if thou dar'st, I'll give thee remedy.

    JULIET. O! bid me leap, rather than marry Paris,
From off the battlements of yonder tower;
Or walk in thievish ways; or bid me lurk
Where serpents are; chain me with roaring bears;
Or shut me nightly in a charnel-house,
O'er-cover'd quite with dead men's rattling bones,
With reeky shanks, and yellow chapless skulls;
Or bid me go into a new-made grave
And hide me with a dead man in his shroud;
Things that, to hear them told, have made me tremble;
And I will do it without fear or doubt,
To live an unstain'd wife to my sweet love.

    FRIAR LAURENCE. Hold, then; go home, be merry, give consent
To marry Paris: Wednesday is to-morrow:
To-morrow night look that thou lie alone,
Let not thy nurse lie with thee in thy chamber:
Take thou this vial, being then in bed,
And this distilled liquor drink thou off;

When presently through all thy veins shall run
A cold and drowsy humour, for no pulse
Shall keep his native progress, but surcease;
No warmth, no breath, shall testify thou liv'st;
The roses in thy lips and cheeks shall fade
To paly ashes; thy eyes' windows fall,
Like death, when he shuts up the day of life;
Each part, depriv'd of supple government,
Shall, stiff and stark and cold, appear like death;
And in this borrow'd likeness of shrunk death
Thou shalt continue two-and-forty hours,
And then awake as from a pleasant sleep.
Now, when the bridegroom in the morning comes
To rouse thee from thy bed, there art thou dead:
Then—as the manner of our country is—
In thy best robes uncover'd on the bier,
Thou shalt be borne to that same ancient vault
Where all the kindred of the Capulets lie.
In the mean time, against thou shalt awake,
Shall Romeo by my letters know our drift,
And hither shall he come; and he and I
Will watch thy waking, and that very night
Shall Romeo bear thee hence to Mantua.
And this shall free thee from this present shame;
If no unconstant toy, nor womanish fear,
Abate thy valour in the acting it.

    JULIET. Give me, give me! O! tell me not of fear!

    FRIAR LAURENCE. Hold; get you gone, be strong and prosper-
ous
In this resolve. I'll send a friar with speed
To Mantua, with my letters to thy lord.

    JULIET. Love, give me strength! and strength shall help afford.
Farewell, dear father!   *[Exeunt.*

Scene II.   The Same. Hall in Capulet's House

Enter CAPULET, LADY CAPULET, NURSE, *and* SERVINGMEN.

CAPULET. So many guests invite as here are writ.

[Exit SERVANT.

Sirrah, go hire me twenty cunning cooks.

SECOND SERVANT. You shall have none ill, sir; for I'll try if they
can lick their fingers.

CAPULET. How canst thou try them so?

SECOND SERVANT. Marry, sir, 'tis an ill cook that cannot lick
his own fingers: therefore he that cannot lick his fingers goes not
with me.

CAPULET. Go, be gone.   *[Exit* SECOND SERVANT.

We shall be much unfurnish'd for this time.

What! is my daughter gone to Friar Laurence?

NURSE. Ay, forsooth.

CAPULET. Well, he may chance to do some good on her:
A peevish self-will'd harlotry it is.

NURSE. See where she comes from shrift with merry look.

Enter JULIET.

CAPULET. How now, my headstrong! where have you been
gadding?

JULIET. Where I have learn'd me to repent the sin
Of disobedient opposition
To you and your behests; and am enjoin'd
By holy Laurence to fall prostrate here,
And beg your pardon. Pardon, I beseech you!
Henceforward I am ever rul'd by you.

CAPULET. Send for the county; go tell him of this:
I'll have this knot knit up to-morrow morning.

JULIET. I met the youthful lord at Laurence' cell;
And gave him what becomed love I might,
Not stepping o'er the bounds of modesty.

CAPULET. Why, I'm glad on't; this is well: stand up:
This is as't should be. Let me see the county;

Ay, marry, go, I say, and fetch him hither.
Now, afore God! this reverend holy friar,
All our whole city is much bound to him.
    JULIET. Nurse, will you go with me into my closet,
To help me sort such needful ornaments
As you think fit to furnish me to-morrow?
    LADY CAPULET. No, not till Thursday; there is time enough.
    CAPULET. Go, nurse, go with her. We'll to church to-morrow.
                          [Exeunt JULIET *and* NURSE.
    LADY CAPULET. We shall be short in our provision:
'Tis now near night.
    CAPULET.   Tush! I will stir about,
And all things shall be well, I warrant thee, wife:
Go thou to Juliet, help to deck up her;
I'll not to bed to-night; let me alone;
I'll play the housewife for this once. What, ho!
They are all forth: well, I will walk myself
To County Paris, to prepare him up
Against to-morrow. My heart is wondrous light,
Since this same wayward girl is so reclaim'd.   *[Exeunt.*

Scene III. *The Same. Juliet's Chamber*

    Enter JULIET *and* NURSE.

    JULIET. Ay, those attires are best; but, gentle nurse,
I pray thee, leave me to myself to-night;
For I have need of many orisons
To move the heavens to smile upon my state,
Which, well thou know'st, is cross and full of sin.

    Enter LADY CAPULET.

    LADY CAPULET. What! are you busy, ho? need you my help?
    JULIET. No, madam; we have cull'd such necessaries
As are behoveful for our state to-morrow:
So please you, let me now be left alone,
And let the nurse this night sit up with you;

For I am sure, you have your hands full all
In this so sudden business.

    LADY CAPULET.   Good-night:
Get thee to bed, and rest; for thou hast need.

                        [Exeunt LADY CAPULET *and* NURSE.

    JULIET. Farewell! God knows when we shall meet again.
I have a faint cold fear thrills through my veins,
That almost freezes up the heat of life:
I'll call them back again to comfort me:
Nurse! What should she do here?
My dismal scene I needs must act alone.
Come, vial.
What if this mixture do not work at all?
Shall I be married then to-morrow morning?
No, no; this shall forbid it: lie thou there.

                        [Laying down a dagger.

What if it be a poison, which the friar
Subtly hath minister'd to have me dead,
Lest in this marriage he should be dishonour'd
Because he married me before to Romeo?
I fear it is: and yet, methinks, it should not,
For he hath still been tried a holy man.
I will not entertain so bad a thought.
How if, when I am laid into the tomb,
I wake before the time that Romeo
Come to redeem me? there's a fearful point!
Shall I not then be stifled in the vault,
To whose foul mouth no healthsome air breathes in,
And there die strangled ere my Romeo comes?
Or, if I live, is it not very like,
The horrible conceit of death and night,
Together with the terror of the place,
As in a vault, an ancient receptacle,
Where, for these many hundred years, the bones
Of all my buried ancestors are pack'd;
Where bloody Tybalt, yet but green in earth,
Lies festering in his shroud; where, as they say,

At some hours in the night spirits resort:
Alack, alack! is it not like that I,
So early waking, what with loathsome smells,
And shrieks like mandrakes' torn out of the earth,
That living mortals, hearing them, run mad:
O! if I wake, shall I not be distraught,
Environed with all these hideous fears,
And madly play with my forefathers' joints,
And pluck the mangled Tybalt from his shroud?
And, in this rage, with some great kinsman's bone,
As with a club, dash out my desperate brains?
O, look! methinks I see my cousin's ghost
Seeking out Romeo, that did spit his body
Upon a rapier's point. Stay, Tybalt, stay!
Romeo, I come! this do I drink to thee.

> [*She falls upon her bed within the curtains.*

Scene IV. *The Same. Hall in Capulet's House*

Enter LADY CAPULET *and* NURSE.

LADY CAPULET. Hold, take these keys, and fetch more spices,
  nurse.
NURSE. They call for dates and quinces in the pastry.

Enter CAPULET.

CAPULET. Come, stir, stir, stir! the second cock hath crow'd,
The curfew bell hath rung, 'tis three o'clock:
Look to the bak'd meats, good Angelica:
Spare not for cost.
NURSE.   Go, go you cot-quean, go;
Get you to bed; faith, you'll be sick to-morrow
For this night's watching.
CAPULET.   No, not a whit; what! I have watch'd ere now
All night for lesser cause, and ne'er been sick.
LADY CAPULET. Ay, you have been a mouse-hunt in your time;
But I will watch you from such watching now.

> [*Exeunt* LADY CAPULET *and* NURSE.

CAPULET. A jealous-hood, a jealous-hood!

Enter three or four SERVINGMEN, *with spits, logs, and baskets.*

Now, fellow,
What's there?

FIRST SERVINGMAN. Things for the cook, sir; but I know not
what.

CAPULET. Make haste, make haste.   [*Exit first* SERVINGMAN.
Sirrah, fetch drier logs:
Call Peter, he will show thee where they are.

SECOND SERVINGMAN. I have a head, sir, that will find out logs,
And never trouble Peter for the matter.   [*Exit.*

CAPULET. Mass, and well said; a merry whoreson, ha!
Thou shalt be logger-head. Good faith! 'tis day:
The county will be here with music straight,
For so he said he would. [*Music within.*] I hear him near.
Nurse! Wife! what, ho! What, nurse, I say!

Re-enter NURSE.

Go waken Juliet, go and trim her up;
I'll go and chat with Paris. Hie, make haste,
Make haste; the bridegroom he is come already:
Make haste, I say.   [*Exeunt.*

Scene V. *The Same. Juliet's Chamber*

Enter NURSE.

NURSE. Mistress! what, mistress! Juliet! fast, I warrant her,
she:
Why, lamb! why, lady! fie, you slug-a-bed!
Why, love, I say! madam! sweet-heart! why, bride
What! not a word? you take your pennyworths now:
Sleep for a week; for the next night, I warrant,
The County Paris hath set up his rest,
That you shall rest but little. God forgive me,
Marry, and amen, how sound is she asleep!

I needs must wake her. Madam, madam, madam!
Ay, let the county take you in your bed;
He'll fright you up, i' faith. Will it not be?
What, dress'd! and in your clothes! and down again!
I must needs wake you. Lady! lady! lady!
Alas! alas! Help! help! my lady's dead!
O! well-a-day, that ever I was born.
Some *aqua-vitæ*, ho! My lord! my lady!

Enter LADY CAPULET.

LADY CAPULET. What noise is here?
NURSE.   O lamentable day!
LADY CAPULET. What is the matter?
NURSE.   Look, look! O heavy day!
LADY CAPULET. O me, O me! my child, my only life,
Revive, look up, or I will die with thee!
Help, help! Call help.

Enter CAPULET.

CAPULET. For shame! bring Juliet forth; her lord is come.
NURSE. She's dead, deceas'd, she's dead; alack the day!
LADY CAPULET. Alack the day! she's dead, she's dead! she's
    dead!
CAPULET. Ha! let me see her. Out, alas! she's cold;
Her blood is settled, and her joints are stiff;
Life and these lips have long been separated:
Death lies on her like an untimely frost
Upon the sweetest flower of all the field.
NURSE. O lamentable day!
LADY CAPULET.   O woeful time!
CAPULET. Death, that hath ta'en her hence to make me wail,
Ties up my tongue, and will not let me speak.

Enter FRIAR LAURENCE, *and* PARIS, *with* MUSICIANS.

FRIAR LAURENCE. Come, is the bride ready to go to church?
CAPULET. Ready to go, but never to return.
O son! the night before thy wedding-day

Hath Death lain with thy wife. There she lies,
Flower as she was, deflowered by him.
Death is my son-in-law, Death is my heir;
My daughter he hath wedded: I will die,
And leave him all; life, living, all is Death's!
    PARIS. Have I thought long to see this morning's face,
And doth it give me such a sight as this?
    LADY CAPULET. Accurs'd, unhappy, wretched, hateful day!
Most miserable hour, that e'er time saw
In lasting labour of his pilgrimage!
But one, poor one, one poor and loving child,
But one thing to rejoice and solace in,
And cruel death hath catch'd it from my sight!
    NURSE. O woe! O woeful, woeful, woeful day!
Most lamentable day, most woeful day,
That ever, ever, I did yet behold!
O day! O day! O day! O hateful day!
Never was seen so black a day as this:
O woeful day, O woeful day!
    PARIS. Beguil'd, divorced, wronged, spited, slain!
Most detestable death, by thee beguil'd,
By cruel cruel thee quite overthrown!
O love! O life! not life, but love in death!
    CAPULET. Despis'd, distressed, hated, martyr'd, kill'd!
Uncomfortable time, why cam'st thou now
To murder, murder our solemnity?
O child! O child! my soul, and not my child!
Dead art thou! dead! alack, my child is dead;
And with my child my joys are buried!
    FRIAR LAURENCE. Peace, ho! for shame! confusion's cure lives
      not
In these confusions. Heaven and yourself
Had part in this fair maid; now heaven hath all,
And all the better is it for the maid:
Your part in her you could not keep from death,
But heaven keeps his part in eternal life.
The most you sought was her promotion,

For 'twas your heaven she should be advanc'd;
And weep ye now, seeing she is advanc'd
Above the clouds, as high as heaven itself?
O! in this love, you love your child so ill,
That you run mad, seeing that she is well:
She's not well married that lives married long;
But she's best married that dies married young.
Dry up your tears, and stick your rosemary
On this fair corse; and, as the custom is,
In all her best array bear her to church;
For though fond nature bids us all lament,
Yet nature's tears are reason's merriment.

    CAPULET. All things that we ordained festival,
Turn from their office to black funeral;
Our instruments to melancholy bells,
Our wedding cheer to a sad burial feast,
Our solemn hymns to sullen dirges change,
Our bridal flowers serve for a buried corse,
And all things change them to the contrary.

    FRIAR LAURENCE. Sir, go you in; and, madam, go with him;
And go, Sir Paris; every one prepare
To follow this fair corse into her grave.
The heavens do lower upon you for some ill;
Move them no more by crossing their high will.

              [*Exeunt* CAPULET, LADY CAPULET, PARIS, *and* FRIAR.

    FIRST MUSICIAN. Faith, we may put up our pipes, and be gone.

    NURSE. Honest good fellows, ah! put up, put up, for, well you
know, this is a pitiful case.   [*Exit.*

    FIRST MUSICIAN. Ay, by my troth, the case may be amended.

    Enter PETER.

    PETER. Musicians! O! musicians, 'Heart's ease, Heart's ease:'
O! an ye will have me live, play 'Heart's ease.'

    FIRST MUSICIAN. Why 'Heart's ease?'

    PETER. O! musicians, because my heart itself plays 'My heart is
full of woe;' O! play me some merry dump, to comfort me.

    SECOND MUSICIAN. Not a dump we; 'tis no time to play now.

PETER. You will not then?

MUSICIANS. No.

PETER. I will then give it you soundly.

FIRST MUSICIAN. What will you give us?

PETER. No money, on my faith! but the gleek; I will give you the minstrel.

FIRST MUSICIAN. Then will I give you the serving-creature.

PETER. Then will I lay the serving-creature's dagger on your pate, I will carry no crotchets: I'll *re* you, I'll *fa* you. Do you note me?

FIRST MUSICIAN. An you *re* us, and *fa* us, you note us.

SECOND MUSICIAN. Pray you, put up your dagger, and put out your wit.

PETER. Then have at you with my wit! I will dry-beat you with an iron wit, and put up my iron dagger. Answer me like men:

> When griping grief the heart doth wound,
> And doleful dumps the mind oppress,
> Then music with her silver sound—

Why 'silver sound?' why 'music with her silver sound?' What say you, Simon Catling?

FIRST MUSICIAN. Marry, sir, because silver hath a sweet sound.

PETER. Pretty! What say you, Hugh Rebeck?

SECOND MUSICIAN. I say 'silver sound,' because musicians sound for silver.

PETER. Pretty too! What say you, James Soundpost?

THIRD MUSICIAN. Faith, I know not what to say.

PETER. O! I cry you mercy; you are the singer: I will say for you. It is, 'music with her silver sound,' because musicians have no gold for sounding:

> Then music with her silver sound
> With speedy help doth lend redress.

[*Exit.*

FIRST MUSICIAN. What a pestilent knave is this same!

SECOND MUSICIAN. Hang him, Jack! Come, we'll in here; tarry for the mourners, and stay dinner. [*Exeunt.*

Act 5

Scene I. Mantua. A Street

Enter ROMEO.

ROMEO. If I may trust the flattering truth of sleep,
My dreams presage some joyful news at hand:
My bosom's lord sits lightly in his throne;
And all this day an unaccustom'd spirit
Lifts me above the ground with cheerful thoughts.
I dreamt my lady came and found me dead;—
Strange dream, that gives a dead man leave to think,—
And breath'd such life with kisses in my lips,
That I reviv'd, and was an emperor.
Ah me! how sweet is love itself possess'd,
When but love's shadows are so rich in joy!

Enter BALTHASAR, *booted.*

News from Verona! How now, Balthasar?
Dost thou not bring me letters from the friar?
How doth my lady? Is my father well?
How fares my Juliet? That I ask again;
For nothing can be ill if she be well.
BALTHASAR. Then she is well, and nothing can be ill;
Her body sleeps in Capel's monument,
And her immortal part with angels lives.
I saw her laid low in her kindred's vault,
And presently took post to tell it you.
O! pardon me for bringing these ill news,
Since you did leave it for my office, sir.

ROMEO. Is it even so? then I defy you, stars!
Thou know'st my lodging: get me ink and paper,
And hire post-horses; I will hence to-night.

BALTHASAR. I do beseech you, sir, have patience:
Your looks are pale and wild, and do import
Some misadventure.

ROMEO.   Tush, thou art deceiv'd;
Leave me, and do the thing I bid thee do.
Hast thou no letters to me from the friar?

BALTHASAR. No, my good lord.

ROMEO.   No matter; get thee gone,
And hire those horses: I'll be with thee straight.

[*Exit* BALTHASAR.

Well, Juliet, I will lie with thee to-night.
Let's see for means: O mischief! thou art swift
To enter in the thoughts of desperate men.
I do remember an apothecary,
And hereabouts he dwells, which late I noted
In tatter'd weeds, with overwhelming brows,
Culling of simples; meagre were his looks,
Sharp misery had worn him to the bones:
And in his needy shop a tortoise hung,
An alligator stuff'd, and other skins
Of ill-shap'd fishes; and about his shelves
A beggarly account of empty boxes,
Green earthen pots, bladders, and musty seeds,
Remnants of packthread, and old cakes of roses,
Were thinly scatter'd, to make up a show.
Noting this penury, to myself I said
And if a man did need a poison now,
Whose sale is present death in Mantua,
Here lives a caitiff wretch would sell it him.
O! this same thought did but fore-run my need,
And this same needy man must sell it me.
As I remember, this should be the house:
Being holiday, the beggar's shop is shut.
What, ho! apothecary!

Enter APOTHECARY.

APOTHECARY.   Who calls so loud?
ROMEO. Come hither, man. I see that thou art poor;
Hold, there is forty ducats; let me have
A dram of poison, such soon-speeding gear
As will disperse itself through all the veins
That the life-weary taker may fall dead,
And that the trunk may be discharg'd of breath
As violently as hasty powder fir'd
Doth hurry from the fatal cannon's womb.
APOTHECARY. Such mortal drugs I have; but Mantua's law
Is death to any he that utters them.
ROMEO. Art thou so bare, and full of wretchedness,
And fear'st to die? famine is in thy cheeks,
Need and oppression starveth in thine eyes,
Contempt and beggary hang upon thy back;
The world is not thy friend nor the world's law:
The world affords no law to make thee rich;
Then be not poor, but break it, and take this.
APOTHECARY. My poverty, but not my will, consents.
ROMEO. I pay thy poverty, and not thy will.
APOTHECARY. Put this in any liquid thing you will,
And drink it off; and, if you had the strength
Of twenty men, it would dispatch you straight.
ROMEO. There is thy gold, worse poison to men's souls,
Doing more murders in this loathsome world
Than these poor compounds that thou mayst not sell:
I sell thee poison, thou hast sold me none.
Farewell; buy food, and get thyself in flesh.
Come, cordial and not poison, go with me
To Juliet's grave, for there must I use thee.   [*Exeunt.*

Scene II. Verona. Friar Laurence's Cell

Enter FRIAR JOHN.

FRIAR JOHN. Holy Franciscan friar! brother, ho!

Enter FRIAR LAURENCE.

FRIAR LAURENCE. This same should be the voice of Friar John.
Welcome from Mantua: what says Romeo?
Or, if his mind be writ, give me his letter.

FRIAR JOHN. Going to find a bare-foot brother out,
One of our order, to associate me,
Here in this city visiting the sick,
And finding him, the searchers of the town,
Suspecting that we both were in a house
Where the infectious pestilence did reign,
Seal'd up the doors, and would not let us forth;
So that my speed to Mantua there was stay'd.

FRIAR LAURENCE. Who bare my letter then to Romeo?

FRIAR JOHN. I could not send it, here it is again,
Nor get a messenger to bring it thee,
So fearful were they of infection.

FRIAR LAURENCE. Unhappy fortune! by my brotherhood
The letter was not nice, but full of charge
Of dear import; and the neglecting it
May do much danger. Friar John, go hence;
Get me an iron crow, and bring it straight
Unto my cell.

FRIAR JOHN. Brother, I'll go and bring it thee.   [*Exit.*

FRIAR LAURENCE. Now must I to the monument alone;
Within these three hours will fair Juliet wake:
She will beshrew me much that Romeo
Hath had no notice of these accidents;
But I will write again to Mantua,
And keep her at my cell till Romeo come:
Poor living corse, clos'd in a dead man's tomb!   [*Exit.*

Scene III. The Same. A Churchyard; in it a Monument belonging to the Capulets

Enter PARIS, *and his* PAGE, *bearing flowers and a torch.*

PARIS. Give me thy torch, boy: hence, and stand aloof;
Yet put it out, for I would not be seen.
Under yond yew-trees lay thee all along,
Holding thine ear close to the hollow ground:
So shall no foot upon the churchyard tread,
Being loose, unfirm with digging up the graves,
But thou shalt hear it: whistle then to me,
As signal that thou hear'st something approach.
Give me those flowers. Do as I bid thee; go.
 PAGE. [*Aside.*] I am almost afraid to stand alone
Here in the churchyard; yet I will adventure.   [*Retires.*
 PARIS. Sweet flower, with flowers thy bridal bed I strew,
 O woe! thy canopy is dust and stones;
Which with sweet water nightly I will dew,
 Or, wanting that, with tears distill'd by moans:
The obsequies that I for thee will keep
Nightly shall be to strew thy grave and weep.
        [*The* PAGE *whistles.*
The boy gives warning something doth approach.
What cursed foot wanders this way to-night,
To cross my obsequies and true love's rite?
What! with a torch?—muffle me, night, awhile.   [*Retires.*

Enter ROMEO *and* BALTHASAR, *with a torch, mattock, &c.*

ROMEO. Give me that mattock, and the wrenching iron.
Hold, take this letter; early in the morning
See thou deliver it to my lord and father.
Give me the light: upon thy life I charge thee,
Whate'er thou hear'st or seest, stand all aloof,
And do not interrupt me in my course.
Why I descend into this bed of death,

Is partly, to behold my lady's face;
But chiefly to take thence from her dead finger
A precious ring, a ring that I must use
In dear employment: therefore hence, be gone:
But, if thou, jealous, dost return to pry
In what I further shall intend to do,
By heaven, I will tear thee joint by joint,
And strew this hungry churchyard with thy limbs.
The time and my intents are savage-wild,
More fierce and more inexorable far
Than empty tigers or the roaring sea.

    BALTHASAR. I will be gone, sir, and not trouble you.

    ROMEO. So shalt thou show me friendship. Take thou that:
Live, and be prosperous; and farewell, good fellow.

    BALTHASAR. [*Aside.*] For all this same, I'll hide me here
      about:
His looks I fear, and his intents I doubt.   [*Retires.*

    ROMEO. Thou detestable maw, thou womb of death,
Gorg'd with the dearest morsel of the earth,
Thus I enforce thy rotten jaws to open,   [*Opens the tomb.*
And, in despite, I'll cram thee with more food!

    PARIS. This is that banish'd haughty Montague,
That murder'd my love's cousin, with which grief
It is supposed the fair creature died;
And here is come to do some villainous shame
To the dead bodies: I will apprehend him.—   [*Comes forward.*
Stop thy unhallow'd toil, vile Montague,
Can vengeance be pursu'd further than death?
Condemned villain, I do apprehend thee:
Obey, and go with me; for thou must die.

    ROMEO. I must, indeed; and therefore came I hither.
Good gentle youth, tempt not a desperate man;
Fly hence and leave me: think upon these gone;
Let them affright thee. I beseech thee, youth,
Put not another sin upon my head
By urging me to fury: O! be gone:
By heaven, I love thee better than myself.

For I come hither arm'd against myself:
Stay not, be gone; live, and hereafter say
A madman's mercy bade thee run away.
 PARIS. I do defy thy conjurations,
And apprehend thee for a felon here.
 ROMEO. Wilt thou provoke me? then have at thee, boy!
              [*They fight.*
 PAGE. O Lord! they fight: I will go call the watch. [*Exit.*
 PARIS. [*Falls.*] O, I am slain!—If thou be merciful,
Open the tomb, lay me with Juliet.   [*Dies.*
 ROMEO. In faith, I will. Let me peruse this face:
Mercutio's kinsman, noble County Paris!
What said my man when my betossed soul
Did not attend him as we rode? I think
He told me Paris should have married Juliet:
Said he not so? or did I dream it so?
Or am I mad, hearing him talk of Juliet,
To think it was so? O! give me thy hand,
One writ with me in sour misfortune's book:
I'll bury thee in a triumphant grave;
A grave? O, no! a lanthorn, slaughter'd youth,
For here lies Juliet, and her beauty makes
This vault a feasting presence full of light.
Death, lie thou there, by a dead man interr'd,
       [*Laying* PARIS *in the tomb.*
How oft when men are at the point of death
Have they been merry! which their keepers call
A lightning before death: O! how may I
Call this a lightning? O my love! my wife!
Death, that hath suck'd the honey of thy breath,
Hath had no power yet upon thy beauty:
Thou art not conquer'd; beauty's ensign yet
Is crimson in thy lips and in thy cheeks,
And death's pale flag is not advanced there.
Tybalt, liest thou there in thy bloody sheet?
O! what more favour can I do to thee,
Than with that hand that cut thy youth in twain

To sunder his that was thine enemy?
Forgive me, cousin! Ah! dear Juliet,
Why art thou yet so fair? Shall I believe
That unsubstantial Death is amorous,
And that the lean abhorred monster keeps
Thee here in dark to be his paramour?
For fear of that I still will stay with thee,
And never from this palace of dim night
Depart again: here, here will I remain
With worms that are thy chambermaids; O! here
Will I set up my everlasting rest,
And shake the yoke of inauspicious stars
From this world-wearied flesh. Eyes, look your last!
Arms, take your last embrace! and, lips, O you
The doors of breath, seal with a righteous kiss
A dateless bargain to engrossing death!
Come, bitter conduct, come, unsavoury guide!
Thou desperate pilot, now at once run on
The dashing rocks thy sea-sick weary bark!
Here's to my love! [*Drinks.*] O true apothecary!
Thy drugs are quick. Thus with a kiss I die.   [*Dies.*

Enter, at the other end of the Churchyard, FRIAR LAURENCE,
with a lanthorn, crow, and spade.

FRIAR LAURENCE. Saint Francis be my speed! how oft to-night
Have my old feet stumbled at graves! Who's there?
BALTHASAR. Here's one, a friend, and one that knows you well.
FRIAR LAURENCE. Bliss be upon you! Tell me, good my friend,
What torch is yond, that vainly lends his light
To grubs and eyeless skulls? as I discern,
It burneth in the Capel's monument.
BALTHASAR. It doth so, holy sir; and there's my master,
One that you love.
FRIAR LAURENCE. Who is it?
BALTHASAR.   Romeo.
FRIAR LAURENCE. How long hath he been there?
BALTHASAR.   Full half an hour.

121482

FRIAR LAURENCE. Go with me to the vault.

BALTHASAR.   I dare not, sir.
My masters knows not but I am gone hence;
And fearfully did menace me with death
If I did stay to look on his intents.

FRIAR LAURENCE. Stay then, I'll go alone. Fear comes upon
   me;
O! much I fear some ill unlucky thing.

BALTHASAR. As I did sleep under this yew-tree here,
I dreamt my master and another fought,
And that my master slew him.

FRIAR LAURENCE. [*Advances.*] Romeo!
Alack, alack! what blood is this which stains
The stony entrance of this sepulchre?
What mean these masterless and gory swords
To lie discolour'd by this place of peace?   [*Enters the tomb.*
Romeo! O, pale! Who else? what! Paris too?
And steep'd in blood? Ah! what an unkind hour
Is guilty of this lamentable chance.
The lady stirs.   [JULIET *wakes.*

JULIET. O, comfortable friar! where is my lord?
I do remember well where I should be,
And there I am. Where is my Romeo?   [*Noise within.*

FRIAR LAURENCE. I hear some noise. Lady, come from that nest
Of death, contagion, and unnatural sleep:
A greater power than we can contradict
Hath thwarted our intents: come, come away.
Thy husband in thy bosom there lies dead;
And Paris too: come, I'll dispose of thee
Among a sisterhood of holy nuns.
Stay not to question, for the watch is coming;
Come, go, good Juliet.—[*Noise again.*] I dare no longer stay.

JULIET. Go, get thee hence, for I will not away.
                              [*Exit* FRIAR LAURENCE.
What's here? a cup, clos'd in my true love's hand?
Poison, I see, hath been his timeless end.
O churl! drunk all, and left no friendly drop

To help me after! I will kiss thy lips;
Haply, some poison yet doth hang on them,
To make me die with a restorative.   *[Kisses him.*
Thy lips are warm!
    FIRST WATCH. [*Within.*] Lead, boy: which way?
    JULIET. Yea, noise? then I'll be brief. O happy dagger!
                          [Snatching ROMEO's *dagger.*
This is thy sheath; [*Stabs herself.*] there rest, and let me die.
                [Falls on ROMEO's *body and dies.*

    Enter WATCH, *with the* PAGE *of* PARIS.

    PAGE. This is the place; there where the torch doth burn.
    FIRST WATCH. The ground is bloody; search about the church-
    yard.
Go, some of you; whoe'er you find, attach.
                   [Exeunt some of the WATCH.
Pitiful sight! here lies the county slain,
And Juliet bleeding, warm, and newly dead,
Who here hath lain these two days buried.
Go, tell the prince, run to the Capulets,
Raise up the Montagues, some others search:
                   [Exeunt others of the WATCH.
We see the ground whereon these woes do lie;
But the true ground of all these piteous woes
We cannot without circumstance descry.

    Re-enter some of the WATCH, *with* BALTHASAR.

    SECOND WATCH. Here's Romeo's man; we found him in the
    churchyard.
    FIRST WATCH. Hold him in safety, till the prince come hither.

    Re-enter other of the WATCH, *with* FRIAR LAURENCE.

    THIRD WATCH. Here is a friar, that trembles, sighs, and weeps;
We took this mattock and this spade from him,
As he was coming from this churchyard side.
    FIRST WATCH. A great suspicion: stay the friar too.

    Enter the PRINCE *and* ATTENDANTS.

PRINCE. What misadventure is so early up,
That calls our person from our morning's rest?

Enter CAPULET, LADY CAPULET, *and Others.*

CAPULET. What should it be, that they so shriek abroad?
LADY CAPULET. The people in the street cry Romeo,
Some Juliet, and some Paris; and all run
With open outcry toward our monument.
PRINCE. What fear is this which startles in our ears?
FIRST WATCH. Sovereign, here lies the County Paris slain;
And Romeo dead; and Juliet, dead before,
Warm and new kill'd.
PRINCE. Search, seek, and know how this foul murder comes.
FIRST WATCH. Here is a friar, and slaughter'd Romeo's man;
With instruments upon them, fit to open
These dead men's tombs.
CAPULET. O, heaven!—O wife! look how our daughter bleeds!
This dagger hath mista'en!—for, lo, his house
Is empty on the back of Montague—
And is mis-sheathed in my daughter's bosom.
LADY CAPULET. O me! this sight of death is as a bell,
That warns my old age to a sepulchre.

Enter MONTAGUE *and Others.*

PRINCE. Come, Montague: for thou art early up,
To see thy son and heir more early down.
MONTAGUE. Alas! my liege, my wife is dead to-night;
Grief of my son's exile hath stopp'd her breath.
What further woe conspires against mine age?
PRINCE. Look, and thou shalt see.
MONTAGUE. O thou untaught! what manners is in this,
To press before thy father to a grave?
PRINCE. Seal up the mouth of outrage for a while,
Till we can clear these ambiguities,
And know their spring, their head, their true descent;
And then will I be general of your woes,
And lead you even to death: meantime forbear,

And let mischance be slave to patience.
Bring forth the parties of suspicion.

FRIAR LAURENCE. I am the greatest, able to do least,
Yet most suspected, as the time and place
Doth make against me, of this direful murder;
And here I stand, both to impeach and purge
Myself condemned and myself excus'd.

PRINCE. Then say at once what thou dost know in this.

FRIAR LAURENCE. I will be brief, for my short date of breath
Is not so long as is a tedious tale.
Romeo, there dead, was husband to that Juliet;
And she, there dead, that Romeo's faithful wife:
I married them; and their stolen marriage-day
Was Tybalt's doomsday, whose untimely death
Banish'd the new-made bridegroom from this city;
For whom, and not for Tybalt, Juliet pin'd.
You, to remove that siege of grief from her,
Betroth'd, and would have married her perforce,
To County Paris: then comes she to me,
And, with wild looks bid me devise some mean
To rid her from this second marriage,
Or in my cell there would she kill herself.
Then gave I her,—so tutor'd by my art,—
A sleeping potion; which so took effect
As I intended, for it wrought on her
The form of death: meantime I writ to Romeo
That he should hither come as this dire night,
To help to take her from her borrow'd grave,
Being the time the potion's force should cease.
But he which bore my letter, Friar John,
Was stay'd by accident, and yesternight
Return'd my letter back. Then, all alone,
At the prefixed hour of her waking,
Came I to take her from her kindred's vault,
Meaning to keep her closely at my cell,
Till I conveniently could send to Romeo:
But, when I came,—some minute ere the time

Of her awakening,—here untimely lay
The noble Paris and true Romeo dead.
She wakes; and I entreated her come forth,
And bear this work of heaven with patience;
But then a noise did scare me from the tomb,
And she, too desperate, would not go with me,
But, as it seems, did violence on herself.
All this I know; and to the marriage
Her nurse is privy: and, if aught in this
Miscarried by my fault, let my old life
Be sacrific'd, some hour before his time,
Unto the rigour of severest law.

PRINCE. We still have known thee for a holy man.
Where's Romeo's man? what can he say in this?

BALTHASAR. I brought my master news of Juliet's death;
And then in post he came from Mantua
To this same place, to this same monument.
This letter he early bid me give his father,
And threaten'd me with death, going in the vault,
If I departed not and left him there.

PRINCE. Give me the letter; I will look on it.
Where is the county's page that rais'd the watch?
Sirrah, what made your master in this place?

PAGE. He came with flowers to strew his lady's grave,
And bid me stand aloof, and so I did;
Anon, comes one with light to ope the tomb;
And by and by my master drew on him;
And then I ran away to call the watch.

PRINCE. This letter doth make good the friar's words,
Their course of love, the tidings of her death:
And here he writes that he did buy a poison
Of a poor 'pothecary, and therewithal
Came to this vault to die, and lie with Juliet.
Where be these enemies?—Capulet! Montague!
See what a scourge is laid upon your hate,
That heaven finds means to kill your joys with love;
And I, for winking at your discords too,

Have lost a brace of kinsmen: all are punish'd.

CAPULET. O brother Montague! give me thy hand:
This is my daughter's jointure, for no more
Can I demand.

MONTAGUE. But I can give thee more;
For I will raise her statue in pure gold;
That while Verona by that name is known,
There shall no figure at such rate be set
As that of true and faithful Juliet.

CAPULET. As rich shall Romeo by his lady lie;
Poor sacrifices of our enmity!

PRINCE. A glooming peace this morning with it brings;
The sun, for sorrow, will not show his head:
Go hence, to have more talk of these sad things:
Some shall be pardon'd, and some punished:
For never was a story of more woe
Than this of Juliet and her Romeo.   [*Exeunt.*

Othello, the Moor of Venice

INTRODUCTION

Written. 1604 (?)

Published, in quarto, and in the first folio, 1623.

Source of the Plot. The tale appears in *The Hecatomithi* of G. B. Giraldi Cinthio. Shakespeare follows Cinthio in the main; but a few details suggest that he knew the story in an ampler version.

The Fable. Iago, ensign to Othello, the Moor of Venice, is jealous of Cassio, his lieutenant. He plots to oust Cassio from the lieutenancy.

Othello marries Desdemona, and sails with her to the wars in Cyprus. Iago resolves to make use of Desdemona to cause Cassio's downfall.

He procures Cassio's discharge from the lieutenancy by involving him in a drunken brawl. Cassio beseeches Desdemona to intercede with Othello for him. Iago hints to Othello that she has good reason to wish Cassio to be restored. He suggests that Cassio is her lover. Partly by fortune, partly by craft, he succeeds in establishing in Othello's mind the conviction that Desdemona is guilty.

Othello smothers Desdemona, learns, too late, that he has been deceived, and kills himself. Cassio's character is cleared. Iago is led away to torture.

This most skilful work is perhaps the most frequently performed of the plays of Shakespeare's greatest period. Its theme, put briefly, is the working of jealous suspicion in a mean and in a generous mind.

As in the *Merchant of Venice*, the mean mind has been made mean by injustice, supposed injustice or the poisoning of false report, all three powerful causes of vengeful devilry in men. Iago, a seasoned soldier of shrewd intelligence, has been passed over for promotion, and Cassio preferred to him for other than military reasons. The appointment of Cassio seems to have been unwise, but being, presumably, highly connected, his destiny tends to preferment: Iago's tends towards frustration, a consequent bitter brooding, and longing for vengeance.

A groundless suspicion that the Moor has wronged him further, determines him to be revenged upon his employer as well as upon his supplanter. A weak intellect who comes to him for help serves him as a tool. He begins to persuade his employer that the supplanter and the newly-married wife are lovers.

He succeeds in this, through his natural adroitness, the working of chance, and the generosity of Othello, who has too much passion to be anything but blind under passionate influence like love or jealousy. The mean man's want of emotion keeps always the conduct of the vengeance precise and clear. Cassio is disgraced. Roderigo, having been fooled to the top of his bent, is killed. Desdemona is smothered. Othello is ruined.

There is a phrase still sometimes heard: "sinner's luck," suggesting that the Devil will always make sin easy. Certainly Iago has sinner's luck; but of course, he plays a cool game with a hot opponent.

That working of an invisible judge, which we call Chance, "life's justicer," lays the villainy bare at the instant of its perfection. Emilia, Iago's wife, a common nature, with no more intelligence than a want of illusion, enters a moment too late to stay the slaughter, but too soon for Iago's purpose. She is the one person in the play certain to be loyal to Desdemona. She is the one person in the play who, judging from her feelings, will judge rightly. The finest part of the play is that scene in which her passionate instinct sees through the web woven about Othello by an intellect that has put aside all that is passionate and instinctive.

The influence and importance of the little thing in the great

Ann Hathaway's cottage. Shakespeare wooed and won his future bride in this thatch-roofed house.

event is marked in this scene as in half-a-dozen other scenes in the greater tragedies. We are all or may at any time become immensely important to the play of the world. Had Emilia come a minute sooner or a minute later the end of the play would have been very different. Desdemona would have lived to repent her marriage at leisure, or she would have gone to her grave branded.

Perhaps Shakespeare had in lively memory some recent great successes among his fellow-players. He had seen the tense success of the clashes between Brutus and Cassius, and Octavius and Mark Antony. He must have had in his mind the thought of a play of personal intrigue in which a volcanic player like —— would be beset by an icy secret sinister player like —— and wonderful effects would be produced. In his mind, and in the Elizabethan mind, the two men were evenly matched, both equally important to the scene, both familiar characters in Tudor society, and their inter-play the vital theme in the tragedy. Doubtless his first Othello and Iago were picked artists, heads of their profession, the one tremendous, the other terrible. Men went to see them both in a whirl overwhelming.

Modern sentiment is somewhat against Desdemona. There is now much prejudice and some law against mixture of colour in marriage. She is forgiven, if not praised, for getting away from her father, Brabantio, but there is a feeling that having shown this sense, she would and should have shown it further in her causing prompt changes in Othello's staff. In the odd world of the theatre the Ensign's wife, Emilia, seems to have become her maid-servant, or bat-woman.

I have seen various performances of the play; and have moving memories of one Othello; but always the outstanding figure of the play, the one character always superbly and shatteringly played, is that of Emilia. In her honesty and fire, she makes every Desdemona like a doll and every Iago like a husband.

The poetry of Othello is nearly as well known as that of *Hamlet*. Many quotations from the play have passed into the speech of the people. A play of intrigue does not give the fullest opportunity for great poetry; but supreme things are spoken throughout the action. Othello's cry—

> It is the very error of the moon;
> She comes more near the earth than she was wont,
> And makes men mad

is one of the most perfect of all the perfect things in the tragedies.

DRAMATIS PERSONÆ

DUKE OF VENICE
BRABANTIO, a Senator. Other Senators
GRATIANO, Brother to Brabantio
LODOVICO, Kinsman to Brabantio
OTHELLO, a noble Moor; in the service of the Venetian State
CASSIO, his Lieutenant
IAGO, his Ancient
RODERIGO, a Venetian Gentleman
MONTANO, Othello's predecessor in the Government of Cyprus
CLOWN, Servant to Othello
DESDEMONA, Daughter to Brabantio, and Wife to Othello
EMILIA, Wife to Iago
BIANCA, Mistress to Cassio
SAILOR, OFFICERS, GENTLEMEN, MESSENGERS, MUSICIANS, HERALDS,
    ATTENDANTS

SCENE. *For the first Act, in Venice; during the rest of the Play,
at a Sea-port in Cyprus*

109

Act 1

Scene I. Venice. A Street

Enter RODERIGO *and* IAGO.

RODERIGO. Tush! Never tell me; I take it much unkindly
That thou, Iago, who hast had my purse
As if the strings were thine, shouldst know of this.
IAGO. 'Sblood, but you will not hear me:
If ever I did dream of such a matter,
Abhor me.
RODERIGO. Thou told'st me thou didst hold him in thy hate.
IAGO. Despise me if I do not. Three great ones of the city,
In personal suit to make me his lieutenant,
Off-capp'd to him; and, by the faith of man,
I know my price, I am worth no worse a place;
But he, as loving his own pride and purposes,
Evades them, with a bombast circumstance
Horribly stuff'd with epithets of war;
And, in conclusion,
Nonsuits my mediators; for, 'Certes,' says he,
'I have already chose my officer.'
And what was he?
Forsooth, a great arithmetician,
One Michael Cassio, a Florentine,
A fellow almost damn'd in a fair wife;
That never set a squadron in the field,
Nor the division of a battle knows
More than a spinster; unless the bookish theoric,
Wherein the toged consuls can propose

As masterly as he: mere prattle, without practice,
Is all his soldiership. But he, sir, had the election;
And I—of whom his eyes had seen the proof
At Rhodes, at Cyprus, and on other grounds
Christian and heathen—must be be-lee'd and calm'd
By debitor and creditor; this counter-caster,
He, in good time, must his lieutenant be,
And I—God bless the mark!—his Moorship's ancient.

    RODERIGO. By heaven, I rather would have been his hangman.

    IAGO. Why, there's no remedy: 'tis the curse of the service,
Preferment goes by letter and affection,
Not by the old gradation, where each second
Stood heir to the first. Now, sir, be judge yourself,
Whe'r I in any just term am affin'd
To love the Moor.

    RODERIGO.   I would not follow him then.

    IAGO. O! sir, content you;
I follow him to serve my turn upon him;
We cannot all be masters, nor all masters
Cannot be truly follow'd. You shall mark
Many a duteous and knee-crooking knave,
That, doting on his own obsequious bondage,
Wears out his time, much like his master's ass,
For nought but provender, and when he's old, cashier'd;
Whip me such honest knaves. Others there are
Who, trimm'd in forms and visages of duty,
Keep yet their hearts attending on themselves,
And, throwing but shows of service on their lords,
Do well thrive by them, and when they have lin'd their coats
Do themselves homage: these fellows have some soul;
And such a one do I profess myself. For, sir,
It is as sure as you are Roderigo,
Were I the Moor, I would not be Iago:
In following him, I follow but myself;
Heaven is my judge, not I for love and duty,
But seeming so, for my peculiar end:
For when my outward action doth demonstrate

The native act and figure of my heart
In compliment extern, 'tis not long after
But I will wear my heart upon my sleeve
For daws to peck at: I am not what I am.

RODERIGO. What a full fortune does the thick-lips owe,
If he can carry't thus!

IAGO.   Call up her father;
Rouse him, make after him, poison his delight,
Proclaim him in the streets, incense her kinsmen,
And, though he in a fertile climate dwell,
Plague him with flies; though that his joy be joy,
Yet throw such changes of vexation on't
As it may lose some colour.

RODERIGO. Here is her father's house; I'll call aloud.

IAGO. Do; with like timorous accent and dire yell
As when, by night and negligence, the fire
Is spied in populous cities.

RODERIGO. What, ho! Brabantio! Signior Brabantio, ho!

IAGO. Awake! what, ho! Brabantio! thieves! thieves! thieves!
Look to your house, your daughter, and your bags!
Thieves! thieves!

Enter BRABANTIO, *above, at a window.*

BRABANTIO. What is the reason of this terrible summons?
What is the matter there?

RODERIGO. Signior, is all your family within?

IAGO. Are your doors lock'd?

BRABANTIO.   Why? wherefore ask you this?

IAGO. 'Zounds! sir, you're robb'd; for shame, put on your
gown;
Your heart is burst, you have lost half your soul;
Even now, now, very now, an old black ram
Is tupping your white ewe. Arise, arise!
Awake the snorting citizens with the bell,
Or else the devil will make a grandsire of you.
Arise, I say.

BRABANTIO. What! have you lost your wits?

RODERIGO. Most reverend signior, do you know my voice?

BRABANTIO. Not I, what are you?

RODERIGO. My name is Roderigo.

BRABANTIO.   The worser welcome:
I have charg'd thee not to haunt about my doors:
In honest plainness thou hast heard me say
My daughter is not for thee; and now, in madness,
Being full of supper and distempering draughts,
Upon malicious knavery dost thou come
To start my quiet.

RODERIGO. Sir, sir, sir!

BRABANTIO.   But thou must needs be sure
My spirit and my place have in them power
To make this bitter to thee.

RODERIGO.   Patience, good sir.

BRABANTIO. What tell'st thou me of robbing? this is Venice;
My house is not a grange.

RODERIGO.   Most grave Brabantio,
In simple and pure soul I come to you.

IAGO. 'Zounds! sir, you are one of those that will not serve
God if the devil bid you. Because we come to do you service and
you think we are ruffians, you'll have your daughter covered
with a Barbary horse; you'll have your nephews neigh to you;
you'll have coursers for cousins and gennets for germans.

BRABANTIO. What profane wretch art thou?

IAGO. I am one, sir, that comes to tell you, your daughter and
the Moor are now making the beast with two backs.

BRABANTIO. Thou art a villain.

IAGO.   You are—a senator.

BRABANTIO. This thou shalt answer; I know thee, Roderigo.

RODERIGO. Sir, I will answer any thing. But, I beseech you,
If't be your pleasure and most wise consent,—
As partly, I find, it is,—that your fair daughter,
At this odd-even and dull-watch o' the night,
Transported with no worse nor better guard
But with a knave of common hire, a gondolier,
To the gross clasps of a lascivious Moor,—

If this be known to you, and your allowance,
We then have done you bold and saucy wrongs;
But if you know not this, my manners tell me
We have your wrong rebuke. Do not believe,
That, from the sense of all civility,
I thus would play and trifle with your reverence:
Your daughter, if you have not given her leave,
I say again, hath made a gross revolt;
Tying her duty, beauty, wit and fortunes
In an extravagant and wheeling stranger
Of here and every where. Straight satisfy yourself:
If she be in her chamber or your house,
Let loose on me the justice of the state
For thus deluding you.

    BRABANTIO.   Strike on the tinder, ho!
Give me a taper! call up all my people!
This accident is not unlike my dream;
Belief of it oppresses me already.
Light, I say! light!   *[Exit, from above.*

    IAGO.   Farewell, for I must leave you:
It seems not meet nor wholesome to my place
To be produc'd, as, if I stay, I shall,
Against the Moor; for, I do know the state,
However this may gall him with some check,
Cannot with safety cast him; for he's embark'd
With such loud reason to the Cyprus wars,—
Which even now stand in act,—that, for their souls,
Another of his fathom they have none.
To lead their business; in which regard,
Though I do hate him as I do hell-pains,
Yet, for necessity of present life,
I must show out a flag and sign of love,
Which is indeed but sign. That you shall surely find him,
Lead to the Sagittary the raised search;
And there will I be with him. So, farewell.   *[Exit.*

    Enter below, BRABANTIO, *and* SERVANTS *with torches.*

BRABANTIO. It is too true an evil: gone she is,
And what's to come of my despised time
Is nought but bitterness. Now, Roderigo,
Where didst thou see her? O, unhappy girl!
With the Moor, sayst thou? Who would be a father!
How didst thou know 'twas she? O, she deceives me
Past thought. What said she to you? Get more tapers!
Raise all my kindred! Are they married, think you?
    RODERIGO. Truly, I think they are.
    BRABANTIO. O heaven! How got she out? O, treason of the
    blood:
Fathers, from hence trust not your daughters' minds
By what you see them act. Are there not charms
By which the property of youth and maidhood
May be abus'd? Have you not read, Roderigo,
Of some such thing?
    RODERIGO.   Yes, sir, I have indeed.
    BRABANTIO. Call up my brother. O! that you had had her.
Some one way, some another! Do you know
Where we may apprehend her and the Moor?
    RODERIGO. I think I can discover him, if you please
To get good guard and go along with me.
    BRABANTIO. Pray you, lead on. At every house I'll call;
I may command at most. Get weapons, ho!
And raise some special officers of night.
On, good Roderigo; I'll deserve your pains.   [*Exeunt.*

Scene II. *Another Street*

Enter OTHELLO, IAGO, *and* ATTENDANTS, *with torches.*

    IAGO. Though in the trade of war I have slain men,
Yet do I hold it very stuff o' the conscience
To do no contriv'd murder: I lack iniquity
Sometimes to do me service. Nine or ten times
I had thought to have yerk'd him here under the ribs.
    OTHELLO. 'Tis better as it is.

IAGO.   Nay, but he prated,
And spoke such scurvy and provoking terms
Against your honour
That, with the little godliness I have,
I did full hard forbear him. But, I pray, sir,
Are you fast married? Be assur'd of this,
That the magnifico is much belov'd,
And hath in his effect a voice potential
As double as the duke's; he will divorce you,
Or put upon you what restraint and grievance
The law—with all his might to enforce it on—
Will give him cable.

OTHELLO.   Let him do his spite:
My services which I have done the signiory
Shall out-tongue his complaints. 'Tis yet to know,
Which when I know that boasting is an honour
I shall promulgate, I fetch my life and being
From men of royal siege, and my demerits
May speak unbonneted to as proud a fortune
As this that I have reach'd; for know, Iago,
But that I love the gentle Desdemona,
I would not my unhoused free condition
Put into circumscription and confine
For the sea's worth. But, look! what lights come yond?

IAGO. Those are the raised father and his friends:
You were best go in.

OTHELLO.   Not I; I must be found:
My parts, my title, and my perfect soul
Shall manifest me rightly. Is it they?

IAGO. By Janus, I think no.

Enter CASSIO *and certain* OFFICERS, *with torches.*

OTHELLO. The servants of the duke, and my lieutenant.
The goodness of the night upon you, friends!
What is the news?

CASSIO.   The duke does greet you, general,
And he requires your haste-post-haste appearance,

Even on the instant.

OTHELLO.   What is the matter, think you?

CASSIO. Something from Cyprus, as I may divine.
It is a business of some heat; the galleys
Have sent a dozen sequent messengers
This very night at one another's heels,
And many of the consuls, rais'd and met,
Are at the duke's already. You have been hotly call'd for;
When, being not at your lodging to be found,
The senate hath sent about three several quests
To search you out.

OTHELLO.   'Tis well I am found by you.
I will but spend a word here in the house,
And go with you.   [*Exit.*

CASSIO.   Ancient, what makes he here?

IAGO. Faith, he to-night hath boarded a land carrack;
If it prove lawful prize, he's made for ever.

CASSIO. I do not understand.

IAGO.   He's married.

CASSIO.   To who?

    Re-enter OTHELLO.

IAGO. Marry, to—Come, captain, will you go?

OTHELLO.   Have with you.

CASSIO. Here comes another troop to seek for you.

IAGO. It is Brabantio. General, be advis'd;
He comes to bad intent.

    Enter BRABANTIO, RODERIGO, *and* OFFICERS, *with torches and
    weapons.*

OTHELLO.   Holla! stand there!

RODERIGO. Signior, it is the Moor.

BRABANTIO.   Down with him, thief!
             [*They draw on both sides.*

IAGO. You, Roderigo! come sir, I am for you.

OTHELLO. Keep up your bright swords, for the dew will rust
    them.

Good signior, you shall more command with years
Than with your weapons.
    BRABANTIO. O thou foul thief! where hast thou stow'd my
        daughter?
Damn'd as thou art, thou hast enchanted her;
For I'll refer me to all things of sense,
If she in chains of magic were not bound,
Whether a maid so tender, fair, and happy,
So opposite to marriage that she shunn'd
The wealthy curled darlings of our nation,
Would ever have, to incur a general mock,
Run from her guardage to the sooty bosom
Of such a thing as thou; to fear, not to delight.
Judge me the world, if 'tis not gross in sense
That thou hast practis'd on her with foul charms,
Abus'd her delicate youth with drugs or minerals
That weaken motion: I'll have't disputed on;
'Tis probable, and palpable to thinking.
I therefore apprehend and do attach thee
For an abuser of the world, a practiser
Of arts inhibited and out of warrant.
Lay hold upon him: if he do resist,
Subdue him at his peril.
    OTHELLO.   Hold your hands,
Both you of my inclining, and the rest:
Were it my cue to fight, I should have known it
Without a prompter. Where will you that I go
To answer this your charge?
    BRABANTIO.   To prison; till fit time
Of law and course of direct session
Call thee to answer.
    OTHELLO.   What if I do obey?
How may the duke be therewith satisfied,
Whose messengers are here about my side,
Upon some present business of the state
To bring me to him?
    OFFICER.   'Tis true, most worthy signior;

The duke's in council, and your noble self,
I am sure, is sent for.

BRABANTIO.   How! the duke in council!
In this time of the night! Bring him away.
Mine's not an idle cause: the duke himself,
Or any of my brothers of the state,
Cannot but feel this wrong as 'twere their own;
For if such actions may have passage free,
Bond-slaves and pagans shall our statesmen be.   [*Exeunt.*

*Scene III.   A Council Chamber. The Duke and
        Senators sitting at a table.
        Officers attending*

DUKE. There is no composition in these news
That gives them credit.

FIRST SENATOR. Indeed, they are disproportion'd;
My letters say a hundred and seven galleys.

DUKE. And mine, a hundred and forty.

SECOND SENATOR.   And mine, two hundred:
But though they jump not on a just account,—
As in these cases, where the aim reports,
'Tis oft with difference,—yet do they all confirm
A Turkish fleet, and bearing up to Cyprus.

DUKE. Nay, it is possible enough to judgment:
I do not so secure me in the error,
But the main article I do approve
In fearful sense.

SAILOR. [*Within.*] What, ho! what, ho! what, ho!

OFFICER. A messenger from the galleys.

   Enter a SAILOR.

DUKE.   Now, what's the business?

SAILOR. The Turkish preparation makes for Rhodes;
So was I bid report here to the state
By Signior Angelo.

DUKE. How say you by this change?

FIRST SENATOR.   This cannot be,
By no assay of reason; 'tis a pageant
To keep us in false gaze. When we consider
The importancy of Cyprus to the Turk,
And let ourselves again but understand,
That as it more concerns the Turk than Rhodes,
So may he with more facile question bear it,
For that it stands not in such war-like brace,
But altogether lacks the abilities
That Rhodes is dress'd in: if we make thought of this,
We must not think the Turk is so unskilful
To leave that latest which concerns him first,
Neglecting an attempt of ease and gain,
To wake and wage a danger profitless.
    DUKE. Nay, in all confidence, he's not for Rhodes.
    OFFICER. Here is more news.

        Enter a MESSENGER.

    MESSENGER. The Ottomites, reverend and gracious,
Steering with due course toward the isle of Rhodes,
Have there injointed them with an after fleet.
    FIRST SENATOR. Ay, so I thought. How many, as you guess?
    MESSENGER. Of thirty sail; and now they do re-stem
Their backward course, bearing with frank appearance
Their purposes toward Cyprus. Signior Montano,
Your trusty and most valiant servitor,
With his free duty recommends you thus,
And prays you to believe him.
    DUKE. 'Tis certain then, for Cyprus.
Marcus Luccicos, is not he in town?
    FIRST SENATOR. He's now in Florence.
    DUKE. Write from us to him; post-post-haste dispatch.
    FIRST SENATOR. Here comes Brabantio and the valiant Moor.

        Enter BRABANTIO, OTHELLO, IAGO, RODERIGO, *and* OFFICERS.

    DUKE. Valiant Othello, we must straight employ you
Against the general enemy Ottoman.

[*To* BRABANTIO.] I did not see you; welcome, gentle signior;
We lack'd your counsel and your help to-night.

BRABANTIO. So did I yours. Good your grace, pardon me;
Neither my place nor aught I heard of business
Hath rais'd me from my bed, nor doth the general care
Take hold of me, for my particular grief
Is of so flood-gate and o'erbearing nature
That it engluts and swallows other sorrows
And it is still itself.

DUKE.   Why, what's the matter?

BRABANTIO. My daughter! O! my daughter.

DUKE.   ⎫
SENATORS. ⎬   Dead?

BRABANTIO.   Ay, to me;
She is abus'd, stol'n from me, and corrupted
By spells and medicines bought of mountebanks;
For nature so preposterously to err,
Being not deficient, blind, or lame of sense,
Sans witchcraft could not.

DUKE. Whoe'er he be that in this foul proceeding
Hath thus beguil'd your daughter of herself
And you of her, the bloody book of law
You shall yourself read in the bitter letter
After your own sense; yea, though our proper son
Stood in your action.

BRABANTIO.   Humbly I thank your Grace.
Here is the man, this Moor; whom now, it seems,
Your special mandate for the state affairs,
Hath hither brought.

DUKE.   ⎫
SENATORS. ⎬   We are very sorry for it.

DUKE. [*To* OTHELLO.] What, in your own part, can you say to
    this?

BRABANTIO. Nothing, but this is so.

OTHELLO. Most potent, grave, and reverend signiors,
My very noble and approv'd good masters,
That I have ta'en away this old man's daughter,

It is most true; true, I have married her:
The very head and front of my offending
Hath this extent, no more. Rude am I in my speech.
And little bless'd with the soft phrase of peace;
For since these arms of mine had seven years' pith,
Till now some nine moons wasted, they have us'd
Their dearest action in the tented field;
And little of this great world can I speak,
More than pertains to feats of broil and battle;
And therefore little shall I grace my cause
In speaking for myself. Yet, by your gracious patience,
I will a round unvarnish'd tale deliver
Of my whole course of love; what drugs, what charms,
What conjuration, and what mighty magic,
For such proceeding I am charg'd withal,
I won his daughter.

    BRABANTIO.   A maiden never bold;
Of spirit so still and quiet, that her motion
Blush'd at herself; and she, in spite of nature,
Of years, of country, credit, every thing,
To fall in love with what she fear'd to look on!
It is a judgment maim'd and most imperfect
That will confess perfection so could err
Against all rules of nature, and must be driven
To find out practices of cunning hell,
Why this should be. I therefore vouch again
That with some mixtures powerful o'er the blood,
Or with some dram conjur'd to this effect,
He wrought upon her.

    DUKE.   To vouch this, is no proof,
Without more certain and more overt test
Than these thin habits and poor likelihoods
Of modern seeming do prefer against him.

    FIRST SENATOR. But, Othello, speak:
Did you by indirect and forced courses
Subdue and poison this young maid's affections;
Or came it by request and such fair question

As soul to soul affordeth?

OTHELLO.   I do beseech you,
Send for the lady to the Sagittary,
And let her speak of me before her father:
If you do find me foul in her report,
The trust, the office I do hold of you,
Not only take away, but let your sentence
Even fall upon my life.

DUKE.   Fetch Desdemona hither.

OTHELLO. Ancient, conduct them; you best know the place.

                              [*Exeunt* IAGO *and* ATTENDANTS.

And, till she come, as truly as to heaven
I do confess the vices of my blood,
So justly to your grave ears I'll present
How I did thrive in this fair lady's love,
And she in mine.

DUKE. Say it, Othello.

OTHELLO. Her father lov'd me; oft invited me,
Still question'd me the story of my life
From year to year, the battles, sieges, fortunes
That I have pass'd.
I ran it through, even from my boyish days
To the very moment that he bade me tell it;
Wherein I spake of most disastrous chances,
Of moving accidents by flood and field,
Of hair-breadth 'scapes i' the imminent deadly breach,
Of being taken by the insolent foe
And sold to slavery, of my redemption thence
And portance in my travel's history;
Wherein of antres vast and desarts idle,
Rough quarries, rocks and hills whose heads touch heaven,
It was my hint to speak, such was the process;
And of the Cannibals that each other eat,
The Anthropophagi, and men whose heads
Do grow beneath their shoulders. This to hear
Would Desdemona seriously incline;
But still the house-affairs would draw her thence;

Which ever as she could with haste dispatch,
She'd come again, and with a greedy ear
Devour up my discourse. Which I observing,
Took once a pliant hour, and found good means
To draw from her a prayer of earnest heart
That I would all my pilgrimage dilate,
Whereof by parcels she had something heard,
But not intentively: I did consent;
And often did beguile her of her tears,
When I did speak of some distressful stroke
That my youth suffer'd. My story being done,
She gave me for my pains a world of sighs:
She swore, in faith, 'twas strange, 'twas passing strange;
'Twas pitiful, 'twas wondrous pitiful:
She wish'd she had not heard it, yet she wish'd
That heaven had made her such a man; she thank'd me,
And bade me, if I had a friend that lov'd her,
I should but teach him how to tell my story,
And that would woo her. Upon this hint I spake:
She lov'd me for the dangers I had pass'd,
And I lov'd her that she did pity them.
This only is the witchcraft I have us'd:
Here comes the lady; let her witness it.

Enter DESDEMONA, IAGO, *and* ATTENDANTS.

DUKE. I think this tale would win my daughter too.
Good Brabantio,
Take up this mangled matter at the best;
Men do their broken weapons rather use
Than their bare hands.

BRABANTIO.   I pray you, hear her speak:
If she confess that she was half the wooer,
Destruction on my head, if my bad blame
Light on the man! Come hither, gentle mistress:
Do you perceive in all this noble company
Where most you owe obedience?

DESDEMONA.   My noble father,

I do perceive here a divided duty:
To you I am bound for life and education;
My life and education both do learn me
How to respect you; you are the lord of duty,
I am hitherto your daughter: but here's my husband;
And so much duty as my mother show'd
To you, preferring you before her father,
So much I challenge that I may profess
Due to the Moor my lord.

BRABANTIO.   God be with you! I have done.
Please it your Grace, on to the state affairs:
I had rather to adopt a child than get it.
Come hither, Moor:
I here do give thee that with all my heart
Which, but thou has already, with all my heart
I would keep from thee. For your sake, jewel,
I am glad at soul I have no other child;
For thy escape would teach me tyranny,
To hang clogs on them. I have done, my lord.

DUKE. Let me speak like yourself and lay a sentence,
Which as a grize or step, may help these lovers
Into your favour.
When remedies are past, the griefs are ended
By seeing the worst, which late on hopes depended.
To mourn a mischief that is past and gone
Is the next way to draw new mischief on.
What cannot be preserv'd when Fortune takes,
Patience her injury a mockery makes.
The robb'd that smiles steals something from the thief;
He robs himself that spends a bootless grief.

BRABANTIO. So let the Turk of Cyprus us beguile;
We lose it not so long as we can smile.
He bears the sentence well that nothing bears
But the free comfort which from thence he hears;
But he bears both the sentence and the sorrow
That, to pray grief, must of poor patience borrow.
These sentences, to sugar, or to gall,

Being strong on both sides, are equivocal:
But words are words; I never yet did hear
That the bruis'd heart was pierced through the ear.
I humbly beseech you, proceed to the affairs of state.

DUKE. The Turk with a most mighty preparation makes for Cyprus. Othello, the fortitude of the place is best known to you; and though we have there a substitute of most allowed sufficiency, yet opinion, a sovereign mistress of effects, throws a more safer voice on you: you must therefore be content to slubber the gloss of your new fortunes with this more stubborn and boisterous expedition.

OTHELLO. The tyrant custom, most grave senators,
Hath made the flinty and steel couch of war
My thrice-driven bed of down: I do agnize
A natural and prompt alacrity
I find in hardness, and do undertake
These present wars against the Ottomites.
Most humbly therefore bending to your state,
I crave fit disposition for my wife,
Due reference of place and exhibition,
With such accommodation and besort
As levels with her breeding.

DUKE.   If you please,
Be't at her father's.

BRABANTIO.   I'll not have it so.

OTHELLO. Nor I.

DESDEMONA. Nor I; I would not there reside,
To put my father in impatient thoughts
By being in his eye. Most gracious duke,
To my unfolding lend your gracious ear;
And let me find a charter in your voice
To assist my simpleness.

DUKE. What would you, Desdemona?

DESDEMONA. That I did love the Moor to live with him,
My downright violence and storm of fortunes
May trumpet to the world; my heart's subdu'd
Even to the very quality of my lord;

I saw Othello's visage in his mind,
And to his honours and his valiant parts
Did I my soul and fortunes consecrate.
So that, dear lords, if I be left behind,
A moth of peace, and he go to the war,
The rites for which I love him are bereft me,
And I a heavy interim shall support
By his dear absence. Let me go with him.

   OTHELLO. Let her have your voices.
Vouch with me, heaven, I therefore beg it not
To please the palate of my appetite,
Nor to comply with heat,—the young affects
In me defunct,—and proper satisfaction,
But to be free and bounteous to her mind;
And heaven defend your good souls that you think
I will your serious and great business scant
For she is with me. No, when light-wing'd toys
Of feather'd Cupid seel with wanton dullness
My speculative and offic'd instruments,
That my disports corrupt and taint my business,
Let housewives make a skillet of my helm,
And all indign and base adversities
Make head against my estimation!

   DUKE. Be it as you shall privately determine,
Either for her stay or going. The affair cries haste,
And speed must answer it.

   FIRST SENATOR. You must away to-night.

   OTHELLO.   With all my heart.

   DUKE. At nine i' the morning here we'll meet again.
Othello, leave some officer behind,
And he shall our commission bring to you;
With such things else of quality and respect
As doth import you.

   OTHELLO.   So please your Grace, my ancient;
A man he is of honesty and trust:
To his conveyance I assign my wife,
With what else needful your good grace shall think

To be sent after me.

DUKE.   Let it be so.
Good night to every one. [*To* BRABANTIO.] And, noble signior,
If virtue no delighted beauty lack,
Your son-in-law is far more fair than black.

FIRST SENATOR. Adieu, brave Moor! use Desdemona well.

BRABANTIO. Look to her, Moor, if thou hast eyes to see:
She has deceiv'd her father, and may thee.

[*Exeunt* DUKE, SENATORS, OFFICERS, &c.

OTHELLO. My life upon her faith! Honest Iago,
My Desdemona must I leave to thee:
I prithee, let thy wife attend on her;
And bring them after in the best advantage.
Come, Desdemona; I have but an hour
Of love, of worldly matters and direction,
To spend with thee: we must obey the time.

[*Exeunt* OTHELLO *and* DESDEMONA.

RODERIGO. Iago!

IAGO. What sayst thou, noble heart?

RODERIGO. What will I do, think'st thou?

IAGO. Why, go to bed, and sleep.

RODERIGO. I will incontinently drown myself.

IAGO. Well, if thou dost, I shall never love thee after. Why,
thou silly gentleman!

RODERIGO. It is silliness to live when to live is torment; and
then have we a prescription to die when death is our physician.

IAGO. O! villainous; I have looked upon the world for four
times seven years, and since I could distinguish betwixt a benefit
and an injury, I never found man that knew how to love himself. Ere I would say, I would drown myself for the love of a
guinea-hen, I would change my humanity with a baboon.

RODERIGO. What should I do? I confess it is my shame to be so
fond; but it is not in my virtue to amend it.

IAGO. Virtue! a fig! 'tis in ourselves that we are thus, or thus.
Our bodies are our gardens, to the which our wills are garden-
ers; so that if we will plant nettles or sow lettuce, set hyssop and
weed up thyme, supply it with one gender of herbs or distract

it with many, either to have it sterile with idleness or manured with industry, why, the power and corrigible authority of this lies in our wills. If the balance of our lives had not one scale of reason to poise another of sensuality, the blood and baseness of our natures would conduct us to most preposterous conclusions; but we have reason to cool our raging motions, our carnal stings, our unbitted lusts, whereof I take this that you call love to be a sect or scion.

RODERIGO. It cannot be.

IAGO. It is merely a lust of the blood and a permission of the will. Come, be a man. Drown thyself! drown cats and blind puppies. I have professed me thy friend, and I confess me knit to thy deserving with cables of perdurable toughness; I could never better stead thee than now. Put money in thy purse; follow these wars; defeat thy favour with a usurped beard; I say, put money in thy purse. It cannot be that Desdemona should long continue her love to the Moor,—put money in thy purse,—nor he his to her. It was a violent commencement in her, and thou shalt see an answerable sequestration; put but money in thy purse. These Moors are changeable in their wills;—fill thy purse with money: —the food that to him now is as luscious as locusts, shall be to him shortly as bitter as coloquintida. She must change for youth: when she is sated with his body, she will find the error of her choice. She must have change, she must: therefore put money in thy purse. If thou wilt needs damn thyself, do it a more delicate way than drowning. Make all the money thou canst. If sanctimony and a frail vow betwixt an erring barbarian and a supersubtle Venetian be not too hard for my wits and all the tribe of hell, thou shalt enjoy her; therefore make money. A pox of drowning thyself! it is clean out of the way: seek thou rather to be hanged in compassing thy joy than to be drowned and go without her.

RODERIGO. Wilt thou be fast to my hopes, if I depend on the issue?

IAGO. Thou art sure of me: go, make money. I have told thee often, and I re-tell thee again and again, I hate the Moor: my cause is hearted: thine hath no less reason. Let us be conjunctive

in our revenge against him; if thou canst cockold him, thou dost
thyself a pleasure, me a sport. There are many events in the
womb of time which will be delivered. Traverse; go: provide
thy money. We will have more of this to-morrow. Adieu.

RODERIGO. Where shall we meet i' the morning?

IAGO. At my lodging.

RODERIGO. I'll be with thee betimes.

IAGO. Go to; farewell. Do you hear, Roderigo?

RODERIGO. What say you?

IAGO. No more of drowning, do you hear?

RODERIGO. I am changed. I'll sell all my land.

IAGO. Go to; farewell! put money enough in your purse.

[*Exit* RODERIGO.

Thus do I ever make my fool my purse;
For I mine own gain'd knowledge should profane,
If I would time expend with such a snipe
But for my sport and profit. I hate the Moor,
And it is thought abroad that 'twixt my sheets
He has done my office: I know not if't be true,
But I, for mere suspicion in that kind,
Will do as if for surety. He holds me well;
The better shall my purpose work on him.
Cassio's a proper man; let me see now:
To get his place; and to plume up my will
In double knavery; how, how? Let's see:
After some time to abuse Othello's ear
That he is too familiar with his wife:
He hath a person and a smooth dispose
To be suspected; framed to make women false.
The Moor is of a free and open nature,
That thinks men honest that but seem to be so,
And will as tenderly be led by the nose
As asses are.
I have't; it is engender'd: hell and night
Must bring this monstrous birth to the world's light.   [*Exit.*

Act 2

Scene I. A Sea-port Town in Cyprus. An open place near the Quay

Enter MONTANO *and two* GENTLEMEN.

MONTANO. What from the cape can you discern at sea?

FIRST GENTLEMAN. Nothing at all: it is a high-wrought flood;
I cannot 'twixt the heaven and the main
Descry a sail.

MONTANO. Methinks the wind hath spoke aloud at land;
A fuller blast ne'er shook our battlements;
If it hath ruffian'd so upon the sea,
What ribs of oak, when mountains melt on them,
Can hold the mortise? what shall we hear of this?

SECOND GENTLEMAN. A segregation of the Turkish fleet;
For do but stand upon the foaming shore,
The chidden billow seems to pelt the clouds;
The wind-shak'd surge, with high and monstrous mane,
Seems to cast water on the burning bear
And quench the guards of the ever-fixed pole:
I never did like molestation view
On the enchafed flood.

MONTANO.   If that the Turkish fleet
Be not enshelter'd and embay'd, they are drown'd;
It is impossible they bear it out.

Enter a third GENTLEMAN.

THIRD GENTLEMAN. News, lads! our wars are done.
The desperate tempest hath so bang'd the Turks
That their designment halts; a noble ship of Venice

131

Hath seen a grievous wrack and sufferance
On most part of their fleet.

    MONTANO. How! is this true?

    THIRD GENTLEMAN.   The ship is here put in,
A Veronesa; Michael Cassio,
Lieutenant to the war-like Moor Othello,
Is come on shore: the Moor himself's at sea,
And is in full commission here for Cyprus.

    MONTANO. I am glad on 't; 'tis a worthy governor.

    THIRD GENTLEMAN. But this same Cassio, though he speak of comfort
Touching the Turkish loss, yet he looks sadly
And prays the Moor be safe; for they were parted
With foul and violent tempest.

    MONTANO.   Pray heaven he be;
For I have serv'd him, and the man commands
Like a full soldier. Let's to the sea-side, ho!
As well to see the vessel that's come in
As to throw out our eyes for brave Othello,
Even till we make the main and the aerial blue
An indistinct regard.

    THIRD GENTLEMAN. Come, let's do so;
For every minute is expectancy
Of more arrivance.

    Enter CASSIO.

    CASSIO. Thanks, you the valiant of this war-like isle,
That so approve the Moor. O! let the heavens
Give him defence against the elements,
For I have lost him on a dangerous sea.

    MONTANO. Is he well shipp'd?

    CASSIO. His bark is stoutly timber'd, and his pilot
Of very expert and approv'd allowance;
Therefore my hopes, not surfeited to death,
Stands in hold cure.   [*Within*, 'A sail!—a sail!—a sail!'

    Enter a MESSENGER.

CASSIO. What noise?

MESSENGER. The town is empty; on the brow o' the sea
Stand ranks of people, and they cry, 'A sail!'

CASSIO. My hopes do shape him for the governor.

[*Guns heard.*

SECOND GENTLEMAN. They do discharge their shot of courtesy;
Our friends at least.

CASSIO.　　　　I pray you, sir, go forth,
And give us truth who 'tis that is arriv'd.

SECOND GENTLEMAN. I shall.

[*Exit.*

MONTANO. But, good lieutenant, is your general wiv'd?

CASSIO. Most fortunately: he hath achiev'd a maid
That paragons description and wild fame;
One that excels the quirks of blazoning pens,
And in th' essential vesture of creation
Does tire the ingener.

Re-enter SECOND GENTLEMAN.

　　　　　　　　　How now! who has put in?

SECOND GENTLEMAN. 'Tis one Iago, ancient to the general.

CASSIO. He has had most favourable and happy speed:
Tempests themselves, high seas, and howling winds,
The gutter'd rocks, and congregated sands,
Traitors ensteep'd to clog the guiltless keel,
As having sense of beauty, do omit
Their mortal natures, letting go safely by
The divine Desdemona.

MONTANO.　　　　What is she?

CASSIO. She that I spake of, our great captain's captain,
Left in the conduct of the bold Iago,
Whose footing here anticipates our thoughts
A se'nnight's speed. Great Jove, Othello guard,
And swell his sail with thine own powerful breath,
That he may bless this bay with his tall ship,
Make love's quick pants in Desdemona's arms,
Give renew'd fire to our extincted spirits,
And bring all Cyprus comfort!

Enter DESDEMONA, EMILIA, IAGO, RODERIGO, *and* ATTENDANTS.

         O! behold,
The riches of the ship is come on shore.
Ye men of Cyprus, let her have your knees.
Hail to thee, lady! and the grace of heaven,
Before, behind thee, and on every hand,
Enwheel thee round!
  DESDEMONA.   I thank you, valiant Cassio.
What tidings can you tell me of my lord?
  CASSIO. He is not yet arriv'd; nor know I aught
But that he's well, and will be shortly here.
  DESDEMONA. O! but I fear—How lost you company?
  CASSIO. The great contention of the sea and skies
Parted our fellowship. But hark! a sail.
      [*Cry within*, 'A sail!—a sail!' *Guns heard.*
  SECOND GENTLEMAN. They give their greeting to the citadel:
This likewise is a friend.
  CASSIO.   See for the news! [*Exit* GENTLEMAN.
Good ancient, you are welcome:—[*To* EMILIA.] welcome, mis-
  tress.
Let it not gall your patience, good Iago,
That I extend my manners; 'tis my breeding
That gives me this bold show of courtesy. [*Kissing her.*
  IAGO. Sir, would she give you so much of her lips
As of her tongue she oft bestows on me,
You'd have enough.
  DESDEMONA. Alas! she has no speech.
  IAGO. In faith, too much;
I find it still when I have list to sleep:
Marry, before your ladyship, I grant,
She puts her tongue a little in her heart,
And chides with thinking.
  EMILIA. You have little cause to say so.
  IAGO. Come on, come on; you are pictures out of doors,
Bells in your parlours, wild cats in your kitchens,
Saints in your injuries, devils being offended,

Players in your housewifery, and housewives in your beds.

DESDEMONA. O! fie upon thee, slanderer.

IAGO. Nay, it is true, or else I am a Turk:
You rise to play and go to bed to work.

EMILIA. You shall not write my praise.

IAGO.   No, let me not.

DESDEMONA. What wouldst thou write of me, if thou shouldst
praise me?

IAGO. O gentle lady, do not put me to't,
For I am nothing if not critical.

DESDEMONA. Come on; assay. There's one gone to the harbour?

IAGO. Ay, madam.

DESDEMONA. I am not merry, but I do beguile
The thing I am by seeming otherwise.
Come, how wouldst thou praise me?

IAGO. I am about it; but indeed my invention
Comes from my pate as birdlime does from frize;
It plucks out brains and all: but my muse labours,
And thus she is deliver'd.
If she be fair and wise, fairness and wit,
The one's for use, the other useth it.

DESDEMONA. Well prais'd! How if she be black and witty?

IAGO. If she be black, and thereto have a wit,
She'll find a white that shall her blackness fit.

DESDEMONA. Worse and worse.

EMILIA. How if fair and foolish?

IAGO. She never yet was foolish that was fair,
For even her folly help'd her to an heir.

DESDEMONA. These are old fond paradoxes to make fools
laugh i' the alehouse. What miserable praise hast thou for her
that's foul and foolish?

IAGO. There's none so foul and foolish thereunto
But does foul pranks which fair and wise ones do.

DESDEMONA. O heavy ignorance! thou praisest the worst best.
But what praise couldst thou bestow on a deserving woman
indeed, one that in the authority of her merit, did justly put on
the vouch of very malice itself?

IAGO. She that was ever fair and never proud,
Had tongue at will and yet was never loud,
Never lack'd gold and yet went never gay,
Fled from her wish and yet said 'Now I may,'
She that being anger'd, her revenge being nigh,
Bade her wrong stay and her displeasure fly,
She that in wisdom never was so frail
To change the cod's head for the salmon's tail,
She that could think and ne'er disclose her mind,
See suitors following and not look behind,
She was a wight, if ever such wight were,—

DESDEMONA. To do what?

IAGO. To suckle fools and chronicle small beer.

DESDEMONA. O most lame and impotent conclusion! Do not learn of him, Emilia, though he be thy husband. How say you, Cassio? is he not a most profane and liberal counsellor?

CASSIO. He speaks home, madam; you may relish him more in the soldier than in the scholar.

IAGO. [Aside.] He takes her by the palm; ay, well said, whisper; with as little a web as this will I ensnare as great a fly as Cassio. Ay, smile upon her, do; I will gyve thee in thine own courtship. You say true, 'tis so, indeed. If such tricks as these strip you out of your lieutenantry, it had been better you had not kissed your three fingers so oft, which now again you are most apt to play the sir in. Very good; well kissed! and excellent courtesy! 'tis so, indeed. Yet again your fingers to your lips? would they were clyster-pipes for your sake! [A trumpet heard.] The Moor! I know his trumpet.

CASSIO. 'Tis truly so.

DESDEMONA. Let's meet him and receive him.

CASSIO. Lo! where he comes.

Enter OTHELLO *and* ATTENDANTS.

OTHELLO. O my fair warrior!

DESDEMONA.   My dear Othello!

OTHELLO. It gives me wonder great as my content
To see you here before me. O my soul's joy!

If after every tempest come such calms,
May the winds blow till they have waken'd death!
And let the labouring bark climb hills of seas
Olympus-high, and duck again as low
As hell's from heaven! If it were now to die,
'Twere now to be most happy, for I fear
My soul hath her content so absolute
That not another comfort like to this
Succeeds in unknown fate.

DESDEMONA.   The heavens forbid
But that our loves and comforts should increase
Even as our days do grow!

OTHELLO.   Amen to that, sweet powers!
I cannot speak enough of this content;
It stops me here; it is too much of joy:
And this, and this, the greatest discords be,   [*Kissing her.*
That e'er our hearts shall make!

IAGO.   [*Aside.*] O! you are well tun'd now,
But I'll set down the pegs that make this music,
As honest as I am.

OTHELLO.   Come, let us to the castle.
News, friends; our wars are done, the Turks are drown'd.
How does my old acquaintance of this isle?
Honey, you shall be well desir'd in Cyprus;
I have found great love amongst them. O my sweet,
I prattle out of fashion, and I dote
In mine own comforts. I prithee, good Iago,
Go to the bay and disembark my coffers.
Bring thou the master to the citadel;
He is a good one, and his worthiness
Does challenge much respect. Come, Desdemona,
Once more well met at Cyprus.

[*Exeunt all except* IAGO *and* RODERIGO.

IAGO. Do thou meet me presently at the harbour. Come
hither. If thou be'st valiant, as they say base men being in love
have then a nobility in their natures more than is native to
them, list me. The lieutenant to-night watches on the court of

guard: first, I must tell thee this, Desdemona is directly in love
with him.

RODERIGO. With him! why, 'tis not possible.

IAGO. Lay thy finger thus, and let thy soul be instructed. Mark
me with what violence she first loved the Moor but for bragging
and telling her fantastical lies; and will she love him still for
prating? let not thy discreet heart think it. Her eye must be fed;
and what delight shall she have to look on the devil? When the
blood is made dull with the act of sport, there should be, again
to inflame it, and to give satiety a fresh appetite, loveliness in
favour, sympathy in years, manners, and beauties; all which the
Moor is defective in. Now, for want of these required con-
veniences, her delicate tenderness will find itself abused, begin
to heave the gorge, disrelish and abhor the Moor; very nature
will instruct her in it, and compel her to some second choice.
Now, sir, this granted, as it is a most pregnant and unforced
position, who stands so eminently in the degree of this fortune as
Cassio does? a knave very voluble, no further conscionable than
in putting on the mere form of civil and humane seeming, for
the better compassing of his salt and most hidden loose affection?
why, none; why, none: a slipper and subtle knave, a finder-out
of occasions, that has an eye can stamp and counterfeit advantages, though true advantage never present itself; a devilish
knave! Besides, the knave is handsome, young, and hath all those
requisites in him that folly and green minds look after; a pestilent complete knave! and the woman hath found him already.

RODERIGO. I cannot believe that in her; she is full of most
blessed condition.

IAGO. Blessed fig's end! the wine she drinks is made of grapes;
if she had been blessed she would never have loved the Moor;
blessed pudding! Didst thou not see her paddle with the palm
of his hand? didst not mark that?

RODERIGO. Yes, that I did; but that was but courtesy.

IAGO. Lechery, by this hand! an index and obscure prologue
to the history of lust and foul thoughts. They met so near with
their lips, that their breaths embraced together. Villanous
thoughts, Roderigo! when these mutualities so marshal the way,

A nineteenth-century etching of Othello in Venice, relating his adventures to Desdemona and her father. "She lov'd me for the dangers I had pass'd, And I lov'd her that she did pity them." Act I, Scene III.

hard at hand comes the master and main exercise, the incorporate conclusion. Pish! But, sir, be you ruled by me: I have brought you from Venice. Watch you to-night; for the command, I'll lay't upon you: Cassio knows you not. I'll not be far from you: do you find some occasion to anger Cassio, either by speaking too loud, or tainting his discipline; or from what other course you please, which the time shall more favourably minister.

RODERIGO. Well.

IAGO. Sir, he is rash and very sudden in choler, and haply may strike at you: provoke him, that he may; for even out of that will I cause these of Cyprus to mutiny, whose qualification shall come into no true taste again but by the displanting of Cassio. So shall you have a shorter journey to your desires by the means I shall then have to prefer them; and the impediment most profitably removed, without the which there were no expectation of our prosperity.

RODERIGO. I will do this, if I can bring it to any opportunity.

IAGO. I warrant thee. Meet me by and by at the citadel: I must fetch his necessaries ashore. Farewell.

RODERIGO. Adieu.   [*Exit.*

IAGO. That Cassio loves her, I do well believe it;
That she loves him, 'tis apt, and of great credit:
The Moor, howbeit that I endure him not,
Is of a constant, loving, noble nature;
And I dare think he'll prove to Desdemona
A most dear husband. Now, I do love her too;
Not out of absolute lust,—though peradventure
I stand accountant for as great a sin,—
But partly led to diet my revenge,
For that I do suspect the lusty Moor
Hath leap'd into my seat; the thought whereof
Doth like a poisonous mineral gnaw my inwards;
And nothing can or shall content my soul
Till I am even'd with him, wife for wife;
Or failing so, yet that I put the Moor
At least into a jealousy so strong

That judgment cannot cure. Which thing to do,
If this poor trash of Venice, whom I trash
For his quick hunting, stand the putting-on,
I'll have our Michael Cassio on the hip;
Abuse him to the Moor in the rank garb,
For I fear Cassio with my night-cap too,
Make the Moor thank me, love me, and reward me
For making him egregiously an ass
And practising upon his peace and quiet
Even to madness. 'Tis here, but yet confus'd:
Knavery's plain face is never seen till us'd.   [*Exit.*

Scene II. *A Street*

Enter a HERALD *with a proclamation; People following.*

HERALD. It is Othello's pleasure, our noble and valiant general, that, upon certain tidings now arrived, importing the mere perdition of the Turkish fleet, every man put himself into triumph; some to dance, some to make bonfires, each man to what sport and revels his addiction leads him; for, besides these beneficial news, it is the celebration of his nuptial. So much was his pleasure should be proclaimed. All offices are open, and there is full liberty of feasting from this present hour of five till the bell have told eleven. Heaven bless the isle of Cyprus and our noble general Othello!   [*Exeunt.*

Scene III. *A Hall in the Castle*

Enter OTHELLO, DESDEMONA, CASSIO, *and* ATTENDANTS.

OTHELLO. Good Michael, look you to the guard to-night:
Let's teach ourselves that honourable stop,
Not to outsport discretion.
    CASSIO. Iago hath direction what to do;
But, notwithstanding, with my personal eye

Will I look to't.

OTHELLO.   Iago is most honest.
Michael, good night; to-morrow with your earliest
Let me have speech with you. [*To* DESDEMONA.] Come, my dear
     love,
The purchase made, the fruits are to ensue;
That profit's yet to come 'twixt me and you.
Good night.   [*Exeunt* OTHELLO, DESDEMONA, *and* ATTENDANTS.

Enter IAGO.

CASSIO. Welcome, Iago; we must to the watch.

IAGO. Not this hour, lieutenant; 'tis not yet ten o' the clock.
Our general cast us thus early for the love of his Desdemona,
who let us not therefore blame; he hath not yet made wanton
the night with her, and she is sport for Jove.

CASSIO. She's a most exquisite lady.

IAGO. And, I'll warrant her, full of game.

CASSIO. Indeed, she is a most fresh and delicate creature.

IAGO. What an eye she has! methinks it sounds a parley of
provocation.

CASSIO. An inviting eye; and yet methinks right modest.

IAGO. And when she speaks, is it not an alarum to love?

CASSIO. She is indeed perfection.

IAGO. Well, happiness to their sheets! Come, lieutenant, I
have a stoup of wine, and here without are a brace of Cyprus
gallants that would fain have a measure to the health of black
Othello.

CASSIO. Not to-night, good Iago: I have very poor and unhappy brains for drinking: I could well wish courtesy would
invent some other custom of entertainment.

IAGO. O! they are our friends; but one cup: I'll drink for you.

CASSIO. I have drunk but one cup to-night, and that was
craftily qualified too, and, behold, what innovation it makes
here: I am unfortunate in the infirmity, and dare not task my
weakness with any more.

IAGO. What, man! 'tis a night of revels; the gallants desire it.

CASSIO. Where are they?

IAGO. Here at the door; I pray you, call them in.

CASSIO. I'll do't; but it dislikes me.   [*Exit.*

IAGO. If I can fasten but one cup upon him,
With that which he hath drunk to-night already,
He'll be as full of quarrel and offence
As my young mistress' dog. Now, my sick fool Roderigo,
Whom love has turn'd almost the wrong side out,
To Desdemona hath to-night carous'd
Potations pottle deep; and he's to watch.
Three lads of Cyprus, noble swelling spirits,
That hold their honours in a wary distance,
The very elements of this war-like isle,
Have I to-night fluster'd with flowing cups,
And they watch too. Now, 'mongst this flock of drunkards,
Am I to put our Cassio in some action
That may offend the isle. But here they come.
If consequence do but approve my dream,
My boat sails freely, both with wind and stream.

Re-enter CASSIO, *with him* MONTANO, *and* GENTLEMEN. SER-
VANT *following with wine.*

CASSIO. 'Fore God, they have given me a rouse already.

MONTANO. Good faith, a little one; not past a pint, as I am a
soldier.

IAGO. Some wine, ho!

　　　　And let me the canakin clink, clink;
　　　　And let me the canakin clink:
　　　　　　A soldier's a man;
　　　　　　A life's but a span;
　　　　Why then let a soldier drink.

Some wine, boys!

CASSIO. 'Fore God, an excellent song.

IAGO. I learned it in England, where indeed they are most potent in potting; your Dane, your German, and your swag-bellied
Hollander,—drink, ho!—are nothing to your English.

CASSIO. Is your Englishman so expert in his drinking?

IAGO. Why, he drinks you with facility your Dane dead drunk; he sweats not to overthrow your Almain; he gives your Hollander a vomit ere the next pottle can be filled.

CASSIO. To the health of our general!

MONTANO. I am for it, lieutenant; and I'll do you justice.

IAGO. O sweet England!

> King Stephen was a worthy peer,
>> His breeches cost him but a crown;
> He held them sixpence all too dear,
>> With that he call'd the tailor lown.
> He was a wight of high renown,
>> And thou art but a low degree:
> 'Tis pride that pulls the country down,
>> Then take thine auld cloak about thee.

Some wine, ho!

CASSIO. Why, this is a more exquisite song than the other.

IAGO. Will you hear't again?

CASSIO. No; for I hold him to be unworthy of his place that does those things. Well, God's above all; and there be souls must be saved, and there be souls must not be saved.

IAGO. It's true, good lieutenant.

CASSIO. For mine own part,—no offence to the general, nor any man of quality,—I hope to be saved.

IAGO. And so do I too, lieutenant.

CASSIO. Ay; but, by your leave, not before me; the lieutenant is to be saved before the ancient. Let's have no more of this; let's to our affairs. God forgive us our sins! Gentlemen, let's look to our business. Do not think, gentlemen, I am drunk: this is my ancient; this is my right hand, and this is my left hand. I am not drunk now; I can stand well enough, and speak well enough.

ALL. Excellent well.

CASSIO. Why, very well, then; you must not think then that I am drunk.   [*Exit.*

MONTANO. To the platform, masters; come, let's set the watch.

IAGO. You see this fellow that is gone before;
He is a soldier fit to stand by Cæsar

And give direction; and do but see his vice;
'Tis to his virtue a just equinox,
The one as long as the other; 'tis pity of him.
I fear the trust Othello puts him in,
On some odd time of his infirmity,
Will shake this island.

MONTANO.   But is he often thus?

IAGO. 'Tis evermore the prologue to his sleep:
He'll watch the horologe a double set,
If drink rock not his cradle.

MONTANO.   It were well
The general were put in mind of it.
Perhaps he sees it not; or his good nature
Prizes the virtue that appears in Cassio,
And looks not on his evils. Is not this true?

    Enter RODERIGO.

IAGO. [*Aside to him.*] How now, Roderigo!
I pray you, after the lieutenant; go.   [*Exit* RODERIGO.

MONTANO. And 'tis great pity that the noble Moor
Should hazard such a place as his own second
With one of an ingraft infirmity;
It were an honest action to say
So to the Moor.

IAGO.   Not I, for this fair island:
I do love Cassio well, and would do much
To cure him of this evil. But hark! what noise?

                    [*Cry within,* 'Help! Help!'

    Re-enter CASSIO, *driving in* RODERIGO.

CASSIO. You rogue! you rascal!

MONTANO.   What's the matter, lieutenant?

CASSIO. A knave teach me my duty!
I'll beat the knave into a twiggen bottle.

RODERIGO. Beat me!

CASSIO.   Dost thou prate, rogue?

                    [*Striking* RODERIGO.

MONTANO. [*Staying him.*] Nay, good lieutenant;
I pray you, sir, hold your hand.
 CASSIO.   Let me go, sir,
Or I'll knock you o'er the mazzard.
 MONTANO.   Come, come; you're drunk.
 CASSIO. Drunk!   [*They fight.*
 IAGO. [*Aside to* RODERIGO.] Away, I say! go out, and cry a
  mutiny.   [*Exit* RODERIGO.
Nay, good lieutenant! God's will, gentlemen!
Help, ho! Lieutenant! sir! Montano! sir!
Help, masters! Here's a goodly watch indeed!   [*Bell rings.*
Who's that that rings the bell? *Diablo*, ho!
The town will rise: God's will! lieutenant, hold!
You will be sham'd for ever.

 Re-enter OTHELLO *and* ATTENDANTS.

 OTHELLO.   What is the matter here?
 MONTANO. 'Zounds! I bleed still; I am hurt to the death.
 OTHELLO. Hold, for your lives!
 IAGO. Hold, ho, lieutenant! Sir! Montano! gentlemen!
Have you forgot all sense of place and duty?
Hold! the general speaks to you; hold for shame!
 OTHELLO. Why, how now, ho! from whence ariseth this?
Are we turn'd Turks, and to ourselves do that
Which heaven hath forbid the Ottomites?
For Christian shame put by this barbarous brawl;
He that stirs next to carve for his own rage
Holds his soul light; he dies upon his motion.
Silence that dreadful bell! it frights the isle
From her propriety. What is the matter, masters?
Honest Iago, that look'st dead with grieving,
Speak, who began this? on thy love, I charge thee.
 IAGO. I do not know; friends all but now, even now,
In quarter and in terms like bride and groom
Devesting them for bed; and then, but now,—
As if some planet had unwitted men,—
Swords out, and tilting one at other's breast,

In opposition bloody. I cannot speak
Any beginning to this peevish odds,
And would in action glorious I had lost
Those legs that brought me to a part of it!

OTHELLO. How comes it, Michael, you are thus forgot?

CASSIO. I pray you, pardon me; I cannot speak.

OTHELLO. Worthy Montano, you were wont be civil;
The gravity and stillness of your youth
The world hath noted, and your name is great
In mouths of wisest censure: what's the matter,
That you unlace your reputation thus
And spend your rich opinion for the name
Of a night-brawler? give me answer to it.

MONTANO. Worthy Othello, I am hurt to danger;
Your officer, Iago, can inform you,
While I spare speech, which something now offends me,
Of all that I do know; nor know I aught
By me that's said or done amiss this night,
Unless self-charity be sometimes a vice,
And to defend ourselves it be a sin
When violence assails us.

OTHELLO.   Now, by heaven,
My blood begins my safer guides to rule,
And passion, having my best judgment collied,
Assays to lead the way. If I once stir,
Or do but lift this arm, the best of you
Shall sink in my rebuke. Give me to know
How this foul rout began, who set it on;
And he that is approv'd in this offence,
Though he had twinn'd with me—both at a birth—
Shall lose me. What! in a town of war,
Yet wild, the people's hearts brimful of fear,
To manage private and domestic quarrel,
In night, and on the court and guard of safety!
'Tis monstrous. Iago, who began't?

MONTANO. If partially affin'd, or leagu'd in office,
Thou dost deliver more or less than truth,

In the 1800's American actor Edwin Booth achieved great success as both Othello and Iago. Here he is seen in the role of Iago.

Thou art no soldier.

    IAGO.   Touch me not so near;
I had rather have this tongue cut from my mouth
Than it should do offence to Michael Cassio;
Yet, I persuade myself, to speak the truth
Shall nothing wrong him. Thus it is, general.
Montano and myself being in speech,
There comes a fellow crying out for help,
And Cassio following with determin'd sword
To execute upon him. Sir, this gentleman
Steps in to Cassio, and entreats his pause;
Myself the crying fellow did pursue,
Lest by his clamour, as it so fell out,
The town might fall in fright; he, swift of foot,
Outran my purpose, and I return'd the rather
For that I heard the clink and fall of swords,
And Cassio high in oath, which till to-night
I ne'er might say before. When I came back,—
For this was brief,—I found them close together,
At blow and thrust, even as again they were
When you yourself did part them.
More of this matter can I not report:
But men are men; the best sometimes forget:
Though Cassio did some little wrong to him,
As men in rage strike those that wish them best,
Yet, surely Cassio, I believe, receiv'd
From him that fled some strange indignity,
Which patience could not pass.

    OTHELLO.   I know, Iago,
Thy honesty and love doth mince this matter,
Making it light to Cassio. Cassio, I love thee;
But never more be officer of mine.

    Enter DESDEMONA, *attended.*

Look! if my gentle love be not rais'd up;
[*To* CASSIO.] I'll make thee an example.

    DESDEMONA.   What's the matter?

OTHELLO. All's well now, sweeting; come away to bed.
Sir, for your hurts, myself will be your surgeon.
Lead him off.   [MONTANO *is led off.*
Iago, look with care about the town,
And silence those whom this vile brawl distracted.
Come, Desdemona; 'tis the soldiers' life,
To have their balmy slumbers wak'd with strife.
                         [*Exeunt all but* IAGO *and* CASSIO.
    IAGO. What! are you hurt, lieutenant?
    CASSIO. Ay; past all surgery.
    IAGO. Marry, heaven forbid!
    CASSIO. Reputation, reputation, reputation! O! I have lost my
reputation. I have lost the immortal part of myself, and what
remains is bestial. My reputation, Iago, my reputation!
    IAGO. As I am an honest man, I thought you had received
some bodily wound; there is more offence in that than in reputation. Reputation is an idle and most false imposition; oft got
without merit, and lost without deserving: you have lost no
reputation at all, unless you repute yourself such a loser. What!
man; there are ways to recover the general again; you are but
now cast in his mood, a punishment more in policy than in
malice; even so as one would beat his offenceless dog to affright
an imperious lion. Sue to him again, and he is yours.
    CASSIO. I will rather sue to be despised than to deceive so good
a commander with so slight, so drunken, and so indiscreet an
officer. Drunk! and speak parrot! and squabble, swagger, swear,
and discourse fustian with one's own shadow! O thou invisible
spirit of wine! if thou hast no name to be known by, let us call
thee devil!
    IAGO. What was he that you followed with your sword? What
had he done to you?
    CASSIO. I know not.
    IAGO. Is't possible?
    CASSIO. I remember a mass of things, but nothing distinctly;
a quarrel, but nothing wherefore. O God! that men should put
an enemy in their mouths to steal away their brains; that we

should, with joy, pleasance, revel, and applause, transform ourselves into beasts.

IAGO. Why, but you are now well enough; how came you thus
recovered?

CASSIO. It hath pleased the devil drunkenness to give place to
the devil wrath; one unperfectness shows me another, to make
me frankly despise myself.

IAGO. Come, you are too severe a moraler. As the time, the
place, and the condition of this country stands, I could heartily
wish this had not befallen, but since it is as it is, mend it for
your own good.

CASSIO. I will ask him for my place again; he shall tell me I
am a drunkard! Had I as many mouths as Hydra, such an answer would stop them all. To be now a sensible man, by and by
a fool, and presently a beast! O strange! Every inordinate cup
is unblessed and the ingredient is a devil.

IAGO. Come, come; good wine is a good familiar creature if it
be well used; exclaim no more against it. And, good lieutenant,
I think you think I love you.

CASSIO. I have well approved it, sir. I drunk!

IAGO. You or any man living may be drunk at some time,
man. I'll tell you what you shall do. Our general's wife is now
the general: I may say so in this respect, for that he hath devoted
and given up himself to the contemplation, mark, and denote-
ment of her parts and graces: confess yourself freely to her; importune her; she'll help to put you in your place again. She is
of so free, so kind, so apt, so blessed a disposition, that she holds
it a vice in her goodness not to do more than she is requested.
This broken joint between you and her husband entreat her to
splinter; and my fortunes against any lay worth naming, this
crack of your love shall grow stronger than it was before.

CASSIO. You advise me well.

IAGO. I protest, in the sincerity of love and honest kindness.

CASSIO. I think it freely; and betimes in the morning I will
beseech the virtuous Desdemona to undertake for me. I am
desperate of my fortunes if they check me here.

IAGO. You are in the right. Good night, lieutenant; I must to the watch.

CASSIO. Good night, honest Iago!   [*Exit.*

IAGO. And what's he then that says I play the villain?
When this advice is free I give and honest,
Probal to thinking and indeed the course
To win the Moor again? For 'tis most easy
The inclining Desdemona to subdue
In any honest suit; she's fram'd as fruitful
As the free elements. And then for her
To win the Moor, were't to renounce his baptism,
All seals and symbols of redeemed sin,
His soul is so enfetter'd to her love,
That she may make, unmake, do what she list,
Even as her appetite shall play the god
With his weak function. How am I then a villain
To counsel Cassio to this parallel course,
Directly to his good? Divinity of hell!
When devils will the blackest sins put on,
They do suggest at first with heavenly shows,
As I do now; for while this honest fool
Plies Desdemona to repair his fortunes,
And she for him pleads strongly to the Moor,
I'll pour this pestilence into his ear
That she repeals him for her body's lust;
And, by how much she strives to do him good,
She shall undo her credit with the Moor.
So will I turn her virtue into pitch,
And out of her own goodness make the net
That shall enmesh them all.

    Re-enter RODERIGO.

                                   How now, Roderigo!

RODERIGO. I do follow here in the chase, not like a hound that hunts, but one that fills up the cry. My money is almost spent; I have been to-night exceedingly well cudgelled; and I think the issue will be, I shall have so much experience for my pains; and

so, with no money at all and a little more wit, return again to
Venice.

IAGO. How poor are they that have not patience!
What wound did ever heal but by degrees?
Thou know'st we work by wit and not by witchcraft,
And wit depends on dilatory time.
Does't not go well? Cassio hath beaten thee,
And thou by that small hurt hast cashiered Cassio.
Though other things grow fair against the sun,
Yet fruits that blossom first will first be ripe:
Content thyself awhile. By the mass, 'tis morning;
Pleasure and action make the hours seem short.
Retire thee; go where thou art billeted:
Away, I say; thou shalt know more hereafter:
Nay, get thee gone. [*Exit* RODERIGO.] Two things are to be done,
My wife must move for Cassio to her mistress;
I'll set her on;
Myself the while to draw the Moor apart,
And bring him jump when he may Cassio find
Soliciting his wife: ay, that's the way:
Dull not device by coldness and delay.   [*Exit.*

Act 3

Scene I. Cyprus. Before the Castle

Enter CASSIO, *and some* MUSICIANS.

CASSIO. Masters, play here, I will content your pains;
Something that's brief; and bid 'Good morrow, general.'

[*Music.*

Enter CLOWN.

CLOWN. Why, masters, have your instruments been in Naples,
that they speak i' the nose thus?
FIRST MUSICIAN. How, sir, how?
CLOWN. Are these, I pray you, wind-instruments?
FIRST MUSICIAN. Ay, marry, are they, sir.
CLOWN. O! thereby hangs a tail.
FIRST MUSICIAN. Whereby hangs a tale, sir?
CLOWN. Marry, sir, by many a wind-instrument that I know.
But, masters, here's money for you; and the general so likes your
music, that he desires you, for love's sake, to make no more noise
with it.
FIRST MUSICIAN. Well, sir, we will not.
CLOWN. If you have any music that may not be heard, to't
again; but, as they say, to hear music the general does not greatly
care.
FIRST MUSICIAN. We have none such, sir.
CLOWN. Then put up your pipes in your bag, for I'll away.
Go; vanish into air; away!   [*Exeunt* MUSICIANS.
CASSIO. Dost thou hear, mine honest friend?
CLOWN. No, I hear not your honest friend; I hear you.

CASSIO. Prithee, keep up thy quillets. There's a poor piece of
gold for thee. If the gentlewoman that attends the general's wife
be stirring, tell her there's one Cassio entreats her a little favour
of speech: wilt thou do this?

CLOWN. She is stirring, sir: if she will stir hither,
I shall seem to notify unto her.

CASSIO. Do, good my friend.   [*Exit* CLOWN.

   Enter IAGO.

                    In happy time, Iago.

IAGO. You have not been a-bed, then?

CASSIO. Why, no; the day had broke
Before we parted. I have made bold, Iago,
To send in to your wife; my suit to her
Is, that she will to virtuous Desdemona
Procure me some access.

IAGO.   I'll send her to you presently;
And I'll devise a mean to draw the Moor
Out of the way, that your converse and business
May be more free.

CASSIO. I humbly thank you for't.   [*Exit* IAGO.
                    I never knew
A Florentine more kind and honest.

   Enter EMILIA.

EMILIA. Good morrow, good lieutenant: I am sorry
For your displeasure; but all will soon be well.
The general and his wife are talking of it,
And she speaks for you stoutly: the Moor replies
That he you hurt is of great fame in Cyprus
And great affinity, and that in wholesome wisdom
He might not but refuse you; but he protests he loves you,
And needs no other suitor but his likings
To take the saf'st occasion by the front
To bring you in again.

CASSIO.   Yet, I beseech you,
If you think fit, or that it may be done,

Give me advantage of some brief discourse
With Desdemona alone.

    EMILIA.   Pray you, come in:
I will bestow you where you shall have time
To speak your bosom freely.

    CASSIO.   I am much bound to you.

                                   [Exeunt.

Scene II. *A Room in the Castle*

Enter OTHELLO, IAGO, *and* GENTLEMEN.

    OTHELLO. These letters give, Iago, to the pilot,
And by him do my duties to the senate;
That done, I will be walking on the works;
Repair there to me.

    IAGO.   Well, my good lord, I'll do't.

    OTHELLO. This fortification, gentlemen, shall we see't?

    GENTLEMEN. We'll wait upon your lordship.   *[Exeunt.*

Scene III. *Before the Castle*

Enter DESDEMONA, CASSIO, *and* EMILIA.

    DESDEMONA. Be thou assur'd, good Cassio, I will do
All my abilities in thy behalf.

    EMILIA. Good madam, do: I warrant it grieves my husband,
As if the case were his.

    DESDEMONA. O! that's an honest fellow. Do not doubt, Cassio,
But I will have my lord and you again
As friendly as you were.

    CASSIO.   Bounteous madam,
Whatever shall become of Michael Cassio,
He's never anything but your true servant.

    DESDEMONA. I know't; I thank you. You do love my lord;
You have known him long; and be you well assur'd
He shall in strangeness stand no further off
Than in a politic distance.

CASSIO. Ay, but lady,
That policy may either last so long,
Or feed upon much nice and waterish diet,
Or breed itself so out of circumstance,
That, I being absent and my place supplied,
My general will forget my love and service.

DESDEMONA. Do not doubt that; before Emilia here
I give thee warrant of thy place. Assure thee,
If I do vow a friendship, I'll perform it
To the last article; my lord shall never rest;
I'll watch him tame, and talk him out of patience;
His bed shall seem a school, his board a shrift;
I'll intermingle every thing he does
With Cassio's suit. Therefore be merry, Cassio;
For thy solicitor shall rather die
Than give thy cause away.

Enter OTHELLO, *and* IAGO *at a distance.*

EMILIA. Madam, here comes my lord.
CASSIO. Madam, I'll take my leave.
DESDEMONA. Why, stay, and hear me speak.
CASSIO. Madam, not now; I am very ill at ease,
Unfit for mine own purposes.
DESDEMONA. Well, do your discretion.　　　[*Exit* CASSIO.
IAGO. Ha! I like not that.
OTHELLO.　　　　　　What dost thou say?
IAGO. Nothing, my lord: or if—I know not what.
OTHELLO. Was not that Cassio parted from my wife?
IAGO. Cassio, my lord? No, sure, I cannot think it
That he would steal away so guilty-like,
Seeing you coming.
OTHELLO.　　　　I do believe 'twas he.
DESDEMONA. How now, my lord!
　　I have been talking with a suitor here,
A man that languishes in your displeasure.
OTHELLO. Who is't you mean?
DESDEMONA. Why, your lieutenant, Cassio. Good my lord,

If I have any grace or power to move you,
His present reconciliation take;
For if he be not one that truly loves you,
That errs in ignorance and not in cunning,
I have no judgment in an honest face.
I prithee call him back.

OTHELLO.   Went he hence now?

DESDEMONA. Ay, sooth; so humbled,
That he hath left part of his grief with me,
To suffer with him. Good love, call him back.

OTHELLO. Not now, sweet Desdemona; some other time.

DESDEMONA. But shall't be shortly?

OTHELLO.   The sooner, sweet, for you.

DESDEMONA. Shall't be to-night at supper?

OTHELLO.   No, not to-night.

DESDEMONA. To-morrow dinner then?

OTHELLO.   I shall not dine at home;
I meet the captains at the citadel.

DESDEMONA. Why then, to-morrow night; or Tuesday morn;
On Tuesday noon, or night; on Wednesday morn:
I prithee name the time, but let it not
Exceed three days: in faith, he's penitent;
And yet his trespass, in our common reason,—
Save that they say, the wars must make examples
Out of their best,—is not almost a fault
To incur a private check. When shall he come?
Tell me, Othello: I wonder in my soul,
What you could ask me that I should deny,
Or stand so mammering on. What! Michael Cassio,
That came a wooing with you, and so many a time,
When I have spoke of you dispraisingly,
Hath ta'en your part; to have so much to do
To bring him in! Trust me, I could do much.—

OTHELLO. Prithee, no more; let him come when he will;
I will deny thee nothing.

DESDEMONA.   Why, this is not a boon;
'Tis as I should entreat you wear your gloves,

Or feed on nourishing dishes, or keep you warm,
Or sue to you to do a peculiar profit
To your own person; nay, when I have a suit
Wherein I mean to touch your love indeed,
It shall be full of poise and difficult weight,
And fearful to be granted.

OTHELLO.   I will deny thee nothing:
Whereon, I do beseech thee, grant me this,
To leave me but a little to myself.

DESDEMONA. Shall I deny you? no, farewell, my lord.

OTHELLO. Farewell, my Desdemona; I'll come to thee straight.

DESDEMONA. Emilia, come. Be as your fancies teach you;
Whate'er you be, I am obedient.   [*Exit, with* EMILIA.

OTHELLO. Excellent wretch! Perdition catch my soul
But I do love thee! and when I love thee not,
Chaos is come again.

IAGO. My noble lord,—

OTHELLO.   What dost thou say, Iago?

IAGO. Did Michael Cassio, when you woo'd my lady,
Know of your love?

OTHELLO. He did, from first to last: why dost thou ask?

IAGO. But for a satisfaction of my thought;
No further harm.

OTHELLO.   Why of thy thought, Iago?

IAGO. I did not think he had been acquainted with her.

OTHELLO. O! yes; and went between us very oft.

IAGO. Indeed!

OTHELLO. Indeed! ay, indeed; discern'st thou aught in that?
Is he not honest?

IAGO.   Honest, my lord?

OTHELLO.   Honest! ay, honest.

IAGO. My lord, for aught I know.

OTHELLO. What dost thou think?

IAGO.   Think, my lord!

OTHELLO.   Think, my lord!
By heaven, he echoes me,
As if there were some monster in his thought

Too hideous to be shown. Thou dost mean something:
I heard thee say but now, thou lik'dst not that,
When Cassio left my wife; what didst not like?
And when I told thee he was of my counsel
In my whole course of wooing, thou criedst, 'Indeed!'
And didst contract and purse thy brow together,
As if thou then hadst shut up in thy brain
Some horrible conceit. If thou dost love me,
Show me thy thought

    IAGO. My lord, you know I love you.

    OTHELLO.   I think thou dost;
And, for I know thou art full of love and honesty,
And weigh'st thy words before thou giv'st them breath,
Therefore these stops of thine fright me the more;
For such things in a false disloyal knave
Are tricks of custom, but in a man that's just
They are close delations, working from the heart
That passion cannot rule.

    IAGO.   For Michael Cassio,
I dare be sworn I think that he is honest.

    OTHELLO. I think so too.

    IAGO.   Men should be what they seem;
Or those that be not, would they might seem none!

    OTHELLO. Certain, men should be what they seem.

    IAGO. Why then, I think Cassio's an honest man.

    OTHELLO. Nay, yet there's more in this.
I pray thee, speak to me as to thy thinkings,
As thou dost ruminate, and give thy worst of thoughts
The worst of words.

    IAGO.   Good my lord, pardon me;
Though I am bound to every act of duty,
I am not bound to that all slaves are free to.
Utter my thoughts? Why, say they are vile and false;
As where's that palace whereinto foul things
Sometimes intrude not? who has a breast so pure
But some uncleanly apprehensions
Keep leets and law days, and in session sit

With meditations lawful?

OTHELLO. Thou dost conspire against thy friend, Iago,
If thou but think'st him wrong'd, and mak'st his ear
A stranger to thy thoughts.

IAGO.   I do beseech you,
Though I perchance am vicious in my guess,—
As, I confess, it is my nature's plague
To spy into abuses, and oft my jealousy
Shapes faults that are not,—that your wisdom yet,
From one that so imperfectly conceits,
Would take no notice, nor build yourself a trouble
Out of his scattering and unsure observance.
It were not for you quiet nor your good,
Nor for my manhood, honesty, or wisdom,
To let you know my thoughts.

OTHELLO.   What dost thou mean?

IAGO. Good name in man and woman, dear my lord,
Is the immediate jewel of their souls:
Who steals my purse steals trash; 'tis something, nothing;
'Twas mine, 'tis his, and has been slave to thousands;
But he that filches from me my good name
Robs me of that which not enriches him,
And makes me poor indeed.

OTHELLO. By heaven, I'll know thy thoughts.

IAGO. You cannot, if my heart were in your hand;
Nor shall not, whilst 'tis in my custody.

OTHELLO. Ha!

IAGO.   O! beware, my lord, of jealousy;
It is the green-ey'd monster which doth mock
The meat it feeds on; that cuckold lives in bliss
Who, certain of his fate, loves not his wronger;
But, O! what damned minutes tells he o'er
Who dotes, yet doubts; suspects, yet soundly loves!

OTHELLO. O misery!

IAGO. Poor and content is rich, and rich enough,
But riches fineless is as poor as winter
To him that ever fears he shall be poor.

Good heaven, the souls of all my tribe defend
From jealousy!
    OTHELLO.   Why, why is this?
Think'st thou I'd make a life of jealousy,
To follow still the changes of the moon
With fresh suspicions? No; to be once in doubt
Is once to be resolved. Exchange me for a goat
When I shall turn the business of my soul
To such exsufflicate and blown surmises,
Matching thy inference. 'Tis not to make me jealous
To say my wife is fair, feeds well, loves company,
Is free of speech, sings, plays, and dances well;
Where virtue is, these are more virtuous:
Nor from mine own weak merits will I draw
The smallest fear, or doubt of her revolt;
For she had eyes, and chose me. No, Iago;
I'll see before I doubt; when I doubt, prove;
And, on the proof, there is no more but this,
Away at once with love or jealousy!
    IAGO. I am glad of it; for now I shall have reason
To show the love and duty that I bear you
With franker spirit; therefore, as I am bound,
Receive it from me; I speak not yet of proof.
Look to your wife; observe her well with Cassio;
Wear your eye thus, not jealous nor secure:
I would not have your free and noble nature
Out of self-bounty be abus'd; look to't:
I know our country disposition well;
In Venice they do let heaven see the pranks
They dare not show their husbands; their best conscience
Is not to leave't undone, but keep't unknown.
    OTHELLO. Dost thou say so?
    IAGO. She did deceive her father, marrying you;
And when she seem'd to shake and fear your looks,
She lov'd them most.
    OTHELLO.   And so she did.
    IAGO.   Why, go to, then;

She that so young could give out such a seeming,
To seel her father's eyes up close as oak,
He thought 'twas witchcraft; but I am much to blame;
I humbly do beseech you of your pardon
For too much loving you.

OTHELLO.　　　　　　　I am bound to thee for ever.

IAGO. I see, this hath a little dash'd your spirits.

OTHELLO. Not a jot, not a jot.

IAGO.　　　　　　　　　I' faith, I fear it has.
I hope you will consider what is spoke
Comes from my love. But, I do see you're mov'd;
I am to pray you not to strain my speech
To grosser issues nor to larger reach
Than to suspicion.

OTHELLO. I will not.

IAGO.　　　　　　　Should you do so, my lord,
My speech should fall into such vile success
As my thoughts aim not at. Cassio's my worthy friend—
My lord, I see you're mov'd.

OTHELLO.　　　　　　　No, not much mov'd:
I do not think but Desdemona's honest.

IAGO. Long live she so! and long live you to think so!

OTHELLO. And, yet, how nature erring from itself,—

IAGO. Ay, there's the point: as, to be bold with you,
Not to affect many proposed matches
Of her own clime, complexion, and degree,
Whereto, we see, in all things nature tends;
Foh! one may smell in such, a will most rank,
Foul disproportion, thoughts unnatural.
But pardon me; I do not in position
Distinctly speak of her, though I may fear
Her will, recoiling to her better judgment,
May fail to match you with her country forms
And happily repent.

OTHELLO.　　　　Farewell, farewell:
If more thou dost perceive, let me know more;
Set on thy wife to observe. Leave me, Iago.

IAGO. My lord, I take my leave.   [*Going.*

OTHELLO. Why did I marry? This honest creature, doubtless,
Sees and knows more, much more, than he unfolds.

IAGO. [*Returning.*] My lord, I would I might entreat your
honour
To scan this thing no further; leave it to time.
Although 'tis fit that Cassio have his place,
For, sure he fills it up with great ability,
Yet, if you please to hold him off awhile,
You shall by that perceive him and his means:
Note if your lady strain his entertainment
With any strong or vehement importunity;
Much will be seen in that. In the mean time,
Let me be thought too busy in my fears,
As worthy cause I have to fear I am,
And hold her free, I do beseech your honour.

OTHELLO. Fear not my government.

IAGO. I once more take my leave.   [*Exit.*

OTHELLO. This fellow's of exceeding honesty,
And knows all qualities, with a learned spirit,
Of human dealings; if I do prove her haggard,
Though that her jesses were my dear heartstrings,
I'd whistle her off and let her down the wind,
To prey at fortune. Haply, for I am black,
And have not those soft parts of conversation
That chamberers have, or, for I am declin'd
Into the vale of years—yet that's not much—
She's gone, I am abus'd; and my relief
Must be to loathe her. O curse of marriage!
That we can call these delicate creatures ours,
And not their appetites. I had rather be a toad,
And live upon the vapour of a dungeon,
Than keep a corner in the thing I love
For others' uses. Yet, 'tis the plague of great ones;
Prerogativ'd are they less than the base;
'Tis destiny unshunnable, like death:
Even then this forked plague is fated to us

Courtesy Stage Photo Company

A scene from *Othello* with Paul Robeson in the title role, London, 1930.

When we do quicken.

Look! where she comes.

If she be false, O! then heaven mocks itself.

I'll not believe it.

Re-enter DESDEMONA *and* EMILIA.

DESDEMONA.   How now, my dear Othello!

Your dinner and the generous islanders

By you invited, do attend your presence.

OTHELLO. I am to blame.

DESDEMONA.   Why do you speak so faintly?

Are you not well?

OTHELLO. I have a pain upon my forehead here.

DESDEMONA. Faith, that's with watching; 'twill away again:

Let me but bind it hard, within this hour

It will be well.

OTHELLO.   Your napkin is too little:

[*She drops her handkerchief.*

Let it alone. Come, I'll go in with you.

DESDEMONA. I am very sorry that you are not well.

[*Exeunt* OTHELLO *and* DESDEMONA.

EMILIA. I am glad I have found this napkin;

This was her first remembrance from the Moor;

My wayward husband hath a hundred times

Woo'd me to steal it, but she so loves the token,

For he conjur'd her she should ever keep it,

That she reserves it evermore about her

To kiss and talk to. I'll have the work ta'en out,

And give't Iago:

What he will do with it heaven knows, not I;

I nothing but to please his fantasy.

Enter IAGO.

IAGO. How now! what do you here alone?

EMILIA. Do not you chide; I have a thing for you.

IAGO. A thing for me? It is a common thing—

EMILIA. Ha!

IAGO. To have a foolish wife.

EMILIA. O! is that all? What will you give me now
For that same handkerchief?

IAGO.   What handkerchief?

EMILIA. What handkerchief!
Why, that the Moor first gave to Desdemona:
That which so often you did bid me steal.

IAGO. Hast stol'n it from her?

EMILIA. No, faith; she let it drop by negligence,
And, to the advantage, I, being there, took't up.
Look, here it is.

IAGO.   A good wench; give it me.

EMILIA. What will you do with't, that you have been so ear-
    nest
To have me filch it?

IAGO. Why, what's that to you?   [Snatches it.

EMILIA. If it be not for some purpose of import
Give't me again; poor lady! she'll run mad
When she shall lack it.

IAGO. Be not acknown on't; I have use for it.
Go, leave me.   [Exit EMILIA.
I will in Cassio's lodging lose this napkin,
And let him find it; trifles light as air
Are to the jealous confirmations strong
As proofs of holy writ; this may do something.
The Moor already changes with my poison:
Dangerous conceits are in their natures poisons,
Which at the first are scarce found to distaste,
But with a little act upon the blood,
Burn like the mines of sulphur. I did say so:
Look! where he comes!

    Enter OTHELLO.

                    Not poppy, nor mandragora,
Nor all the drowsy syrups of the world,
Shall ever medicine thee to that sweet sleep
Which thou ow'dst yesterday.

OTHELLO.   Ha! ha! false to me?

IAGO. Why, how now, general! no more of that.

OTHELLO. Avaunt! be gone! thou hast set me on the rack;
I swear 'tis better to be much abus'd
Than but to know't a little.

IAGO.   How now, my lord!

OTHELLO. What sense had I of her stol'n hours of lust?
I saw't not, thought it not, it harm'd not me;
I slept the next night well, was free and merry;
I found not Cassio's kisses on her lips;
He that is robb'd, not wanting what is stol'n,
Let him not know't and he's not robb'd at all.

IAGO. I am sorry to hear this.

OTHELLO. I had been happy, if the general camp,
Pioners and all, had tasted her sweet body,
So I had nothing known. O! now, for ever
Farewell the tranquil mind; farewell content!
Farewell the plumed troop and the big wars
That make ambition virtue! O, farewell!
Farewell the neighing steed, and the shrill trump,
The spirit-stirring drum, the ear-piercing fife,
The royal banner, and all quality,
Pride, pomp, and circumstance of glorious war!
And, O you mortal engines, whose rude throats
The immortal Jove's dread clamours counterfeit,
Farewell! Othello's occupation's gone!

IAGO. Is it possible, my lord?

OTHELLO. Villain, be sure thou prove my love a whore,
Be sure of it; give me the ocular proof;
Or, by the worth of mine eternal soul,
Thou hadst been better have been born a dog
Than answer my wak'd wrath.

IAGO.   Is't come to this?

OTHELLO. Make me to see't; or, at the least, so prove it,
That the probation bear no hinge nor loop
To hang a doubt on; or woe upon thy life!

IAGO. My noble lord,—

OTHELLO. If thou dost slander her and torture me,
Never pray more; abandon all remorse;
On horror's head horrors accumulate;
Do deeds to make heaven weep, all earth amaz'd;
For nothing canst thou to damnation add
Greater than that.

IAGO.   O grace! O heaven forgive me!
Are you a man! have you a soul or sense?
God be wi' you; take mine office. O wretched fool!
That liv'st to make thine honesty a vice.
O monstrous world! Take note, take note, O world!
To be direct and honest is not safe.
I thank you for this profit, and, from hence
I'll love no friend, sith love breeds such offence.

OTHELLO. Nay, stay; thou shouldst be honest.

IAGO. I should be wise; for honesty's a fool,
And loses that it works for.

OTHELLO.   By the world,
I think my wife be honest and think she is not;
I think that thou art just and think thou art not.
I'll have some proof. Her name, that was as fresh
As Dian's visage, is now begrim'd and black
As mine own face. If there be cords or knives,
Poison or fire or suffocating streams,
I'll not endure it. Would I were satisfied!

IAGO. I see, sir, you are eaten up with passion.
I do repent me that I put it to you.
You would be satisfied?

OTHELLO.   Would! nay, I will.

IAGO. And may; but how? how satisfied, my lord?
Would you, the supervisor, grossly gape on;
Behold her tupp'd?

OTHELLO.   Death and damnation! O!

IAGO. It were a tedious difficulty, I think,
To bring them to that prospect; damn them then,
If ever mortal eyes do see them bolster
More than their own! What then? how then?

What shall I say? Where's satisfaction?
It is impossible you should see this,
Were they as prime as goats, as hot as monkeys,
As salt as wolves in pride, and fools as gross
As ignorance made drunk; but yet, I say,
If imputation, and strong circumstances,
Which lead directly to the door of truth,
Will give you satisfaction, you may have it.

   OTHELLO. Give me a living reason she's disloyal.

   IAGO. I do not like the office;
But, sith I am enter'd in this cause so far,
Prick'd to't by foolish honesty and love,
I will go on. I lay with Cassio lately;
And, being troubled with a raging tooth,
I could not sleep.
There are a kind of men so loose of soul
That in their sleeps will mutter their affairs;
One of this kind is Cassio.
In sleep I heard him say, 'Sweet Desdemona,
Let us be wary, let us hide our loves!'
And then, sir, would he gripe and wring my hand,
Cry, 'O, sweet creature!' and then kiss me hard,
As if he pluck'd up kisses by the roots,
That grew upon my lips; then laid his leg
Over my thigh, and sigh'd, and kiss'd; and then
Cried, 'Cursed fate, that gave thee to the Moor!'

   OTHELLO. O monstrous! monstrous!

   IAGO.   Nay, this was but his dream.

   OTHELLO. But this denoted a foregone conclusion:
'Tis a shrewd doubt, though it be but a dream.

   IAGO. And this may help to thicken other proofs
That do demonstrate thinly.

   OTHELLO.   I'll tear her all to pieces.

   IAGO. Nay, but be wise; yet we see nothing done;
She may be honest yet. Tell me but this:
Have you not sometimes seen a handkerchief
Spotted with strawberries in your wife's hand?

OTHELLO. I gave her such a one; 'twas my first gift.

IAGO. I know not that; but such a handkerchief—
I am sure it was your wife's—did I to-day
See Cassio wipe his beard with.

OTHELLO.   If it be that,—

IAGO. If it be that, or any that was hers,
It speaks against her with the other proofs.

OTHELLO. O! that the slave had forty thousand lives;
One is too poor, too weak for my revenge.
Now do I see 'tis true. Look here, Iago;
All my fond love thus do I blow to heaven:
'Tis gone.
Arise, black vengeance, from the hollow hell!
Yield up, O love! thy crown and hearted throne
To tyrannous hate. Swell, bosom, with thy fraught,
For 'tis of aspics' tongues!

IAGO.   Yet be content.

OTHELLO. O! blood, blood, blood!

IAGO. Patience, I say; your mind, perhaps, may change.

OTHELLO. Never, Iago. Like to the Pontick sea,
Whose icy current and compulsive course
Ne'er feels retiring ebb, but keeps due on
To the Propontic and the Hellespont,
Even so my bloody thoughts, with violent pace,
Shall ne'er look back, ne'er ebb to humble love,
Till that a capable and wide revenge
Swallow them up.   [*Kneels.*
                    Now, by yond marble heaven,
In the due reverence of a sacred vow
I here engage my words.

IAGO.   Do not rise yet.   [*Kneels.*
Witness, you ever-burning lights above!
You elements that clip us round about!
Witness, that here Iago doth give up
The execution of his wit, hands, heart,
To wrong'd Othello's service! Let him command,
And to obey shall be in me remorse,

What bloody business ever.

OTHELLO.   I greet thy love,
Not with vain thanks, but with acceptance bounteous,
And will upon the instant put thee to't:
Within these three days let me hear thee say
That Cassio's not alive.

IAGO. My friend is dead; 'tis done at your request:
But let her live.

OTHELLO. Damn her, lewd minx! O, damn her!
Come, go with me apart; I will withdraw
To furnish me with some swift means of death
For the fair devil. Now art thou my lieutenant.

IAGO. I am your own for ever.   [*Exeunt.*

Scene IV. Before the Castle

Enter DESDEMONA, EMILIA, *and* CLOWN.

DESDEMONA. Do you know, sirrah, where Lieutenant Cassio lies?

CLOWN. I dare not say he lies any where.

DESDEMONA. Why, man?

CLOWN. He is a soldier; and for one to say a soldier lies, is stabbing.

DESDEMONA. Go to; where lodges he?

CLOWN. To tell you where he lodges is to tell you where I lie.

DESDEMONA. Can anything be made of this?

CLOWN. I know not where he lodges, and for me to devise a lodging, and say he lies here or he lies there, were to lie in mine own throat.

DESDEMONA. Can you inquire him out, and be edified by report?

CLOWN. I will catechize the world for him; that is, make questions, and by them answer.

DESDEMONA. Seek him, bid him come hither; tell him I have moved my lord in his behalf, and hope all will be well.

CLOWN. To do this is within the compass of man's wit, and

therefore I will attempt the doing it. [*Exit.*

DESDEMONA. Where should I lose that handkerchief, Emilia?

EMILIA. I know not, madam.

DESDEMONA. Believe me, I had rather have lost my purse
Full of cruzadoes; and, but my noble Moor
Is true of mind, and made of no such baseness
As jealous creatures are, it were enough
To put him to ill thinking.

EMILIA. Is he not jealous?

DESDEMONA. Who! he? I think the sun where he was born
Drew all such humours from him.

EMILIA. Look! where he comes.

DESDEMONA. I will not leave him now till Cassio
Be call'd to him.

Enter OTHELLO.

How is't with you, my lord?

OTHELLO. Well, my good lady. [*Aside.*] O! hardness to dissemble.

How do you, Desdemona?

DESDEMONA. Well, my good lord.

OTHELLO. Give me your hand. This hand is moist, my lady.

DESDEMONA. It yet has felt no age nor known no sorrow.

OTHELLO. This argues fruitfulness and liberal heart;
Hot, hot, and moist; this hand of yours requires
A sequester from liberty, fasting and prayer,
Much castigation, exercise devout;
For here's a young and sweating devil here,
That commonly rebels. 'Tis a good hand,
A frank one.

DESDEMONA. You may, indeed, say so;
For 'twas that hand that gave away my heart.

OTHELLO. A liberal hand; the hearts of old gave hands,
But our new heraldry is hands not hearts.

DESDEMONA. I cannot speak of this. Come now, your promise.

OTHELLO. What promise, chuck?

DESDEMONA. I have sent to bid Cassio come speak with you.

OTHELLO. I have a salt and sorry rheum offends me.
Lend me thy handkerchief.

DESDEMONA.   Here, my lord.

OTHELLO. That which I gave you.

DESDEMONA.   I have it not about me.

OTHELLO. Not?

DESDEMONA. No, indeed, my lord.

OTHELLO.   That is a fault.
That handkerchief
Did an Egyptian to my mother give;
She was a charmer, and could almost read
The thoughts of people; she told her, while she kept it,
'Twould make her amiable and subdue my father
Entirely to her love, but if she lost it
Or made a gift of it, my father's eye
Should hold her loathed, and his spirits should hunt
After new fancies. She dying gave it me;
And bid me, when my fate would have me wive,
To give it her. I did so: and take heed on't;
Make it a darling like your precious eye;
To lose't or give't away, were such perdition
As nothing else could match.

DESDEMONA.   Is't possible?

OTHELLO. 'Tis true; there's magic in the web of it;
A sibyl, that had number'd in the world
The sun to course two hundred compasses,
In her prophetic fury sew'd the work;
The worms were hallow'd that did breed the silk,
And it was dy'd in mummy which the skilful
Conserv'd of maidens' hearts.

DESDEMONA.   Indeed! is't true?

OTHELLO. Most veritable; therefore look to't well.

DESDEMONA. Then would to heaven that I had never seen it!

OTHELLO. Ha! wherefore?

DESDEMONA. Why do you speak so startingly and rash?

OTHELLO. Is't lost? is't gone? speak, is it out o' the way?

DESDEMONA. Heaven bless us!

OTHELLO.   Say you?

DESDEMONA. It is not lost: but what an if it were?

OTHELLO. How!

DESDEMONA. I say, it is not lost.

OTHELLO.   Fetch't, let me see't.

DESDEMONA. Why, so I can, sir, but I will not now.
This is a trick to put me from my suit:
Pray you let Cassio be receiv'd again.

OTHELLO. Fetch me the handkerchief; my mind misgives.

DESDEMONA. Come, come;
You'll never meet a more sufficient man.

OTHELLO. The handkerchief!

DESDEMONA.   I pray, talk me of Cassio.

OTHELLO. The handkerchief!

DESDEMONA.   A man that all his time
Hath founded his good fortunes on your love,
Shar'd dangers with you,—

OTHELLO. The handkerchief!

DESDEMONA.   In sooth you are to blame.

OTHELLO. Away!   [*Exit.*

EMILIA. Is not this man jealous?

DESDEMONA. I ne'er saw this before.
Sure, there's some wonder in this handkerchief;
I am most unhappy in the loss of it.

EMILIA. 'Tis not a year or two shows us a man;
They are all but stomachs, and we all but food;
They eat us hungerly, and when they are full
They belch us. Look you! Cassio and my husband.

        Enter IAGO *and* CASSIO.

IAGO. There is no other way; 'tis she must do't:
And, lo! the happiness: go and importune her.

DESDEMONA. How now, good Cassio! what's the news with
    you?

CASSIO. Madam, my former suit: I do beseech you
That by your virtuous means I may again
Exist, and be a member of his love

Whom I with all the office of my heart
Entirely honour; I would not be delay'd.
If my offence be of such mortal kind
That nor my service past, nor present sorrows,
Nor purpos'd merit in futurity,
Can ransom me into his love again,
But to know so must be my benefit;
So shall I clothe me in a forc'd content,
And shut myself up in some other course
To fortune's alms.

    DESDEMONA.   Alas! thrice-gentle Cassio!
My advocation is not now in tune;
My lord is not my lord; nor should I know him,
Were he in favour as in humour alter'd.
So help me every spirit sanctified,
As I have spoken for you all my best
And stood within the blank of his displeasure
For my free speech. You must awhile be patient;
What I can do I will, and more I will
Than for myself I dare: let that suffice you.

    IAGO. Is my lord angry?

    EMILIA.   He went hence but now,
And, certainly in strange unquietness.

    IAGO. Can he be angry? I have seen the cannon,
When it hath blown his ranks into the air,
And, like the devil, from his very arm
Puff'd his own brother; and can he be angry?
Something of moment then; I will go meet him;
There's matter in't indeed, if he be angry.

    DESDEMONA. I prithee, do so. [*Exit* IAGO.] Something, sure, of
        state,
Either from Venice, or some unhatch'd practice
Made demonstrable here in Cyprus to him,
Hath puddled his clear spirit; and, in such cases
Men's natures wrangle with inferior things,
Though great ones are their object. 'Tis even so;
For let our finger ache, and it indues

Our other healthful members ev'n to that sense
Of pain. Nay, we must think men are not gods,
Nor of them look for such observancy
As fits the bridal. Beshrew me much, Emilia,
I was—unhandsome warrior as I am—
Arraigning his unkindness with my soul;
But now I find I had suborn'd the witness,
And he's indicted falsely.

    EMILIA. Pray heaven it be state-matters, as you think,
And no conception, nor no jealous toy
Concerning you.

    DESDEMONA. Alas the day! I never gave him cause.

    EMILIA. But jealous souls will not be answer'd so;
They are not ever jealous for the cause,
But jealous for they are jealous; 'tis a monster
Begot upon itself, born on itself.

    DESDEMONA. Heaven keep that monster from Othello's mind!

    EMILIA. Lady, amen.

    DESDEMONA. I will go seek him. Cassio, walk hereabout;
If I do find him fit, I'll move your suit
And seek to effect it to my uttermost.

    CASSIO. I humbly thank your ladyship.

                  [*Exeunt* DESDEMONA *and* EMILIA.

    Enter BIANCA.

    BIANCA. Save you, friend Cassio!

    CASSIO.   What make you from home?
How is it with you, my most fair Bianca?
I' faith, sweet love, I was coming to your house.

    BIANCA. And I was going to your lodging, Cassio.
What! keep a week away? seven days and nights?
Eight score eight hours? and lovers' absent hours,
More tedious than the dial eight score times?
O weary reckoning!

    CASSIO.   Pardon me, Bianca,
I have this while with leaden thoughts been press'd,
But I shall, in a more continuate time,

Strike off this score of absence. Sweet Bianca.

                    [*Giving her* DESDEMONA'S *handkerchief.*

Take me this work out.

    BIANCA.   O Cassio! whence came this?

This is some token from a newer friend;

To the felt absence now I feel a cause;

Is't come to this? Well, well.

    CASSIO.   Go to, woman!

Throw your vile guesses in the devil's teeth,

From whence you have them. You are jealous now

That this is from some mistress, some remembrance:

No, in good troth, Bianca.

    BIANCA.   Why, whose is it?

    CASSIO. I know not, sweet; I found it in my chamber.

I like the work well; ere it be demanded,—

As like enough it will,—I'd have it copied;

Take it and do't; and leave me for this time.

    BIANCA. Leave you! wherefore?

    CASSIO. I do attend here on the general,

And think it no addition nor my wish

To have him see me woman'd.

    BIANCA.   Why, I pray you?

    CASSIO. Not that I love you not.

    BIANCA.   But that you do not love me.

I pray you, bring me on the way a little

And say if I shall see you soon at night.

    CASSIO. 'Tis but a little way that I can bring you,

For I attend here; but I'll see you soon.

    BIANCA. 'Tis very good; I must be circumstanc'd.   [*Exeunt.*

Act 4

Scene I. Cyprus. Before the Castle

Enter OTHELLO *and* IAGO.

IAGO. Will you think so?

OTHELLO.   Think so, Iago!

IAGO.   What!

To kiss in private?

OTHELLO.   An unauthoriz'd kiss.

IAGO. Or to be naked with her friend a-bed
An hour or more, not meaning any harm?

OTHELLO. Naked a-bed, Iago, and not mean harm?
It is hypocrisy against the devil:
They that mean virtuously, and yet do so,
The devil their virtue tempts, and they tempt heaven.

IAGO. If they do nothing, 'tis a venial slip;
But if I give my wife a handkerchief,—

OTHELLO. What then?

IAGO. Why, then, 'tis hers, my lord; and, being hers,
She may, I think, bestow't on any man.

OTHELLO. She is protectress of her honour too;
May she give that?

IAGO. Her honour is an essence that's not seen;
They have it very oft that have it not:
But for the handkerchief,—

OTHELLO. By heaven, I would most gladly have forgot it:—
Thou said'st,—O! it comes o'er my memory,
As doth the raven o'er the infected house,
Boding to all,—he had my handkerchief.

176

IAGO. Ay, what of that?

OTHELLO. That's not so good now.

IAGO. What,
If I had said I had seen him do you wrong?
Or heard him say, as knaves be such abroad,
Who having, by their own importunate suit,
Or voluntary dotage of some mistress,
Convinced or supplied them, cannot choose
But they must blab.

OTHELLO. Hath he said any thing?

IAGO. He hath, my lord; but be you well assur'd,
No more than he'll unswear.

OTHELLO. What hath he said?

IAGO. Faith, that he did—I know not what he did.

OTHELLO. What? what?

IAGO. Lie—

OTHELLO. With her?

IAGO. With her, on her; what you will.

OTHELLO. Lie with her! lie on her! We say, lie on her, when
they belie her. Lie with her! that's fulsome. Handkerchief,—
confessions,—handkerchief! To confess, and be hanged for his
labour. First, to be hanged, and then to confess: I tremble at it.
Nature would not invest herself in such shadowing passion without some instruction. It is not words that shake me thus. Pish!
Noses, ears, and lips. Is it possible?—Confess!—Handkerchief!—
O devil!   [*Falls in a trance.*

IAGO. Work on,
My medicine, work! Thus credulous fools are caught;
And many worthy and chaste dames even thus,
All guiltless, meet reproach. What, ho! my lord!
My lord, I say! Othello!

Enter CASSIO.

How now, Cassio!

CASSIO. What's the matter?

IAGO. My lord is fallen into an epilepsy;
This is his second fit; he had one yesterday.

CASSIO. Rub him about the temples.

IAGO.   No, forbear;
The lethargy must have his quiet course,
If not he foams at mouth, and by and by
Breaks out to savage madness. Look! he stirs;
Do you withdraw yourself a little while,
He will recover straight; when he is gone,
I would on great occasion speak with you.   [*Exit* CASSIO.
How is it, general? have you not hurt your head?

OTHELLO. Dost thou mock me?

IAGO.   I mock you! no, by heaven.
Would you would bear your fortune like a man!

OTHELLO. A horned man's a monster and a beast.

IAGO. There's many a beast then, in a populous city,
And many a civil monster.

OTHELLO. Did he confess it?

IAGO.   Good sir, be a man;
Think every bearded fellow that's but yok'd
May draw with you; there's millions now alive
That nightly lie in those unproper beds
Which they dare swear peculiar; your case is better.
O! 'tis the spite of hell, the fiend's arch-mock,
To lip a wanton in a secure couch,
And to suppose her chaste. No, let me know;
And knowing what I am I know what she shall be.

OTHELLO. O! thou art wise; 'tis certain.

IAGO.   Stand you awhile apart;
Confine yourself but in a patient list.
Whilst you were here o'erwhelmed with your grief,—
A passion most unsuiting such a man,—
Cassio came hither; I shifted him away,
And laid good 'scuse upon your ecstasy;
Bade him anon return and here speak with me;
The which he promis'd. Do but encave yourself,
And mark the fleers, the gibes, and notable scorns,
That dwell in every region of his face;
For I will make him tell the tale anew,

Where, how, how oft, how long ago, and when
He hath, and is again to cope your wife:
I say, but mark his gesture. Marry, patience;
Or I shall say you are all in all in spleen,
And nothing of a man.

OTHELLO.   Dost thou hear, Iago?
I will be found most cunning in my patience;
But—dost thou hear?—most bloody.

IAGO.   That's not amiss;
But yet keep time in all. Will you withdraw?

[OTHELLO *goes apart.*

Now will I question Cassio of Bianca,
A housewife that by selling her desires
Buys herself bread and clothes; it is a creature
That dotes on Cassio; as 'tis the strumpet's plague
To beguile many and be beguil'd by one.
He, when he hears of her, cannot refrain
From the excess of laughter. Here he comes:

Re-enter CASSIO.

As he shall smile, Othello shall go mad;
And his unbookish jealousy must construe
Poor Cassio's smiles, gestures, and light behaviour
Quite in the wrong. How do you now, lieutenant?

CASSIO. The worser that you give me the addition
Whose want even kills me.

IAGO. Ply Desdemona well, and you are sure on't.
[*Speaking lower.*] Now, if this suit lay in Bianca's power,
How quickly should you speed!

CASSIO.   Alas! poor caitiff!

OTHELLO. Look! how he laughs already!

IAGO. I never knew woman love man so.

CASSIO. Alas! poor rogue, I think, i' faith, she loves me.

OTHELLO. Now he denies it faintly, and laughs it out.

IAGO. Do you hear, Cassio?

OTHELLO.   Now, he importunes him
To tell it o'er: go to; well said, well said.

IAGO. She gives it out that you shall marry her;
Do you intend it?

CASSIO. Ha, ha, ha!

OTHELLO. Do you triumph, Roman? do you triumph?

CASSIO. I marry her! what? a customer? I prithee, bear some charity to my wit; do not think it so unwholesome. Ha, ha, ha!

OTHELLO. So, so, so, so. They laugh that win.

IAGO. Faith, the cry goes that you shall marry her.

CASSIO. Prithee, say true.

IAGO. I am a very villain else.

OTHELLO. Have you scored me? Well.

CASSIO. This is the monkey's own giving out: she is persuaded I will marry her, out of her own love and flattery, not out of my promise.

OTHELLO. Iago beckons me; now he begins the story.

CASSIO. She was here even now; she haunts me in every place. I was the other day talking on the sea bank with certain Venetians, and thither come this bauble, and, by this hand, she falls me thus about my neck;—

OTHELLO. Crying, 'O dear Cassio!' as it were; his gesture imports it.

CASSIO. So hangs and lolls and weeps upon me; so hales and pulls me; ha, ha, ha!

OTHELLO. Now he tells how she plucked him to my chamber. O! I see that nose of yours, but not the dog I shall throw it to.

CASSIO. Well, I must leave her company.

IAGO. Before me! look, where she comes.

CASSIO. 'Tis such another fitchew! marry, a perfumed one.

Enter BIANCA.

What do you mean by this haunting of me?

BIANCA. Let the devil and his dam haunt you! What did you mean by that same handkerchief you gave me even now? I was a fine fool to take it. I must take out the work! A likely piece of work, that you should find it in your chamber, and not know who left it there! This is some minx's token, and I must take out the work! There, give it your hobby-horse; wheresoever you had it I'll take out no work on't.

CASSIO. How now, my sweet Bianca! how now, how now!

OTHELLO. By heaven, that should be my handkerchief!

BIANCA. An you'll come to supper to-night, you may; an you will not, come when you are next prepared for. [*Exit.*

IAGO. After her, after her.

CASSIO. Faith, I must; she'll rail in the street else.

IAGO. Will you sup there?

CASSIO. Faith, I intend so.

IAGO. Well, I may chance to see you, for I would very fain speak with you.

CASSIO. Prithee, come; will you?

IAGO. Go to; say no more. [*Exit* CASSIO.

OTHELLO. [*Advancing.*] How shall I murder him, Iago?

IAGO. Did you perceive how he laughed at his vice?

OTHELLO. O! Iago!

IAGO. And did you see the handkerchief?

OTHELLO. Was that mine?

IAGO. Yours, by this hand; and to see how he prizes the foolish woman your wife! she gave it him, and he hath given it his whore.

OTHELLO. I would have him nine years a-killing. A fine woman! a fair woman! a sweet woman!

IAGO. Nay, you must forget that.

OTHELLO. Ay, let her rot, and perish, and be damned to-night; for she shall not live. No, my heart is turned to stone; I strike it, and it hurts my hand. O! the world hath not a sweeter creature; she might lie by an emperor's side and command him tasks.

IAGO. Nay, that's not your way.

OTHELLO. Hang her! I do but say what she is. So delicate with her needle! An admirable musician! O, she will sing the savageness out of a bear. Of so high and plenteous wit and invention!

IAGO. She's the worse for all this.

OTHELLO. O! a thousand, a thousand times. And then, of so gentle a condition!

IAGO. Ay, too gentle.

OTHELLO. Nay, that's certain;—but yet the pity of it, Iago! O! Iago, the pity of it, Iago!

IAGO. If you are so fond over her iniquity, give her patent to offend; for, if it touch not you, it comes near nobody.

OTHELLO. I will chop her into messes. Cuckold me!

IAGO. O! 'tis foul in her.

OTHELLO. With mine officer!

IAGO. That's fouler.

OTHELLO. Get me some poison, Iago; this night: I'll not expostulate with her, lest her body and beauty unprovide my mind again. This night, Iago.

IAGO. Do it not with poison, strangle her in her bed, even the bed she hath contaminated.

OTHELLO. Good, good; the justice of it pleases; very good.

IAGO. And for Cassio, let me be his undertaker; you shall hear more by midnight.

OTHELLO. Excellent good. [A trumpet within.]
What trumpet is that same?

IAGO. Something from Venice, sure. 'Tis Lodovico,
Come from the duke; and see, your wife is with him.

Enter LODOVICO, DESDEMONA, *and* ATTENDANTS.

LODOVICO. God save you, worthy general!

OTHELLO.   With all my heart, sir.

LODOVICO. The duke and senators of Venice greet you.
                              [*Gives him a packet.*

OTHELLO. I kiss the instrument of their pleasures.
                              [*Opens the packet, and reads.*

DESDEMONA. And what's the news, good cousin Lodovico?

IAGO. I am very glad to see you, signior;
Welcome to Cyprus.

LODOVICO. I thank you. How does Lieutenant Cassio?

IAGO. Lives, sir.

DESDEMONA. Cousin, there's fall'n between him and my lord
An unkind breach; but you shall make all well.

OTHELLO. Are you sure of that?

DESDEMONA. My lord?

OTHELLO. *This fail you not to do, as you will—*

LODOVICO. He did not call; he's busy in the paper.
Is there division 'twixt my lord and Cassio?

DESDEMONA. A most unhappy one; I would do much
To atone them, for the love I bear to Cassio.

OTHELLO. Fire and brimstone!

DESDEMONA.   My lord?

OTHELLO.   Are you wise?

DESDEMONA. What! is he angry?

LODOVICO.   May be the letter mov'd him;
For, as I think, they do command him home,
Deputing Cassio in his government.

DESDEMONA. Trust me, I am glad on't.

OTHELLO.   Indeed!

DESDEMONA.   My lord?

OTHELLO. I am glad to see you mad.

DESDEMONA.   Why, sweet Othello?

OTHELLO. Devil!   [*Strikes her.*

DESDEMONA.   I have not deserved this.

LODOVICO. My lord, this would not be believ'd in Venice,
Though I should swear I saw't: 'tis very much;
Make her amends, she weeps.

OTHELLO.   O devil, devil!
If that the earth could teem with woman's tears,
Each drop she falls would prove a crocodile.
Out of my sight!

DESDEMONA.   I will not stay to offend you.   [*Going.*

LODOVICO. Truly, an obedient lady;
I do beseech your lordship, call her back.

OTHELLO. Mistress!

DESDEMONA.   My lord?

OTHELLO.   What would you with her, sir?

LODOVICO. Who, I, my lord?

OTHELLO. Ay; you did wish that I would make her turn:
Sir, she can turn, and turn, and yet go on,
And turn again; and she can weep, sir, weep;

And she's obedient, as you say, obedient,
Very obedient. Proceed you in your tears.
Concerning this, sir, O—well-painted passion!—
I am commanded home. Get you away;
I'll send for you anon. Sir, I obey the mandate,
And will return to Venice. Hence! avaunt!   [*Exit* DESDEMONA.
Cassio shall have my place. And, sir, to-night,
I do entreat that we may sup together;
You are welcome, sir, to Cyprus. Goats and monkeys!   [*Exit.*
    LODOVICO. Is this the noble Moor whom our full senate
Call all-in-all sufficient? is this the noble nature
Whom passion could not shake? whose solid virtue
The shot of accident nor dart of chance
Could neither graze nor pierce?
    IAGO.   He is much chang'd.
    LODOVICO. Are his wits safe? is he not light of brain?
    IAGO. He's that he is; I may not breathe my censure.
What he might be, if, what he might, he is not,
I would to heaven he were!
    LODOVICO.   What! strike his wife!
    IAGO. Faith, that was not so well; yet would I knew
That stroke would prove the worst!
    LODOVICO.   Is it his use?
Or did the letters work upon his blood,
And new-create his fault?
    IAGO.   Alas, alas!
It is not honesty in me to speak
What I have seen and known. You shall observe him,
And his own courses will denote him so
That I may save my speech. Do but go after
And mark how he continues.
    LODOVICO. I am sorry that I am deceiv'd in him.   [*Exeunt.*

Scene II. *A Room in the Castle*

Enter OTHELLO *and* EMILIA.

OTHELLO. You have seen nothing, then?

EMILIA. Nor ever heard, nor ever did suspect.

OTHELLO. Yes, you have seen Cassio and her together.

EMILIA. But then I saw no harm, and then I heard
Each syllable that breath made up between them.

OTHELLO. What! did they never whisper?

EMILIA.   Never, my lord.

OTHELLO. Nor send you out o' the way?

EMILIA.   Never.

OTHELLO. To fetch her fan, her gloves, her mask, nor nothing?

EMILIA. Never, my lord.

OTHELLO. That's strange.

EMILIA. I durst, my lord, to wager she is honest,
Lay down my soul at stake: if you think other,
Remove your thought; it doth abuse your bosom.
If any wretch have put this in your head,
Let heaven requite it with the serpent's curse!
For, if she be not honest, chaste, and true,
There's no man happy; the purest of their wives
Is foul as slander.

OTHELLO.   Bid her come hither; go.   [*Exit* EMILIA.
She says enough; yet she's a simple bawd
That cannot say as much. This is a subtle whore,
A closet lock and key of villainous secrets;
And yet she'll kneel and pray; I have seen her do't.

Re-enter EMILIA *with* DESDEMONA.

DESDEMONA. My lord, what is your will?

OTHELLO.   Pray, chuck, come hither.

DESDEMONA. What is your pleasure?

OTHELLO.   Let me see your eyes;
Look in my face.

DESDEMONA.   What horrible fancy's this?

OTHELLO. [*To* EMILIA.] Some of your function, mistress;
Leave procreants alone and shut the door;
Cough or cry 'hem' if any body come;
Your mystery, your mystery; nay, dispatch.   [*Exit* EMILIA.
DESDEMONA. Upon my knees, what doth your speech import?
I understand a fury in your words,
But not the words.
OTHELLO. Why, what art thou?
DESDEMONA.   Your wife, my lord; your true
And loyal wife.
OTHELLO.   Come, swear it, damn thyself;
Lest, being like one of heaven, the devils themselves
Should fear to seize thee; therefore be double-damn'd;
Swear thou art honest.
DESDEMONA.   Heaven doth truly know it.
OTHELLO. Heaven truly knows that thou art false as hell.
DESDEMONA. To whom, my lord? with whom? how am I false?
OTHELLO. Ah! Desdemona; away, away, away!
DESDEMONA. Alas, the heavy day!—Why do you weep?
Am I the motive of these tears, my lord?
If haply you my father do suspect
An instrument of this your calling back,
Lay not your blame on me; if you have lost him,
Why, I have lost him too.
OTHELLO.   Had it pleas'd heaven
To try me with affliction, had he rain'd
All kinds of sores, and shames, on my bare head,
Steep'd me in poverty to the very lips,
Given to captivity me and my utmost hopes,
I should have found in some part of my soul
A drop of patience; but, alas! to make me
The fixed figure for the time of scorn
To point his slow and moving finger at;
Yet could I bear that too; well, very well.
But there, where I have garner'd up my heart,
Where either I must live or bear no life,

The fountain from the which my current runs
Or else dries up; to be discarded thence!
Or keep it as a cistern for foul toads
To knot and gender in! Turn thy complexion there,
Patience, thou young and rose-lipp'd cherubin;
Ay, there, look grim as hell!

DESDEMONA. I hope my noble lord esteems me honest.

OTHELLO. O! ay; as summer flies are in the shambles,
That quicken even with blowing. O thou weed!
Who art so lovely fair and smell'st so sweet
That the sense aches at thee, would thou hadst ne'er been born.

DESDEMONA. Alas! what ignorant sin have I committed?

OTHELLO. Was this fair paper, this most goodly book,
Made to write 'whore' upon? What committed!
Committed! O thou public commoner!
I should make very forges of my cheeks,
That would to cinders burn up modesty,
Did I but speak thy deeds. What committed!
Heaven stops the nose at it and the moon winks,
The bawdy wind that kisses all it meets
Is hush'd within the hollow mine of earth,
And will not hear it. What committed!
Impudent strumpet!

DESDEMONA.   By heaven, you do me wrong.

OTHELLO. Are not you a strumpet?

DESDEMONA.   No, as I am a Christian.
If to preserve this vessel for my lord
From any other foul unlawful touch
Be not to be a strumpet, I am none.

OTHELLO. What! not a whore?

DESDEMONA.   No, as I shall be sav'd.

OTHELLO. Is it possible?

DESDEMONA. O! heaven forgive us.

OTHELLO.   I cry you mercy, then;
I took you for that cunning whore of Venice
That married with Othello. You, mistress,

That have the office opposite to Saint Peter,
And keep the gate of hell!

Re-enter EMILIA.

                    You, you, ay, you!
We have done our course; there's money for your pains.
I pray you, turn the key and keep our counsel.   [*Exit.*
    EMILIA. Alas! what does this gentleman conceive?
How do you, madam? how do you, my good lady?
    DESDEMONA. Faith, half asleep.
    EMILIA. Good madam, what's the matter with my lord?
    DESDEMONA. With who?
    EMILIA. Why, with my lord, madam.
    DESDEMONA. Who is thy lord?
    EMILIA.   He that is yours, sweet lady.
    DESDEMONA. I have none; do not talk to me, Emilia;
I cannot weep, nor answer have I none,
But what should go by water. Prithee, to-night
Lay on my bed my wedding sheets: remember:
And call thy husband hither.
    EMILIA.   Here is a change indeed!   [*Exit.*
    DESDEMONA. 'Tis meet I should be us'd so, very meet.
How have I been behav'd, that he might stick
The small'st opinion on my least misuse?

    Re-enter EMILIA, *with* IAGO.

    IAGO. What is your pleasure, madam? How is it with you?
    DESDEMONA. I cannot tell. Those that do teach young babes
Do it with gentle means and easy tasks;
He might have chid me so; for, in good faith,
I am a child to chiding.
    IAGO.   What's the matter, lady?
    EMILIA. Alas! Iago, my lord hath so bewhor'd her,
Thrown such despite and heavy terms upon her,
As true hearts cannot bear.
    DESDEMONA. Am I that name, Iago?
    IAGO.   What name, fair lady?

DESDEMONA. Such as she says my lord did say I was.

EMILIA. He call'd her whore; a beggar in his drink
Could not have laid such terms upon his callat.

IAGO. Why did he so?

DESDEMONA. I do not know; I am sure I am none such.

IAGO. Do not weep, do not weep. Alas the day!

EMILIA. Has she forsook so many noble matches,
Her father and her country and her friends,
To be call'd whore? would it not make one weep?

DESDEMONA. It is my wretched fortune.

IAGO.   Beshrew him for it!
How comes this trick upon him?

DESDEMONA.   Nay, heaven doth know.

EMILIA. I will be hang'd, if some eternal villain,
Some busy and insinuating rogue,
Some cogging cozening slave, to get some office,
Have not devis'd this slander; I'll be hang'd else.

IAGO. Fie! there is no such man; it is impossible.

DESDEMONA. If any such there be, heaven pardon him!

EMILIA. A halter pardon him, and hell gnaw his bones!
Why should he call her whore? who keeps her company?
What place? what time? what form? what likelihood?
The Moor's abus'd by some most villainous knave,
Some base notorious knave, some scurvy fellow.
O heaven! that such companions thou'dst unfold,
And put in every honest hand a whip
To lash the rascals naked through the world,
Even from the east to the west!

IAGO.   Speak within door.

EMILIA. O! fie upon them. Some such squire he was
That turn'd your wit the seamy wide without,
And made you to suspect me with the Moor.

IAGO. You are a fool; go to.

DESDEMONA.   O good Iago,
What shall I do to win my lord again?
Good friend, go to him; for, by this light of heaven,
I know not how I lost him. Here I kneel:

If e'er my will did trespass 'gainst his love,
Either in discourse of thought or actual deed,
Or that mine eyes, mine ears, or any sense,
Delighted them in any other form;
Or that I do not yet, and ever did,
And ever will, though he do shake me off
To beggarly divorcement, love him dearly,
Comfort forswear me! Unkindness may do much;
And his unkindness may defeat my life,
But never taint my love. I cannot say 'whore:'
It does abhor me I speak the word;
To do the act that might the addition earn
Not the world's mass of vanity could make me.

    IAGO. I pray you be content, 'tis but his humour;
The business of the state does him offence,
And he does chide with you.

    DESDEMONA.   If 'twere no other,—

    IAGO. 'Tis but so, I warrant.   [*Trumpets.*
Hark! how these instruments summon to supper;
The messengers of Venice stay the meat:
Go in, and weep not; all things shall be well.

                [*Exeunt* DESDEMONA *and* EMILIA.

    Enter RODERIGO.

How now, Roderigo!

    RODERIGO. I do not find that thou dealest justly with me.

    IAGO. What in the contrary?

    RODERIGO. Every day thou daffest me with some device, Iago; and rather, as it seems to me now, keepest from me all conveniency, than suppliest me with the least advantage of hope. I will indeed no longer endure it, nor am I yet persuaded to put up in peace what already I have foolishly suffered.

    IAGO. Will you hear me, Roderigo?

    RODERIGO. Faith, I have heard too much, for your words and performances are no kin together.

    IAGO. You charge me most unjustly.

    RODERIGO. With nought but truth. I have wasted myself out

of my means. The jewels you have had from me to deliver to Desdemona would half have corrupted a votarist; you have told me she has received them, and returned me expectations and comforts of sudden respect and acquaintance, but I find none.

IAGO. Well; go to; very well.

RODERIGO. Very well! go to! I cannot go to, man; nor 'tis not very well: by this hand, I say, it is very scurvy, and begin to find myself fobbed in it.

IAGO. Very well.

RODERIGO. I tell you 'tis not very well. I will make myself known to Desdemona; if she will return me my jewels, I will give over my suit and repent my unlawful solicitation; if not, assure yourself I will seek satisfaction of you.

IAGO. You have said now.

RODERIGO. Ay, and said nothing, but what I protest intendment of doing.

IAGO. Why, now I see there's mettle in thee, and even from this instant do build on thee a better opinion than ever before. Give me thy hand, Roderigo; thou hast taken against me a most just exception; but yet, I protest, I have dealt most directly in thy affair.

RODERIGO. It hath not appeared.

IAGO. I grant indeed it hath not appeared, and your suspicion is not without wit and judgment. But, Roderigo, if thou hast that in thee indeed, which I have greater reason to believe now than ever, I mean purpose, courage, and valour, this night show it: if thou the next night following enjoy not Desdemona, take me from this world with treachery and devise engines for my life.

RODERIGO. Well, what is it? is it within reason and compass?

IAGO. Sir, there is special commission come from Venice to depute Cassio in Othello's place.

RODERIGO. Is that true? why, then Othello and Desdemona return again to Venice.

IAGO. O, no! he goes into Mauritania, and takes away with him the fair Desdemona, unless his abode be lingered here by

some accident; wherein none can be so determinate as the removing of Cassio.

RODERIGO. How do you mean, removing of him?

IAGO. Why, by making him uncapable of Othello's place;
knocking out his brains.

RODERIGO. And that you would have me do?

IAGO. Ay; if you dare do yourself a profit and a right. He sups
to-night with a harlotry, and thither will I go to him; he knows
not yet of his honourable fortune. If you will watch his going
thence,—which I will fashion to fall out between twelve and one,
—you may take him at your pleasure; I will be near to second
your attempt, and he shall fall between us. Come, stand not
amazed at it, but go along with me; I will show you such a
necessity in his death that you shall think yourself bound to put
it on him. It is now high supper-time, and the night grows to
waste; about it.

RODERIGO. I will hear further reason for this.

IAGO. And you shall be satisfied. [*Exeunt.*

Scene III. *Another Room in the Castle*

Enter OTHELLO, LODOVICO, DESDEMONA, EMILIA, *and* ATTEN-
DANTS.

LODOVICO. I do beseech you, sir, trouble yourself no further.

OTHELLO. O! pardon me; 'twill do me good to walk.

LODOVICO. Madam, good night; I humbly thank your ladyship.

DESDEMONA. Your honour is most welcome.

OTHELLO.   Will you walk, sir?
O! Desdemona,——

DESDEMONA. My lord?

OTHELLO. Get you to bed on the instant; I will be returned
forthwith; dismiss your attendant there; look it be done.

DESDEMONA. I will, my lord.

               [*Exeunt* OTHELLO, LODOVICO, *and* ATTENDANTS.

EMILIA. How goes it now? he looks gentler than he did.

DESDEMONA. He says he will return incontinent;

He hath commanded me to go to bed,
And bade me to dismiss you.

EMILIA.   Dismiss me!

DESDEMONA. It was his bidding; therefore, good Emilia,
Give me my nightly wearing, and adieu:
We must not now displease him.

EMILIA. I would you had never seen him.

DESDEMONA. So would not I; my love doth so approve him,
That even his stubbornness, his checks and frowns,—
Prithee, unpin me,—have grace and favour in them.

EMILIA. I have laid those sheets you bade me on the bed.

DESDEMONA. All's one. Good faith! how foolish are our minds!
If I do die before thee, prithee, shroud me
In one of those same sheets.

EMILIA.   Come, come, you talk.

DESDEMONA. My mother had a maid call'd Barbara;
She was in love, and he she lov'd prov'd mad
And did forsake her; she had a song of 'willow;'
An old thing 'twas, but it express'd her fortune,
And she died singing it; that song to-night
Will not go from my mind; I have much to do
But to go hang my head all at one side,
And sing it like poor Barbara. Prithee, dispatch.

EMILIA. Shall I go fetch your night-gown?

DESDEMONA.   No, unpin me here.
This Lodovico is a proper man.

EMILIA. A very handsome man.

DESDEMONA. He speaks well.

EMILIA. I know a lady in Venice would have walked barefoot
to Palestine for a touch of his nether lip.

DESDEMONA. The poor soul sat sighing by a sycamore tree,
          Sing all a green willow;
       Her hand on her bosom, her head on her knee,
          Sing willow, willow, willow:
       The fresh streams ran by her, and murmur'd her
          moans;

> Sing willow, willow, willow:
> Her salt tears fell from her, and soften'd the
> stones;—

Lay by these:—

> Sing willow, willow, willow:

Prithee, hie thee; he'll come anon.—

> Sing all a green willow must be my garland.
> Let nobody blame him, his scorn I approve,—

Nay, that's not next. Hark! who is it that knocks?

EMILIA. It is the wind.

DESDEMONA. I call'd my love false love; but what said he then?
> Sing willow, willow, willow:
> If I court moe women, you'll couch with moe
> men.

So, get thee gone; good night. Mine eyes do itch;
Doth that bode weeping?

EMILIA.   'Tis neither here nor there.

DESDEMONA. I have heard it said so. O! these men, these men!
Dost thou in conscience think, tell me, Emilia,
That there be women do abuse their husbands
In such gross kind?

EMILIA.   There be some such, no question.

DESDEMONA. Wouldst thou do such a deed for all the world?

EMILIA. Why, would not you?

DESDEMONA.   No, by this heavenly light!

EMILIA. Nor I neither by this heavenly light;
I might do't as well i' the dark.

DESDEMONA. Wouldst thou do such a deed for all the world?

EMILIA. The world is a huge thing; 'tis a great price
For a small vice.

DESDEMONA.   In troth, I think thou wouldst not.

EMILIA. In troth, I think I should, and undo't when I had
done. Marry, I would not do such a thing for a joint-ring, nor

measures of lawn, nor for gowns, petticoats, nor caps, nor any
petty exhibition; but for the whole world, who would not make
her husband a cuckold to make him a monarch? I should venture
purgatory for't.

DESDEMONA. Beshrew me, if I would do such a wrong
For the whole world.

EMILIA. Why, the wrong is but a wrong i' the world; and having the world for your labour, 'tis a wrong in your own world,
and you might quickly make it right.

DESDEMONA. I do not think there is any such woman.

EMILIA. Yes, a dozen; and as many to the vantage, as would
store the world they played for.
But I do think it is their husbands' faults
If wives do fall. Say that they slack their duties,
And pour our treasures into foreign laps,
Or else break out in peevish jealousies,
Throwing restraint upon us; or, say they strike us,
Or scant our former having in despite;
Why, we have galls, and though we have some grace,
Yet have we some revenge. Let husbands know
Their wives have sense like them; they see and smell,
And have their palates both for sweet and sour,
As husbands have. What is it that they do
When they change us for others? Is it sport?
I think it is; and doth affection breed it?
I think it doth; is't frailty that thus errs?
It is so too; and have not we affections,
Desires for sport, and frailty, as men have?
Then, let them use us well; else let them know,
The ills we do, their ills instruct us so.

DESDEMONA. Good night, good night; heaven me such usage
send,
Not to pick bad from bad, but by bad mend!   [*Exeunt.*

Act 5

Scene I. Cyprus. A Street

Enter IAGO *and* RODERIGO.

IAGO. Here, stand behind this bulk; straight will he come:
Wear thy good rapier bare, and put it home.
Quick, quick; fear nothing; I'll be at thy elbow.
It makes us, or it mars us; think on that,
And fix most firm thy resolution.
    RODERIGO. Be near at hand; I may miscarry in't.
    IAGO. Here, at thy hand: be bold, and take thy stand.
                                 [*Retires.*

RODERIGO. I have no great devotion to the deed;
And yet he has given me satisfying reasons:
'Tis but a man gone: forth, my sword; he dies.
    IAGO. I have rubb'd this young quat almost to the sense,
And he grows angry. Now, whether he kill Cassio,
Or Cassio him, or each do kill the other,
Every way makes my gain: live Roderigo,
He calls me to a restitution large
Of gold and jewels that I bobb'd from him,
As gifts to Desdemona;
It must not be: if Cassio do remain,
He hath a daily beauty in his life
That makes me ugly; and, besides, the Moor
May unfold me to him; there stand I in much peril.
No, he must die. But so; I hear him coming.

Enter CASSIO.

RODERIGO. I know his gait; 'tis he. Villain, thou diest!

                        [Makes a pass at CASSIO.

CASSIO. That thrust had been mine enemy indeed
But that my coat is better than thou know'st;
I will make proof of thine.   *[Draws, and wounds* RODERIGO.

RODERIGO.   O! I am slain.

     *[*IAGO *from behind wounds* CASSIO *in the leg, and exit.*

CASSIO. I am maim'd for ever. Help, ho! murder! murder!

                                      [Falls.

Enter OTHELLO, *at a distance.*

OTHELLO. The voice of Cassio: Iago keeps his word.

RODERIGO. O! villain that I am!

OTHELLO.   It is e'en so.

CASSIO. O, help, ho! light! a surgeon!

OTHELLO. 'Tis he: O brave Iago, honest and just!
That hast such noble sense of thy friend's wrong;
Thou teachest me. Minion, your dear lies dead,
And your unblest fate hies; strumpet, I come!
Forth of my heart those charms, thine eyes, are blotted;
Thy bed lust-stain'd shall with lust's blood be spotted.   *[Exit.*

Enter LODOVICO *and* GRATIANO, *at a distance.*

CASSIO. What ho! no watch? no passage? murder! murder!

GRATIANO. 'Tis some mischance; the cry is very direful.

CASSIO. O, help!

LODOVICO. Hark!

RODERIGO. O wretched villain!

LODOVICO. Two or three groan: it is a heavy night;
These may be counterfeits; let's think't unsafe
To come in to the cry without more help.

RODERIGO. Nobody come? then shall I bleed to death.

LODOVICO. Hark!

Re-enter IAGO, *with a light.*

GRATIANO. Here's one comes in his shirt, with light and weapons.

IAGO. Who's there? whose noise is this that cries on murder?

LODOVICO. We do not know.

IAGO.   Did not you hear a cry?

CASSIO. Here, here! for heaven's sake, help me.

IAGO.   What's the matter?

GRATIANO. This is Othello's ancient, as I take it.

LODOVICO. The same indeed; a very valiant fellow.

IAGO. What are you here that cry so grievously?

CASSIO. Iago? O! I am spoil'd, undone by villains!
Give me some help.

IAGO. O me, lieutenant! what villains have done this?

CASSIO. I think that one of them is hereabout,
And cannot make away.

IAGO.   O treacherous villains!
[To LODOVICO and GRATIANO.] What are you there? come in,
    and give some help.

RODERIGO. O! help me here.

CASSIO. That's one of them.

IAGO.   O murderous slave! O villain!
                                    [Stabs RODERIGO.

RODERIGO. O damn'd Iago! O inhuman dog!

IAGO. Kill men i' the dark! Where be these bloody thieves?
How silent is this town! Ho! murder! murder!
What may you be? are you of good or evil?

LODOVICO. As you shall prove us, praise us.

IAGO. Signior Lodovico?

LODOVICO. He, sir.

IAGO. I cry you mercy. Here's Cassio hurt by villains.

GRATIANO. Cassio!

IAGO. How is it, brother?

CASSIO. My leg is cut in two.

IAGO.   Marry, heaven forbid,
Light, gentlemen; I'll bind it with my shirt.

    Enter BIANCA.

BIANCA. What is the matter, ho? who is't that cried?

IAGO. Who is't that cried!

BIANCA. O my dear Cassio! my sweet Cassio!
O Cassio, Cassio, Cassio!
IAGO. O notable strumpet! Cassio, may you suspect
Who they should be that have thus mangled you?
CASSIO. No.
GRATIANO. I am sorry to find you thus; I have been to seek
you.
IAGO. Lend me a garter. So. O! for a chair,
To bear him easily hence!
BIANCA. Alas! he faints! O Cassio, Cassio, Cassio!
IAGO. Gentlemen all, I do suspect this trash
To be a party in this injury.
Patience awhile, good Cassio. Come, come.
Lend me a light. Know we this face, or no?
Alas! my friend and my dear countryman,
Roderigo? no: yes, sure, O heaven! Roderigo.
GRATIANO. What! of Venice?
IAGO. Even he, sir: did you know him?
GRATIANO.   Know him! ay.
IAGO. Signior Gratiano? I cry you gentle pardon;
These bloody accidents must excuse my manners,
That so neglected you.
GRATIANO.   I am glad to see you.
IAGO. How do you, Cassio? O! a chair, a chair!
GRATIANO. Roderigo!   [*A chair brought in.*
IAGO. He, he, 'tis he.—O! that's well said; the chair:
Some good men bear him carefully from hence;
I'll fetch the general's surgeon. [*To* BIANCA.] For you, mistress,
Save you your labour. He that lies slain here, Cassio,
Was my dear friend. What malice was between you?
CASSIO. None in the world; nor do I know the man.
IAGO. [*To* BIANCA.] What! look you pale? O! bear him out
   o' the air—   [CASSIO *and* RODERIGO *are borne off.*
Stay you, good gentlemen. Look you pale, mistress?—
Do you perceive the gastness of her eye?
Nay, if you stare, we shall hear more anon.
Behold her well; I pray you, look upon her:

Do you see, gentlemen? nay, guiltiness will speak
Though tongues were out of use.

Enter EMILIA.

EMILIA. 'Las! what's the matter? what's the matter, husband?
IAGO. Cassio hath here been set on in the dark
By Roderigo and fellows that are 'scap'd:
He's almost slain, and Roderigo dead.
EMILIA. Alas! good gentleman; alas! good Cassio!
IAGO. This is the fruit of whoring. Prithee, Emilia,
Go know of Cassio where he supp'd to-night.
What! do you shake at that?
BIANCA. He supp'd at my house; but I therefore shake not.
IAGO. O! did he so? I charge you, go with me.
EMILIA. Fie, fie upon thee, strumpet!
BIANCA. I am no strumpet, but of life as honest
As you that thus abuse me.
EMILIA.   As I! foh! fie upon thee!
IAGO. Kind gentlemen, let's go see poor Cassio dress'd.
Come, mistress, you must tell's another tale.
Emilia, run you to the citadel,
And tell my lord and lady what hath happ'd.
Will you go on afore? [*Aside.*] This is the night
That either makes me or fordoes me quite.   [*Exeunt.*

Scene II. *A Bedchamber in the Castle.*
Desdemona in bed asleep.
A light burning

Enter OTHELLO.

OTHELLO. It is the cause, it is the cause, my soul;
Let me not name it to you, you chaste stars!
It is the cause. Yet I'll not shed her blood,
Nor scar that whiter skin of hers than snow,
And smooth as monumental alabaster.
Yet she must die, else she'll betray more men.

Put out the light, and then put out the light:
If I quench thee, thou flaming minister,
I can again thy former light restore,
Should I repent me; but once put out thy light,
Thou cunning'st pattern of excelling nature,
I know not where is that Promethean heat
That can thy light relume. When I have pluck'd the rose,
I cannot give it vital growth again,
It needs must wither: I'll smell it on the tree.   [*Kisses her.*
O balmy breath, that dost almost persuade
Justice to break her sword! One more, one more.
Be thus when thou art dead, and I will kill thee,
And love thee after. One more, and this the last:
So sweet was ne'er so fatal. I must weep,
But they are cruel tears; this sorrow's heavenly,
It strikes where it doth love. She wakes.

DESDEMONA. Who's there? Othello?

OTHELLO.   Ay, Desdemona.

DESDEMONA. Will you come to bed, my lord?

OTHELLO. Have you pray'd to-night, Desdemona?

DESDEMONA.   Ay, my lord.

OTHELLO. If you bethink yourself of any crime
Unreconcil'd as yet to heaven and grace,
Solicit for it straight.

DESDEMONA. Alas, my lord, what may you mean by that?

OTHELLO. Well, do it, and be brief; I will walk by:
I would not kill thy unprepared spirit;
No; heaven forfend! I would not kill thy soul.

DESDEMONA. Talk you of killing?

OTHELLO.   Ay, I do.

DESDEMONA.   Then heaven
Have mercy on me!

OTHELLO.   Amen! with all my heart.

DESDEMONA. If you say so, I hope you will not kill me.

OTHELLO. Hum!

DESDEMONA. And yet I fear you; for you are fatal then
When your eyes roll so. Why I should fear I know not,

Since guiltiness I know not; but yet I feel I fear.

OTHELLO. Think on thy sins.

DESDEMONA.   They are loves I bear to you.

OTHELLO. Ay, and for that thou diest.

DESDEMONA. That death's unnatural that kills for loving.
Alas! why gnaw you so your nether lip?
Some bloody passion shakes your very frame;
These are portents, but yet, I hope, I hope
They do not point on me.

OTHELLO.   Peace, and be still!

DESDEMONA. I will so. What's the matter?

OTHELLO. That handkerchief which I so lov'd and gave thee
Thou gav'st to Cassio.

DESDEMONA.   No, by my life and soul!
Send for the man and ask him.

OTHELLO.   Sweet soul, take heed,
Take heed of perjury; thou'rt on thy death-bed.

DESDEMONA. Ay, but not yet to die.

OTHELLO.   Yes, presently;
Therefore confess thee freely of thy sin;
For to deny each article with oath
Cannot remove nor choke the strong conception
That I do groan withal. Thou art to die.

DESDEMONA. Then Lord have mercy on me!

OTHELLO.   I say, amen.

DESDEMONA. And have you mercy too! I never did
Offend you in my life; never lov'd Cassio
But with such general warranty of heaven
As I might love; I never gave him token.

OTHELLO. By heaven, I saw my handkerchief in's hand.
O perjur'd woman! thou dost stone my heart,
And mak'st me call what I intend to do
A murder, which I thought a sacrifice:
I saw the handkerchief.

DESDEMONA.   He found it then;
I never gave it him. Send for him hither;
Let him confess a truth.

Photo by Richard Tucker

Paul Robeson as Othello and Uta Hagen as Desdemona at Cambridge, Massachusetts, in 1942.

OTHELLO.   He hath confess'd.

DESDEMONA. What, my lord?

OTHELLO. That he hath us'd thee.

DESDEMONA.   How? unlawfully?

OTHELLO. Ay.

DESDEMONA. He will not say so.

OTHELLO.   No; his mouth is stopp'd:
Honest Iago hath ta'en order for't.

DESDEMONA. O! my fear interprets. What! is he dead?

OTHELLO. Had all his hairs been lives, my great revenge
Had stomach for them all.

DESDEMONA. Alas! he is betray'd and I undone.

OTHELLO. Out, strumpet! Weep'st thou for him to my face?

DESDEMONA. O! banish me, my lord, but kill me not!

OTHELLO. Down, strumpet!

DESDEMONA. Kill me to-morrow; let me live to-night!

OTHELLO. Nay, if you strive,—

DESDEMONA. But half an hour!

OTHELLO.   Being done, there is no pause.

DESDEMONA. But while I say one prayer!

OTHELLO.   It is too late.

[*He smothers her.*

EMILIA. [*Within.*] My lord, my lord! what, ho! my lord, my
     lord!

OTHELLO. What noise is this? Not dead? not yet quite dead?
I that am cruel am yet merciful;
I would not have thee linger in thy pain.
So, so.

EMILIA. [*Within.*] What, ho! my lord, my lord!

OTHELLO.   Who's there?

EMILIA. [*Within.*] O! good my lord, I would speak a word
     with you!

OTHELLO. Yes; 'tis Emilia: by and by. She's dead.
'Tis like she comes to speak of Cassio's death;
The noise was high. Ha! no more moving?
Still as the grave. Shall she come in? Were't good?
I think she stirs again: no. What's best to do?

If she come in she'll sure speak to my wife:
My wife! my wife! what wife? I have no wife:
O, insupportable! O heavy hour!
Methinks it should be now a huge eclipse
Of sun and moon, and that the affrighted globe
Should yawn at alteration.

    EMILIA.   [*Within.*] I do beseech you
That I may speak with you, O! good my lord.

    OTHELLO. I had forgot thee: O! come in, Emilia:
Soft, by and by: let me the curtains draw.
Where art thou?   [*Unlocks the door.*

    Enter EMILIA.

                What's the matter with thee now?

    EMILIA. O! my good lord, yonder's foul murder done.

    OTHELLO. What! now?

    EMILIA.   But now, my lord.

    OTHELLO. It is the very error of the moon;
She comes more near the earth than she was wont,
And makes men mad.

    EMILIA. Cassio, my lord, has kill'd a young Venetian
Call'd Roderigo.

    OTHELLO.   Roderigo kill'd!
And Cassio kill'd?

    EMILIA.   No, Cassio is not kill'd.

    OTHELLO. Not Cassio kill'd! then murder's out of tune,
And sweet revenge grows harsh.

    DESDEMONA. O! falsely, falsely murder'd.

    EMILIA.   Alas! what cry is that?

    OTHELLO. That! what?

    EMILIA. Out, and alas! that was my lady's voice:
Help! Help, ho! help! O lady, speak again!
Sweet Desdemona! O! sweet mistress, speak.

    DESDEMONA. A guiltless death I die.

    EMILIA. O! who hath done this deed?

    DESDEMONA. Nobody; I myself; farewell:
Commend me to my kind lord. O! farewell!   [*Dies.*

OTHELLO. Why, how should she be murder'd?

EMILIA.   Alas! who knows?

OTHELLO. You heard her say herself it was not I.

EMILIA. She said so; I must needs report the truth.

OTHELLO. She's like a liar gone to burning hell;
'Twas I that kill'd her.

EMILIA.   O! the more angel she,
And you the blacker devil.

OTHELLO. She turn'd to folly, and she was a whore.

EMILIA. Thou dost belie her, and thou art a devil.

OTHELLO. She was false as water.

EMILIA.   Thou art rash as fire to say
That she was false: O! she was heavenly true.

OTHELLO. Cassio did tup her; ask thy husband else.
O! I were damn'd beneath all depth in hell
But that I did proceed upon just grounds
To this extremity. Thy husband knew it all.

EMILIA. My husband!

OTHELLO. Thy husband.

EMILIA. That she was false to wedlock?

OTHELLO. Ay, with Cassio. Nay, had she been true,
If heaven would make me such another world
Of one entire and perfect chrysolite,
I'd not have sold her for it.

EMILIA. My husband!

OTHELLO.   Ay, 'twas he that told me first:
An honest man he is, and hates the slime
That sticks on filthy deeds.

EMILIA.   My husband!

OTHELLO. What needs this iterance, woman? say thy husband.

EMILIA. O mistress! villany hath made mocks with love.
My husband say that she was false!

OTHELLO.   He, woman;
I say, thy husband: dost understand the word?
My friend, thy husband, honest, honest Iago.

EMILIA. If he say so, may his pernicious soul
Rot half a grain a day! he lies to the heart:

She was too fond of her most filthy bargain.

OTHELLO. Ha!

EMILIA. Do thy worst:
This deed of thine is no more worthy heaven
Than thou wast worthy her.

OTHELLO. Peace! you were best.

EMILIA. Thou hast not half the power to do me harm
As I have to be hurt. O gull! O dolt!
As ignorant as dirt! thou hast done a deed,—
I care not for thy sword; I'll make thee known,
Though I lost twenty lives. Help! help, ho! help!
The Moor has kill'd my mistress! Murder! murder!

Enter MONTANO, GRATIANO, IAGO, *and Others.*

MONTANO. What is the matter? How now, general!

EMILIA. O! are you come, Iago? you have done well,
That men must lay their murders on your neck.

GRATIANO. What is the matter?

EMILIA. Disprove this villain if thou be'st a man:
He says thou told'st him that his wife was false.
I know thou didst not, thou'rt not such a villain.
Speak, for my heart is full.

IAGO. I told him what I thought, and told no more
Than what he found himself was apt and true.

EMILIA. But did you ever tell him she was false?

IAGO. I did.

EMILIA. You told a lie, an odious damned lie;
Upon my soul, a lie, a wicked lie.
She false with Cassio! Did you say with Cassio?

IAGO. With Cassio, mistress. Go to, charm your tongue.

EMILIA. I will not charm my tongue; I am bound to speak.
My mistress here lies murder'd in her bed.

ALL. O heavens forfend!

EMILIA. And your reports have set the murder on.

OTHELLO. Nay, stare not, masters; it is true, indeed.

GRATIANO. 'Tis a strange truth.

MONTANO. O monstrous act!

EMILIA.   Villany! villany! villany!
I think upon't, I think, I smell't; O villany!
I thought so then; I'll kill myself for grief.
O! villany, villany!
   IAGO. What! are you mad? I charge you, get you home.
   EMILIA. Good gentlemen, let me have leave to speak:
'Tis proper I obey him, but not now.
Perchance, Iago, I will ne'er go home.
   OTHELLO. O! O! O!   [*Falls on the bed.*
   EMILIA.   Nay, lay thee down and roar,
For thou hast kill'd the sweetest innocent
That e'er did lift up eye.
   OTHELLO.   O! she was foul.
I scarce did know you, uncle. There lies your niece,
Whose breath, indeed, these hands have newly stopp'd:
I know this act shows terrible and grim.
   GRATIANO. Poor Desdemona! I am glad thy father's dead.
Thy match was mortal to him, and pure grief
Shore his old thread in twain: did he live now,
This sight would make him do a desperate turn,
Yea, curse his better angel from his side,
And fall to reprobation.
   OTHELLO. 'Tis pitiful; but yet Iago knows
That she with Cassio hath the act of shame
A thousand times committed; Cassio confess'd it:
And she did gratify his amorous works
With that recognizance and pledge of love
Which I first gave her. I saw it in his hand:
It was a handkerchief, an antique token
My father gave my mother.
   EMILIA. O heaven! O heavenly powers!
   IAGO.   Come, hold your peace.
   EMILIA. 'Twill out, 'twill out; I hold my peace, sir? no;
No, I will speak as liberal as the north;
Let heaven and men and devils, let them all,
All, all, cry shame against me, yet I'll speak.
   IAGO. Be wise, and get you home.

EMILIA.   I will not.

[IAGO *offers to stab* EMILIA.

GRATIANO.   Fie!
Your sword upon a woman?

EMILIA. O thou dull Moor! that handkerchief thou speak'st of
I found by fortune and did give my husband;
For often, with a solemn earnestness,
More than, indeed, belong'd to such a trifle,
He begg'd of me to steal it.

IAGO.   Villainous whore!

EMILIA. She give it Cassio! no, alas! I found it,
And I did give't my husband.

IAGO.   Filth, thou liest!

EMILIA. By heaven, I do not, I do not, gentlemen.
O murderous coxcomb! what should such a fool
Do with so good a wife?

OTHELLO.   Are there no stones in heaven
But what serve for the thunder? Precious villain!

[*He runs at* IAGO. IAGO *stabs* EMILIA, *and exit.*

GRATIANO. The woman falls: sure, he has kill'd his wife.

EMILIA. Ay, ay; O! lay me by my mistress' side.

GRATIANO. He's gone; but his wife's kill'd.

MONTANO. 'Tis a notorious villain. Take you this weapon,
Which I have here recover'd from the Moor.
Come, guard the door without; let him not pass,
But kill him rather. I'll after that same villain,
For 'tis a damned slave.   [*Exeunt* MONTANO *and* GRATIANO.

OTHELLO.   I am not valiant neither,
But every puny whipster gets my sword.
But why should honour outlive honesty?
Let it go all.

EMILIA.   What did thy song bode, lady?
Hark, canst thou hear me? I will play the swan,
And die in music:—

Willow, willow, willow.

Moor, she was chaste; she lov'd thee, cruel Moor;
So come my soul to bliss as I speak true;
So speaking as I think, I die, I die.   [*Dies.*
    OTHELLO. I have another weapon in this chamber;
It is a sword of Spain, the ice brook's temper.
O! here it is. Uncle, I must come forth.
    GRATIANO. [*Within.*] If thou attempt it, it will cost thee dear:
Thou hast no weapon, and perforce must suffer.
    OTHELLO. Look in upon me then, and speak with me,
Or, naked as I am, I will assault thee.

        Re-enter GRATIANO.

    GRATIANO. What is the matter?
    OTHELLO.   Behold! I have a weapon;
A better never did itself sustain
Upon a soldier's thigh: I have seen the day,
That with this little arm, and this good sword,
I have made my way through more impediments
Than twenty times your stop: but, O vain boast!
Who can control his fate? 'tis not so now.
Be not afraid, though you do see me weapon'd;
Here is my journey's end, here is my butt,
And very sea-mark of my utmost sail.
Do you go back dismay'd? 'tis a lost fear;
Man but a rush against Othello's breast,
And he retires. Where should Othello go?
Now how dost thou look now? O ill-starr'd wench!
Pale as thy smock! when we shall meet at compt,
This look of thine will hurl my soul from heaven,
And fiends will snatch at it. Cold, cold, my girl!
Even like thy chastity.
O! cursed, cursed slave. Whip me, ye devils,
From the possession of this heavenly sight!
Blow me about in winds! roast me in sulphur!
Wash me in steep-down gulfs of liquid fire!
O Desdemona! Desdemona! dead!
Oh! Oh! Oh!

Enter LODOVICO, MONTANO, CASSIO *carried in a chair, and* OFFICERS *with* IAGO, *prisoner.*

LODOVICO. Where is this rash and most unfortunate man?

OTHELLO. That's he that was Othello; here I am.

LODOVICO. Where is that viper? bring the villain forth.

OTHELLO. I look down towards his feet; but that's a fable.
If that thou be'st a devil, I cannot kill thee.   [*Wounds* IAGO.

LODOVICO. Wrench his sword from him.

IAGO.   I bleed, sir; but not kill'd.

OTHELLO. I am not sorry neither; I'd have thee live;
For, in my sense, 'tis happiness to die.

LODOVICO. O thou Othello! that wert once so good,
Fall'n in the practice of a damned slave,
What shall be said to thee?

OTHELLO.   Why, any thing:
An honourable murderer, if you will;
For nought did I in hate, but all in honour.

LODOVICO. This wretch hath part confess'd his villany:
Did you and he consent in Cassio's death?

OTHELLO. Ay.

CASSIO. Dear general, I never gave you cause.

OTHELLO. I do believe it, and I ask your pardon.
Will you, I pray, demand that demi-devil
Why he hath thus ensnar'd my soul and body?

IAGO. Demand me nothing: what you know, you know:
From this time forth I never will speak word.

LODOVICO. What! not to pray?

GRATIANO.   Torments will ope your lips.

OTHELLO. Well, thou dost best.

LODOVICO. Sir, you shall understand what hath befall'n,
Which, as I think, you know not. Here is a letter
Found in the pocket of the slain Roderigo,
And here another; the one of them imports
The death of Cassio to be undertook
By Roderigo.

OTHELLO. O villain!

CASSIO.   Most heathenish and most gross!

LODOVICO. Now here's another discontented paper,
Found in his pocket too; and this, it seems,
Roderigo meant to have sent this damned villain,
But that, belike, Iago in the interim
Came in and satisfied him.

OTHELLO.   O the pernicious caitiff!
How came you, Cassio, by that handkerchief
That was my wife's?

CASSIO.   I found it in my chamber;
And he himself confess'd but even now
That there he dropp'd it for a special purpose
Which wrought to his desire.

OTHELLO.   O fool! fool! fool!

CASSIO. There is besides in Roderigo's letter
How he upbraids Iago that he made him
Brave me upon the watch; whereon it came
That I was cast: and even but now he spake,
After long seeming dead, Iago hurt him,
Iago set him on.

LODOVICO. You must forsake this room and go with us;
Your power and your command is taken off,
And Cassio rules in Cyprus. For this slave,
If there be any cunning cruelty
That can torment him much and hold him long,
It shall be his. You shall close prisoner rest.
Till that the nature of your fault be known
To the Venetian state. Come, bring him away.

OTHELLO. Soft you; a word or two before you go.
I have done the state some service, and they know't;
No more of that. I pray you, in your letters,
When you shall these unlucky deeds relate,
Speak of me as I am; nothing extenuate,
Nor set down aught in malice: then, must you speak
Of one that lov'd not wisely but too well;
Of one not easily jealous, but, being wrought,
Perplex'd in the extreme; of one whose hand,

Like the base Indian, threw a pearl away
Richer than all his tribe; of one whose subdu'd eyes
Albeit unused to the melting mood,
Drop tears as fast as the Arabian trees
Their med'cinable gum. Set you down this;
And say besides, that in Aleppo once,
Where a malignant and a turban'd Turk
Beat a Venetian and traduc'd the state,
I took by the throat the circumcised dog,
And smote him thus.   [*Stabs himself.*

    LODOVICO. O bloody period!

    GRATIANO.   All that's spoke is marr'd.

    OTHELLO. I kiss'd thee ere I kill'd thee; no way but this,
                        [*Falling upon* DESDEMONA.
Killing myself to die upon a kiss.   [*Dies.*

    CASSIO. This did I fear, but thought he had no weapon;
For he was great of heart.

    LODOVICO. [*To* IAGO.] O Spartan dog!
More fell than anguish, hunger, or the sea.
Look on the tragic loading of this bed;
This is thy work; the object poisons sight;
Let it be hid. Gratiano, keep the house,
And seize upon the fortunes of the Moor,
For they succeed on you. To you, lord governor,
Remains the censure of this hellish villain,
The time, the place, the torture; O! enforce it.
Myself will straight aboard, and to the state
This heavy act with heavy heart relate.   [*Exeunt.*

King Lear

INTRODUCTION

Written. 1605–1606.

Published. 1608.

Source of the Plot. The story of Lear is told in Holinshed's *Chronicles,* in a play by an unknown hand, *The True Chronicle History of King Leir,* and in a few stanzas of the tenth canto of the second Book of Spenser's *Faerie Queene.*

The character of Gloucester seems to have been suggested by the character of a blind king in Sir Philip Sidney's *Arcadia.*

The Fable. King Lear, in his old age, determines to give up his kingdom to his three daughters. Before he does so, he tries to assure himself of their love for him. The two elder women, Goneril and Regan, vow that they love him intensely; the youngest, Cordelia, can only tell him that she cares for him as a daughter should. He curses and casts off Cordelia, who is taken to wife by the King of France.

Gloucester, deceived by his bastard Edmund, casts off Edgar his son.

King Lear, thwarted and flouted by Goneril and Regan, goes mad, and wanders away with his Fool. Gloucester, trying to comfort him against the wishes of Goneril and Regan, is betrayed by his bastard Edmund, and blinded. He wanders away with Edgar, who has disguised himself as a madman.

Regan's husband is killed. Seeking to take Edmund in his stead, she rouses the jealousy of Goneril, who has already made advances to him.

Cordelia lands with French troops to repossess Lear of his kingdom. She finds Lear, and comforts him. In an engagement with the sisters' armies, she and Lear are captured.

215

Edmund's baseness is exposed. He is attainted and struck down. Goneril poisons Regan, and kills herself. Edmund, before he dies, reveals that he has given order for Lear and Cordelia to be killed. His news comes too late to save Cordelia. She is brought in dead. Lear dies over her body.

Albany, Goneril's husband, Kent, Lear's faithful servant, and Edgar, Edmund's slayer, are left to set the kingdom in order.

The early history of this island is most obscure and uncertain, but as told in Holinshed it was attractive to the eager writers of the late Tudor time. Without any great faith in the reality of King Brute, and King Lear, of Locrine, Sabrina and Queen Gwendolen we should all be the poorer if the fictions they have inspired were all expunged. King Lear, certainly, is a much more living spirit to us than (shall we say) King John, who is said to have signed our charter of liberty, and King Henry who is said to have defended our faith.

He comes to us as a figure of fable, almost of fairy-story, as the main character in an affecting great play based upon the rage of child against father and the stupidity of father against child.

The stupidity of two fathers is the cause of the evil that makes the play; the stupidity of Lear, who gives away his power and casts out Cordelia; and that of Gloucester who suddenly casts out his son, and makes much of a bastard whom he has not seen for nine years. The stupidity, having given sudden strength to evil hearts, sets going a vitality or storm of wickedness, in which the mad Lear moves, blasted yet unable to die.

In this storm of crime Goneril and Regan rule their father, commit the most ghastly and beastly cruelty, lust after the same man, and die unnaturally (having betrayed each other), the one by her sister's hand, the other by her own. Lear is driven mad. The King of France is forced to war with his wife's sisters. Edmund betrays his half-brother to ruin and his father to blindness. Cornwall is stabbed by his servant, Edgar kills his half-brother. Gloucester, thrust out blind, dies when he finds that his wronged son loves him. Cordelia, fighting against her own blood, is betrayed to death by one who claims to love her sisters.

The honest mild man, Albany, and the honest blunt man, Kent, survive the general ruin. Had Kent been a little milder and Albany a little blunter in the first act, before the fates were given strength, the ruin would not have been. All the unnatural treacherous evil comes to pass, because for a few fatal moments they were true to their natures.

Of the great mature tragedies of this time in Shakespeare's life, it may be said that the central figure in each is that of someone caught in a net. Macbeth is a ruthless man so caught. Hamlet is a wise man so caught, Othello is a passionate and Antony a glorious man so caught. All are caught, all are powerless, and all are superb tragic inventions. King Lear is a grander, ironic invention, who hurts far more than any of these because he is a horribly strong man who is caught and cannot die. He is so strong that he nearly breaks the net, before the folds kill him.

No image in the world is so fierce with imaginative energy. The stormy soul runs out storming in a night of the soul as mad as the elements. With him goes the invention of the Fool, the horribly faithful fool, like conscience or worldly wisdom, to flick him mad with ironic comment and bitter song.

The verse is as great as the invention. It rises and falls with the passion. All the scale of Shakespeare's art is used; the terrible spiritual manner of

> You sulphurous and thought-executing fires,
> Vaunt-couriers to oak-cleaving thunderbolts,

as well as the instinctive manner of a prose coloured to the height with all the traditions of country life.

Dramatic genius has the power of understanding half-a-dozen lives at once in tense, swiftly changing situations. This power is shown at its best in the last act of this play. One of the most wonderful and least praised of the inventions in the last scene is that of the dying Edmund. He has been treacherous to nearly every person in the play. His last treachery, indirectly the cause of his ruin, is still in act, the killing of Cordelia and the King. He has been stricken down. "The wheel has come full circle." He has learned too late that

> The gods are just, and of our pleasant vices
> Make instruments to plague us.

He can hardly hope to live for more than a few minutes; the
death of his last two victims cannot benefit him; a word from
him would save them: no one else can save them. Yet at the
last minute, his one little glimmer of faithfulness keeps the word
unspoken. He is silent for Goneril's sake. If he ever cared for
any one in the world, except himself, he may have cared a little
for Goneril. He thinks of her now. She has gone from him; but
she is on his side, he trusts to her, acts for her, and waits for
some word or token from her. In any case, the death of Lear will
benefit her. It will be to her something saved from the general
wreck, something to the good, in the losing bout. An impulse
stirs him to speak, but he puts it by. He keeps silent about Lear,
till one comes saying that Goneril has killed herself. Still he
does not speak. The news pricks the vanity in him. He strokes
his plumes with a tender thought for that body of his that made
two princesses die for love of him. When he speaks of Lear, it
is too late; the little, little instant which alters destiny has
passed; Cordelia is dead: no mist stains the stone. She will come
no more—

> Never, never, never, never, never!

The heart-breaking scene at the end has been blamed as "too
painful for tragedy." Shakespeare's opinion of what is tragic is
worth that of all his critics together. He gave to every soul in
this play an excessive and terrible vitality. On the excessive terrible soul of Lear he poured such misery that the cracking of
the great heart is a thing of joy, a relief so fierce that the audience should go out in exultation singing—

> O, our lives' sweetness!
> That we the pain of death would hourly die
> Rather than die at once!

Tragedy to the Elizabethan was that terrible fall of greatness
to which the heads on the gates bore witness. All who saw these

plays had seen heads fall. Tragedy to them was a looking at Fate
for a lesson in deportment on life's scaffold; that if they could
not, like the swan, die singing, they could in their hearts exult
that in death they won eternal victory.

> Strike, strike, O strike; fly, fly, commanding soul,
> And on thy wings, for this thy body's breath,
> Bear the eternal victory of death.

DRAMATIS PERSONÆ

LEAR, King of Britain

KING OF FRANCE

DUKE OF BURGUNDY

DUKE OF CORNWALL

DUKE OF ALBANY

EARL OF KENT

EARL OF GLOUCESTER

EDGAR, Son to Gloucester

EDMUND, Bastard Son to Gloucester

CURAN, a Courtier

OSWALD, Steward to Goneril

OLD MAN, Tenant to Gloucester

DOCTOR

FOOL

AN OFFICER, employed by Edmund

A GENTLEMAN, Attendant on Cordelia

A HERALD

SERVANTS to Cornwall

GONERIL,
REGAN, } Daughters to Lear
CORDELIA,

KNIGHTS of Lear's Train, OFFICERS, MESSENGERS, SOLDIERS, and ATTENDANTS

SCENE. *Britain*

Act 1

Scene I. *A Room of State in King Lear's Palace*

Enter KENT, GLOUCESTER, *and* EDMUND.

KENT. I thought the king had more affected the Duke of Albany than Cornwall.

GLOUCESTER. It did always seem so to us; but now, in the division of the kingdom, it appears not which of the dukes he values most; for equalities are so weighed that curiosity in neither can make choice of either's moiety.

KENT. Is not this your son, my lord?

GLOUCESTER. His breeding, sir, hath been at my charge: I have so often blushed to acknowledge him, that now I am brazed to it.

KENT. I cannot conceive you.

GLOUCESTER. Sir, this young fellow's mother could; whereupon she grew round-wombed, and had, indeed, sir, a son for her cradle ere she had a husband for her bed. Do you smell a fault?

KENT. I cannot wish the fault undone, the issue of it being so proper.

GLOUCESTER. But I have a son, sir, by order of law, some year elder than this, who yet is no dearer in my account: though this knave came somewhat saucily into the world before he was sent for, yet was his mother fair; there was good sport at his making, and the whoreson must be acknowledged. Do you know this noble gentleman, Edmund?

EDMUND. No, my lord.

GLOUCESTER. My Lord of Kent: remember him hereafter as my honourable friend.

221

EDMUND. My services to your lordship.

KENT. I must love you, and sue to know you better.

EDMUND. Sir, I shall study deserving.

GLOUCESTER. He hath been out nine years, and away he shall again. The king is coming.

> *Sennet. Enter* LEAR, CORNWALL, ALBANY, GONERIL, REGAN, CORDELIA, *and* ATTENDANTS.

LEAR. Attend the Lords of France and Burgundy, Gloucester.

GLOUCESTER. I shall, my liege.

> [*Exeunt* GLOUCESTER *and* EDMUND.

LEAR. Meantime we shall express our darker purpose.
Give me the map there. Know that we have divided
In three our kingdom; and 'tis our fast intent
To shake all cares and business from our age,
Conferring them on younger strengths, while we
Unburden'd crawl toward death. Our son of Cornwall,
And you, our no less loving son of Albany,
We have this hour a constant will to publish
Our daughters' several dowers, that future strife
May be prevented now. The princes, France and Burgundy,
Great rivals in our youngest daughter's love,
Long in our court have made their amorous sojourn,
And here are to be answer'd. Tell me, my daughters,—
Since now we will divest us both of rule,
Interest of territory, cares of state,—
Which of you shall we say doth love us most?
That we our largest bounty may extend
Where nature doth with merit challenge. Goneril,
Our eldest-born, speak first.

GONERIL. Sir, I love you more than words can wield the mat-
ter;
Dearer than eye-sight, space, and liberty;
Beyond what can be valu'd, rich or rare;
No less than life, with grace, health, beauty, honour;
As much as child e'er lov'd, or father found;
A love that makes breath poor and speech unable;

Beyond all manner of so much I love you.

CORDELIA. [*Aside.*] What shall Cordelia do? Love, and be
silent.

LEAR. Of all these bounds, even from this line to this,
With shadowy forests and with champains rich'd,
With plenteous rivers and wide-skirted meads,
We make thee lady: to thine and Albany's issue
Be this perpetual. What says our second daughter,
Our dearest Regan, wife to Cornwall? Speak.

REGAN. I am made of that self metal as my sister,
And prize me at her worth. In my true heart
I find she names my very deed of love;
Only she comes too short: that I profess
Myself an enemy to all other joys
Which the most precious square of sense possesses
And find I am alone felicitate
In your dear highness' love.

CORDELIA. [*Aside.*] Then, poor Cordelia!
And yet not so; since, I am sure, my love's
More richer than my tongue.

LEAR. To thee and thine, hereditary ever,
Remain this ample third of our fair kingdom,
No less in space, validity, and pleasure,
Than that conferr'd on Goneril. Now, our joy,
Although our last, not least; to whose young love
The vines of France and milk of Burgundy
Strive to be interess'd; what can you say to draw
A third more opulent than your sisters? Speak.

CORDELIA. Nothing, my lord.

LEAR. Nothing?

CORDELIA. Nothing.

LEAR. Nothing will come of nothing: speak again.

CORDELIA. Unhappy that I am, I cannot heave
My heart into my mouth: I love your majesty
According to my bond; nor more nor less.

LEAR. How, how, Cordelia! mend your speech a little,
Lest you may mar your fortunes.

CORDELIA.   Good my lord,
You have begot me, bred me, lov'd me: I
Return those duties back as are right fit,
Obey you, love you, and most honour you.
Why have my sisters husbands, if they say
They love you all? Haply, when I shall wed,
That lord whose hand must take my plight shall carry
Half my love with him, half my care and duty:
Sure I shall never marry like my sisters,
To love my father all.

    LEAR. But goes thy heart with this?

    CORDELIA.   Ay, good my lord.

    LEAR. So young, and so untender?

    CORDELIA. So young, my lord, and true.

    LEAR. Let it be so; thy truth then be thy dower:
For, by the sacred radiance of the sun,
The mysteries of Hecate and the night,
By all the operation of the orbs
From whom we do exist and cease to be,
Here I disclaim all my paternal care,
Propinquity and property of blood,
And as a stranger to my heart and me
Hold thee from this for ever. The barbarous Scythian,
Or he that makes his generation messes
To gorge his appetite, shall to my bosom
Be as well neighbour'd, pitied, and reliev'd,
As thou my sometime daughter.

    KENT.   Good my liege,—

    LEAR. Peace, Kent!
Come not between the dragon and his wrath.
I lov'd her most, and thought to set my rest
On her kind nursery. Hence, and avoid my sight!
So be my grave my peace, as here I give
Her father's heart from her! Call France. Who stirs?
Call Burgundy. Cornwall and Albany,
With my two daughters' dowers digest the third;
Let pride, which she calls plainness, marry her.

I do invest you jointly with my power,
Pre-eminence, and all the large effects
That troop with majesty. Ourself by monthly course,
With reservation of a hundred knights,
By you to be sustain'd, shall our abode
Make with you by due turn. Only we shall retain
The name and all th' addition to a king;
The sway, revenue, execution of the rest,
Beloved sons, be yours: which to confirm,
This coronet part between you.

    KENT.   Royal Lear,
Whom I have ever honour'd as my king,
Lov'd as my father, as my master follow'd,
As my great patron thought on in my prayers,—

    LEAR. The bow is bent and drawn; make from the shaft.

    KENT. Let it fall rather, though the fork invade
The region of my heart: be Kent unmannerly
When Lear is mad. What wouldst thou do, old man?
Think'st thou that duty shall have dread to speak
When power to flattery bows? To plainness honour's bound
When majesty falls to folly. Reserve thy state;
And, in thy best consideration, check
This hideous rashness: answer my life my judgment,
Thy youngest daughter does not love thee least;
Nor are those empty-hearted whose low sound
Reverbs no hollowness.

    LEAR.   Kent, on thy life, no more.

    KENT. My life I never held but as a pawn
To wage against thine enemies; nor fear to lose it,
Thy safety being the motive.

    LEAR.   Out of my sight!

    KENT. See better, Lear; and let me still remain
The true blank of thine eye.

    LEAR. Now, by Apollo,—

    KENT.   Now, by Apollo, king,
Thou swear'st thy gods in vain.

LEAR.   O vassal! miscreant!
                      [*Laying his hand on his sword.*

ALBANY. ⎫
         ⎬ Dear sir, forbear.
CORNWALL. ⎭

KENT. Do;
Kill thy physician, and the fee bestow
Upon the foul disease. Revoke thy gift;
Or, whilst I can vent clamour from my throat,
I'll tell thee thou dost evil.

LEAR.   Hear me, recreant!
On thine allegiance, hear me!
Since thou hast sought to make us break our vow,—
Which we durst never yet,—and, with strain'd pride
To come betwixt our sentence and our power,—
Which nor our nature nor our place can bear,—
Our potency made good, take thy reward.
Five days we do allot thee for provision
To shield thee from diseases of the world;
And, on the sixth, to turn thy hated back
Upon our kingdom: if, on the tenth day following
Thy banish'd trunk be found in our dominions,
The moment is thy death. Away! By Jupiter,
This shall not be revok'd.

KENT. Fare thee well, king; sith thus thou wilt appear,
Freedom lives hence, and banishment is here.
[*To* CORDELIA.] The gods to their dear shelter take thee, maid,
That justly think'st, and hast most rightly said!
[*To* REGAN *and* GONERIL.] And your large speeches may your
    deeds approve,
That good effects may spring from words of love.
Thus Kent, O princes! bids you all adieu;
He'll shape his old course in a country new.   [*Exit.*

    Flourish. Re-enter GLOUCESTER, *with* FRANCE, BURGUNDY,
    and ATTENDANTS.

GLOUCESTER. Here's France and Burgundy, my noble lord.
LEAR. My Lord of Burgundy,

We first address toward you, who with this king
Hath rivall'd for our daughter. What, in the least,
Will you require in present dower with her,
Or cease your quest of love?

BURGUNDY.   Most royal majesty,
I crave no more than hath your highness offer'd,
Nor will you tender less.

LEAR.   Right noble Burgundy,
When she was dear to us we did hold her so.
But now her price is fall'n. Sir, there she stands:
If aught within that little-seeming substance,
Or all of it, with our displeasure piec'd,
And nothing more, may fitly like your Grace,
She's there, and she is yours.

BURGUNDY.   I know no answer.

LEAR. Will you, with those infirmities she owes,
Unfriended, new-adopted to our hate,
Dower'd with our curse, and stranger'd with our oath,
Take her, or leave her?

BURGUNDY.   Pardon me, royal sir;
Election makes not up on such conditions.

LEAR. Then leave her, sir; for, by the power that made me,
I tell you all her wealth.—[*To* FRANCE.] For you, great king,
I would not from your love make such a stray
To match you where I hate; therefore, beseech you
To avert your liking a more worthier way
Than on a wretch whom nature is asham'd
Almost to acknowledge hers.

FRANCE.   This is most strange,
That she, who even but now was your best object,
The argument of your praise, balm of your age,
The best, the dearest, should in this trice of time
Commit a thing so monstrous, to dismantle
So many folds of favour. Sure, her offence
Must be of such unnatural degree
That monsters it, or your fore-vouch'd affection
Fall into taint; which to believe of her,

Must be a faith that reason without miracle
Could never plant in me.

    CORDELIA.   I yet beseech your majesty—
If for I want that glib and oily art
To speak and purpose not; since what I well intend,
I'll do't before I speak—that you make known
It is no vicious blot nor other foulness,
No unchaste action, or dishonour'd step,
That hath depriv'd me of your grace and favour,
But even for want of that for which I am richer,
A still-soliciting eye, and such a tongue
That I am glad I have not, though not to have it
Hath lost me in your liking.

    LEAR.   Better thou
Hadst not been born than not to have pleas'd me better.

    FRANCE. Is it but this? a tardiness in nature
Which often leaves the history unspoke
That it intends to do? My Lord of Burgundy,
What say you to the lady? Love is not love
When it is mingled with regards that stand
Aloof from the entire point. Will you have her?
She is herself a dowry.

    BURGUNDY.   Royal Lear,
Give but that portion which yourself propos'd,
And here I take Cordelia by the hand,
Duchess of Burgundy.

    LEAR. Nothing: I have sworn; I am firm.

    BURGUNDY. I am sorry, then, you have so lost a father
That you must lose a husband.

    CORDELIA.   Peace be with Burgundy!
Since that respects of fortune are his love,
I shall not be his wife.

    FRANCE. Fairest Cordelia, that art most rich, being poor;
Most choice, forsaken; and most lov'd, despis'd!
Thee and thy virtues here I seize upon:
Be it lawful I take up what's cast away.
Gods, gods! 'tis strange that from their cold'st neglect

My love should kindle to inflam'd respect.
Thy dowerless daughter, king, thrown to my chance,
Is queen of us, of ours, and our fair France:
Not all the dukes of waterish Burgundy
Shall buy this unpriz'd precious maid of me.
Bid them farewell, Cordelia, though unkind:
Thou losest here, a better where to find.

LEAR. Thou hast her, France; let her be thine, for we
Have no such daughter, nor shall ever see
That face of hers again, therefore be gone
Without our grace, our love, our benison.
Come, noble Burgundy.

[*Flourish. Exeunt* LEAR, BURGUNDY, CORNWALL, ALBANY,
GLOUCESTER, *and* ATTENDANTS.

FRANCE. Bid farewell to your sisters.

CORDELIA. The jewels of our father, with wash'd eyes
Cordelia leaves you: I know you what you are;
And like a sister am most loath to call
Your faults as they are nam'd. Use well our father:
To your professed bosoms I commit him:
But yet, alas! stood I within his grace,
I would prefer him to a better place.
So farewell to you both.

REGAN. Prescribe not us our duties.

GONERIL. Let your study
Be to content your lord, who hath receiv'd you
At fortune's alms; you have obedience scanted,
And well are worth the want that you have wanted.

CORDELIA. Time shall unfold what plighted cunning hides;
Who covers faults, at last shame them derides.
Well may you prosper!

FRANCE. Come, my fair Cordelia.

[*Exit* FRANCE *and* CORDELIA.

GONERIL. Sister, it is not little I have to say of what most nearly
appertains to us both. I think our father will hence to-night.

REGAN. That's most certain, and with you; next month with
us.

GONERIL. You see how full of changes his age is; the observation we have made of it hath not been little: he always loved our sister most; and with what poor judgment he hath now cast her off appears too grossly.

REGAN. 'Tis the infirmity of his age; yet he hath ever but slenderly known himself.

GONERIL. The best and soundest of his time hath been but rash; then, must we look to receive from his age, not alone the imperfections of long-engraffed condition, but, therewithal the unruly waywardness that infirm and choleric years bring with them.

REGAN. Such unconstant starts are we like to have from him as this of Kent's banishment.

GONERIL. There is further compliment of leave-taking between France and him. Pray you, let us hit together: if our father carry authority with such dispositions as he bears, this last surrender of his will but offend us.

REGAN. We shall further think on't.

GONERIL. We must do something, and i' the heat.   [*Exeunt.*

Scene II. *A Hall in the Earl of Gloucester's Castle*

Enter EDMUND, *with a letter.*

EDMUND. Thou, Nature, art my goddess; to thy law
My services are bound. Wherefore should I
Stand in the plague of custom, and permit
The curiosity of nations to deprive me,
For that I am some twelve or fourteen moonshines
Lag of a brother? Why bastard? wherefore base?
When my dimensions are as well compact,
My mind as generous, and my shape as true,
As honest madam's issue? Why brand they us
With base? with baseness? bastardy? base, base?
Who in the lusty stealth of nature take
More composition and fierce quality
Than doth, within a dull, stale, tired bed,

Go to the creating a whole tribe of fops,
Got 'tween asleep and wake? Well then,
Legitimate Edgar, I must have your land:
Our father's love is to the bastard Edmund
As to the legitimate. Fine word, 'legitimate!'
Well, my legitimate, if this letter speed,
And my invention thrive, Edmund the base
Shall top the legitimate:—I grow, I prosper;
Now, gods, stand up for bastards!

    Enter GLOUCESTER.

    GLOUCESTER. Kent banished thus! And France in choler
      parted!
And the king gone to-night! subscrib'd his power!
Confin'd to exhibition! All this done
Upon the gad! Edmund, how now! what news?
    EDMUND. So please your lordship, none.
                                [Putting up the letter.
    GLOUCESTER. Why so earnestly seek you to put up that letter?
    EDMUND. I know no news, my lord.
    GLOUCESTER. What paper were you reading?
    EDMUND. Nothing, my lord.
    GLOUCESTER. No? What needed then that terrible dispatch of
it into your pocket? the quality of nothing hath not such need
to hide itself. Let's see; come; if it be nothing, I shall not need
spectacles.
    EDMUND. I beseech you, sir, pardon me; it is a letter from my
brother that I have not all o'er-read, and for so much as I have
perused, I find it not fit for your o'er-looking.
    GLOUCESTER. Give me the letter, sir.
    EDMUND. I shall offend, either to detain or give it. The con-
tents, as in part I understand them, are to blame.
    GLOUCESTER. Let's see, let's see.
    EDMUND. I hope, for my brother's justification, he wrote this
but as an essay or taste of my virtue.
    GLOUCESTER. *This policy and reverence of age makes the*
world bitter to the best of our times; keeps our fortunes from us

till our oldness cannot relish them. I begin to find an idle and fond bondage in the oppression of aged tyranny, who sways, not as it hath power, but as it is suffered. Come to me, that of this I may speak more. If our father would sleep till I waked him, you should enjoy half his revenue for ever, and live the beloved of your brother, EDGAR.—Hum! Conspiracy! 'Sleep till I waked him, you should enjoy half his revenue.'—My son Edgar! Had he a hand to write this? a heart and brain to breed it in? When came this to you? Who brought it?

EDMUND. It was not brought me, my lord; there's the cunning of it; I found it thrown in at the casement of my closet.

GLOUCESTER. You know the character to be your brother's?

EDMUND. If the matter were good, my lord, I durst swear it were his; but, in respect of that, I would fain think it were not.

GLOUCESTER. It is his.

EDMUND. It is his hand, my lord; but I hope his heart is not in the contents.

GLOUCESTER. Hath he never heretofore sounded you in this business?

EDMUND. Never, my lord: but I have often heard him maintain it to be fit that, sons at perfect age, and fathers declined, the father should be as ward to the son, and the son manage his revenue.

GLOUCESTER. O villain, villain! His very opinion in the letter! Abhorred villain! Unnatural, detested, brutish villain! worse than brutish! Go, sirrah, seek him; I'll apprehend him. Abominable villain! Where is he?

EDMUND. I do not well know, my lord. If it shall please you to suspend your indignation against my brother till you can derive from him better testimony of his intent, you shall run a certain course; where, if you violently proceed against him, mistaking his purpose, it would make a great gap in your own honour, and shake in pieces the heart of his obedience. I dare pawn down my life for him, that he hath writ this to feel my affection to your honour, and to no other pretence of danger.

GLOUCESTER. Think you so?

EDMUND. If your honour judge it meet, I will place you where

you shall hear us confer of this, and by an auricular assurance
have your satisfaction; and that without any further delay than
this very evening.

GLOUCESTER. He cannot be such a monster—

EDMUND. Nor is not, sure.

GLOUCESTER. —to his father, that so tenderly and entirely loves
him. Heaven and earth! Edmund, seek him out; wind me into
him, I pray you: frame the business after your own wisdom. I
would unstate myself to be in a due resolution.

EDMUND. I will seek him, sir, presently; convey the business
as I shall find means, and acquaint you withal.

GLOUCESTER. These late eclipses in the sun and moon portend
no good to us: though the wisdom of nature can reason it thus
and thus, yet nature finds itself scourged by the sequent effects.
Love cools, friendship falls off, brothers divide: in cities, mu-
tinies; in countries, discord; in palaces, treason; and the bond
cracked between son and father. This villain of mine comes
under the prediction; there's son against father: the king falls
from bias of nature; there's father against child. We have seen
the best of our time: machinations, hollowness, treachery, and
all ruinous disorders, follow us disquietly to our graves. Find out
this villain, Edmund; it shall lose thee nothing: do it carefully.
And the noble and true-hearted Kent banished! his offence,
honesty! 'Tis strange!   [*Exit.*

EDMUND. This is the excellent foppery of the world, that,
when we are sick in fortune,—often the surfeit of our own behaviour,—we make guilty of our disasters the sun, the moon, and
the stars; as if we were villains by necessity, fools by heavenly
compulsion, knaves, thieves, and treachers by spherical pre-
dominance, drunkards, liars, and adulterers by an enforced obedience of planetary influence; and all that we are evil in, by a
divine thrusting on: an admirable evasion of whoremaster man,
to lay his goatish disposition to the charge of a star! My father
compounded with my mother under the dragon's tail, and my
nativity was under *ursa major;* so that it follows I am rough and
lecherous. 'Sfoot! I should have been that I am had the maiden-
liest star in the firmament twinkled on my bastardizing. Edgar—

Enter EDGAR.

and pat he comes, like the catastrophe of the old comedy: my
cue is villainous melancholy, with a sigh like Tom o' Bedlam.
O, these eclipses do portend these divisions! *Fa, sol, la, mi.*

EDGAR. How now, brother Edmund! What serious contemplation are you in?

EDMUND. I am thinking, brother, of a prediction I read this
other day, what should follow these eclipses.

EDGAR. Do you busy yourself with that?

EDMUND. I promise you the effects he writes of succeed unhap-
pily; as of unnaturalness between the child and the parent;
death, dearth, dissolutions of ancient amities; divisions in state;
menaces and maledictions against king and nobles; needless
diffidences, banishment of friends, dissipation of cohorts, nuptial
breaches, and I know not what.

EDGAR. How long have you been a sectary astronomical?

EDMUND. Come, come; when saw you my father last?

EDGAR. The night gone by.

EDMUND. Spake you with him?

EDGAR. Ay, two hours together.

EDMUND. Parted you in good terms? Found you no displeasure
in him by word or countenance?

EDGAR. None at all.

EDMUND. Bethink yourself wherein you may have offended
him; and at my entreaty forbear his presence till some little
time hath qualified the heat of his displeasure, which at this instant so rageth in him that with the mischief of your person it
would scarcely allay.

EDGAR. Some villain hath done me wrong.

EDMUND. That's my fear. I pray you have a continent forbearance till the speed of his rage goes slower, and, as I say, retire
with me to my lodging, from whence I will fitly bring you to
hear my lord speak. Pray you, go; there's my key. If you do stir
abroad, go armed.

EDGAR. Armed, brother!

EDMUND. Brother, I advise you to the best; go armed; I am no

The house in which Shakespeare was born, as it appeared before
restoration in 1864.

honest man if there be any good meaning toward you; I have told
you what I have seen and heard; but faintly, nothing like the
image and horror of it; pray you, away.

EDGAR. Shall I hear from you anon?

EDMUND. I do serve you in this business.   [*Exit* EDGAR.
A credulous father, and a brother noble,
Whose nature is so far from doing harms
That he suspects none; on whose foolish honesty
My practices ride easy! I see the business.
Let me, if not by birth, have lands by wit:
All with me's meet that I can fashion fit.   [*Exit.*

Scene III. *A Room in the Duke of Albany's Palace*

Enter GONERIL *and* OSWALD *her Steward.*

GONERIL. Did my father strike my gentleman for chiding of
his fool?

OSWALD. Ay, madam.

GONERIL. By day and night he wrongs me; every hour
He flashes into one gross crime or other,
That sets us all at odds: I'll not endure it:
His knights grow riotous, and himself upbraids us
On every trifle. When he returns from hunting
I will not speak with him; say I am sick:
If you come slack of former services,
You shall do well; the fault of it I'll answer.

OSWALD. He's coming, madam; I hear him.   [*Horns within.*

GONERIL. Put on what weary negligence you please,
You and your fellows; I'd have it come to question:
If he distaste it, let him to my sister,
Whose mind and mine, I know, in that are one,
Not to be over-rul'd. Idle old man,
That still would manage those authorities
That he hath given away! Now, by my life,
Old fools are babes again, and must be us'd
With checks as flatteries, when they are seen abus'd.
Remember what I have said.

OSWALD. Well, madam.

GONERIL. And let his knights have colder looks among you;
What grows of it, no matter; advise your fellows so:
I would breed from hence occasions, and I shall,
That I may speak: I'll write straight to my sister
To hold my very course. Prepare for dinner.   [*Exeunt.*

Scene IV. *A Hall in the Same*

Enter KENT, *disguised.*

KENT. If but as well I other accents borrow,
That can my speech diffuse, my good intent
May carry through itself to that full issue
For which I raz'd my likeness. Now, banish'd Kent,
If thou canst serve where thou dost stand condemn'd,
So may it come, thy master, whom thou lov'st,
Shall find thee full of labours.

Horns within. Enter LEAR, KNIGHTS, *and* ATTENDANTS.

LEAR. Let me not stay a jot for dinner: go, get it ready. [*Exit
an* ATTENDANT.] How now! what art thou?

KENT. A man, sir.

LEAR. What dost thou profess? What wouldst thou with us?

KENT. I do profess to be no less than I seem; to serve him truly
that will put me in trust; to love him that is honest; to converse
with him that is wise, and says little; to fear judgment; to fight
when I cannot choose; and to eat no fish.

LEAR. What art thou?

KENT. A very honest-hearted fellow, and as poor as the king.

LEAR. If thou be as poor for a subject as he is for a king, thou
art poor enough. What wouldst thou?

KENT. Service.

LEAR. Whom wouldst thou serve?

KENT. You.

LEAR. Dost thou know me, fellow?

KENT. No, sir; but you have that in your countenance which
I would fain call master.

LEAR. What's that?

KENT. Authority.

LEAR. What services canst thou do?

KENT. I can keep honest counsel, ride, run, mar a curious tale in telling it, and deliver a plain message bluntly; that which ordinary men are fit for, I am qualified in, and the best of me is diligence.

LEAR. How old art thou?

KENT. Not so young, sir, to love a woman for singing, nor so old to dote on her for any thing; I have years on my back forty-eight.

LEAR. Follow me; thou shalt serve me: if I like thee no worse after dinner I will not part from thee yet. Dinner, ho! dinner! Where's my knave? my fool? Go you and call my fool hither.

[*Exit an* ATTENDANT.

Enter OSWALD.

You, you, sirrah, where's my daughter?

OSWALD. So please you,— [*Exit.*

LEAR. What says the fellow there? Call the clotpoll back. [*Exit a* KNIGHT.] Where's my fool, ho? I think the world's asleep. How now! where's that mongrel?

Re-enter KNIGHT.

KNIGHT. He says, my lord, your daughter is not well.

LEAR. Why came not the slave back to me when I called him?

KNIGHT. Sir, he answered me in the roundest manner, he would not.

LEAR. He would not!

KNIGHT. My lord, I know not what the matter is; but, to my judgment, your highness is not entertained with that ceremonious affection as you were wont; there's a great abatement of kindness appears as well in the general dependants as in the duke himself also and your daughter.

LEAR. Ha! sayest thou so?

KNIGHT. I beseech you, pardon me, my lord, if I be mistaken;

for my duty cannot be silent when I think your highness wronged.

LEAR. Thou but rememberest me of mine own conception: I have perceived a most faint neglect of late; which I have rather blamed as mine own jealous curiosity than as a very pretence and purpose of unkindness: I will look further into't. But where's my fool? I have not seen him this two days.

KNIGHT. Since my young lady's going into France, sir, the fool hath much pined him away.

LEAR. No more of that; I have noted it well. Go you and tell my daughter I would speak with her.　　　[*Exit an* ATTENDANT.
Go you, call hither my fool.　　　[*Exit an* ATTENDANT.

　　　Re-enter OSWALD.

O! you sir, you, come you hither, sir. Who am I, sir?

OSWALD. My lady's father.

LEAR. 'My lady's father!' my lord's knave: you whoreson dog! you slave! you cur!

OSWALD. I am none of these, my lord; I beseech your pardon.

LEAR. Do you bandy looks with me, you rascal?
　　　[*Striking him.*

OSWALD. I'll not be struck, my lord.

KENT. Nor tripped neither, you base football player.
　　　[*Tripping up his heels.*

LEAR. I thank thee, fellow; thou servest me, and I'll love thee.

KENT. Come, sir, arise, away! I'll teach you differences: away, away! If you will measure your lubber's length again, tarry; but away! Go to; have you wisdom? so.　　　[*Pushes* OSWALD *out.*

LEAR. Now, my friendly knave, I thank thee: there's earnest of thy service.　　　[*Gives* KENT *money.*

　　　Enter FOOL.

FOOL. Let me hire him too: here's my coxcomb.
　　　[*Offers* KENT *his cap.*

LEAR. How now, my pretty knave! how dost thou?

FOOL. Sirrah, you were best take my coxcomb.

KENT. Why, fool?

FOOL. Why? for taking one's part that's out of favour. Nay, an thou canst not smile as the wind sits, thou'lt catch cold shortly: there, take my coxcomb. Why, this fellow has banished two on's daughters, and did the third a blessing against his will: if thou follow him thou must needs wear my coxcomb. How now, nuncle! Would I had two coxcombs and two daughters!

LEAR. Why, my boy?

FOOL. If I gave them all my living, I'd keep my coxcombs myself. There's mine; beg another of thy daughters.

LEAR. Take heed, sirrah; the whip.

FOOL. Truth's a dog must to kennel; he must be whipped out when Lady the brach may stand by the fire and stink.

LEAR. A pestilent gall to me!

FOOL. [*To* KENT.] Sirrah, I'll teach thee a speech.

LEAR. Do.

FOOL. Mark it, nuncle:—

> Have more than thou showest,
> Speak less than thou knowest,
> Lend less than thou owest,
> Ride more than thou goest,
> Learn more than thou trowest,
> Set less than thou throwest;
> Leave thy drink and thy whore,
> And keep in-a-door,
> And thou shalt have more
> Than two tens to a score.

KENT. This is nothing, fool.

FOOL. Then 'tis like the breath of an unfee'd lawyer, you gave me nothing for't. Can you make no use of nothing, nuncle?

LEAR. Why, no, boy; nothing can be made out of nothing.

FOOL. [*To* KENT.] Prithee, tell him, so much the rent of his land comes to: he will not believe a fool.

LEAR. A bitter fool!

FOOL. Dost thou know the difference, my boy, between a bitter fool and a sweet fool?

LEAR. No, lad; teach me.

FOOL. That lord that counsell'd thee
    To give away thy land,
    Come place him here by me,
    Do thou for him stand:
    The sweet and bitter fool
    Will presently appear;
    The one in motley here,
    The other found out there.

LEAR. Dost thou call me fool, boy?

FOOL. All thy other titles thou hast given away; that thou wast born with.

KENT. This is not altogether fool, my lord.

FOOL. No, faith, lords and great men will not let me; if I had a monopoly out, they would have part on't, and ladies too: they will not let me have all fool to myself; they'll be snatching. Nuncle, give me an egg, and I'll give thee two crowns.

LEAR. What two crowns shall they be?

FOOL. Why, after I have cut the egg i' the middle and eat up the meat, the two crowns of the egg. When you clovest thy crown i' the middle, and gavest away both parts, thou borest thine ass on thy back o'er the dirt: thou hadst little wit in thy bald crown when thou gavest thy golden one away. If I speak like myself in this, let him be whipped that first finds it so.

    Fools had ne'er less grace in a year;
      For wise men are grown foppish,
    And know not how their wits to wear,
      Their manners are so apish.

LEAR. When were you wont to be so full of songs, sirrah?

FOOL. I have used it, nuncle, ever since thou madest thy daughters thy mothers; for when thou gavest them the rod and puttest down thine own breeches,

    Then they for sudden joy did weep,
      And I for sorrow sung,
    That such a king should play bo-peep,
      And go the fools among.

Prithee, nuncle, keep a schoolmaster that can teach thy fool to
lie: I would fain learn to lie.

LEAR. An you lie, sirrah, we'll have you whipped.

FOOL. I marvel what kin thou and thy daughters are: they'll
have me whipped for speaking true, thou'lt have me whipped
for lying; and sometimes I am whipped for holding my peace.
I had rather be any kind o' thing than a fool; and yet I would
not be thee, nuncle; thou hast pared thy wit o' both sides, and
left nothing i' the middle: here comes one o' the parings.

Enter GONERIL.

LEAR. How now, daughter! what makes that frontlet on? Methinks you are too much of late i' the frown.

FOOL. Thou wast a pretty fellow when thou hadst no need to
care for her frowning; now thou art an O without a figure. I
am better than thou art now; I am a fool, thou art nothing.
[*To* GONERIL.] Yes, forsooth, I will hold my tongue; so your face
bids me, though you say nothing.

 Mum, mum;

 He that keeps nor crust nor crumb,

 Weary of all, shall want some.

That's a shealed peascod.   [*Pointing to* LEAR.

GONERIL. Not only, sir, this your all-licens'd fool,
But other of your insolent retinue
Do hourly carp and quarrel, breaking forth
In rank and not-to-be-endured riots. Sir,
I had thought, by making this well known unto you,
To have found a safe redress; but now grow fearful,
By what yourself too late have spoke and done,
That you protect this course, and put it on
By your allowance; which if you should, the fault
Would not 'scape censure, nor the redresses sleep,
Which, in the tender of a wholesome weal,
Might in their working do you that offence,
Which else were shame, that then necessity
Will call discreet proceeding.

FOOL. For you trow, nuncle,

The hedge-sparrow fed the cuckoo so long,
That it had it head bit off by it young.
So out went the candle, and we were left darkling.

LEAR. Are you our daughter?

GONERIL. I would you would make use of your good wisdom,
Whereof I know you are fraught; and put away
These dispositions which of late transform you
From what you rightly are.

FOOL. May not an ass know when the cart draws the horse?
Whoop, Jug! I love thee.

LEAR. Does any here know me? This is not Lear:
Does Lear walk thus? speak thus? Where are his eyes?
Either his notion weakens, his discernings
Are lethargied. Ha! waking? 'tis not so.
Who is it that can tell me who I am?

FOOL. Lear's shadow.

LEAR. I would learn that; for, by the marks of sovereignty,
knowledge and reason, I should be false persuaded I had daughters.

FOOL. Which they will make an obedient father.

LEAR. Your name, fair gentlewoman?

GONERIL. This admiration, sir, is much o' the favour
Of other your new pranks. I do beseech you
To understand my purposes aright:
As you are old and reverend, should be wise.
Here do you keep a hundred knights and squires;
Men so disorder'd, so debosh'd, and bold,
That this our court, infected with their manners,
Shows like a riotous inn: epicurism and lust
Make it more like a tavern or a brothel
Than a grac'd palace. The shame itself doth speak
For instant remedy; be then desir'd
By her that else will take the thing she begs,
A little to disquantity your train;
And the remainder, that shall still depend,
To be such men as may besort your age,
Which know themselves and you.

Shakespeare's birthplace after restoration. The house at left was the family residence. The house on the right was used for business by his father, John Shakespeare.

LEAR. Darkness and devils!
Saddle my horses; call my train together.
Degenerate bastard! I'll not trouble thee:
Yet have I left a daughter.

GONERIL. You strike my people, and your disorder'd rabble
Make servants of their betters.

Enter ALBANY.

LEAR. Woe, that too late repents;
[*To* ALBANY.] O! sir, are you come?
Is it your will? Speak, sir. Prepare my horses.
Ingratitude, thou marble-hearted fiend,
More hideous, when thou show'st thee in a child,
Than the sea-monster.

ALBANY. Pray, sir, be patient.

LEAR. [*To* GONERIL.] Detested kite! thou liest:
My train are men of choice and rarest parts,
That all particulars of duty know,
And in the most exact regard support
The worships of their name. O most small fault,
How ugly didst thou in Cordelia show!
Which, like an engine, wrench'd my frame of nature
From the fix'd place, drew from my heart all love,
And added to the gall. O Lear, Lear, Lear!
Beat at this gate, that let thy folly in, [*Striking his head.*
And thy dear judgment out: Go, go, my people.

ALBANY. My lord, I am guiltless, as I am ignorant
Of what hath mov'd you.

LEAR. It may be so, my lord.
Hear, Nature, hear! dear goddess, hear!
Suspend thy purpose, if thou didst intend
To make this creature fruitful!
Into her womb convey sterility!
Dry up in her the organs of increase,
And from her derogate body never spring
A babe to honour her! If she must teem,
Create her child of spleen, that it may live

And be a thwart disnatur'd torment to her!
Let it stamp wrinkles in her brow of youth,
With cadent tears fret channels in her cheeks,
Turn all her mother's pains and benefits
To laughter and contempt, that she may feel
How sharper than a serpent's tooth it is
To have a thankless child! Away, away!   [Exit.
    ALBANY. Now, gods that we adore, whereof comes this?
    GONERIL. Never afflict yourself to know the cause;
But let his disposition have that scope
That dotage gives it.

      Re-enter LEAR.

    LEAR. What! fifty of my followers at a clap,
Within a fortnight?
    ALBANY.   What's the matter, sir?
    LEAR. I'll tell thee. [*To* GONERIL.] Life and death! I am
      asham'd
That thou hast power to shake my manhood thus,
That these hot tears, which break from me perforce,
Should make thee worth them. Blasts and fogs upon thee!
Th' untented woundings of a father's curse
Pierce every sense about thee! Old fond eyes,
Beweep this cause again, I'll pluck ye out,
And cast you, with the waters that you lose,
To temper clay. Yea, is it come to this?
Let it be so: I have another daughter,
Who, I am sure, is kind and comfortable:
When she shall hear this of thee, with her nails
She'll flay thy wolvish visage. Thou shalt find
That I'll resume the shape which thou dost think
I have cast off for ever; thou shalt, I warrant thee.
                [*Exeunt* LEAR, KENT, *and* ATTENDANTS.
    GONERIL. Do you mark that?
    ALBANY. I cannot be so partial, Goneril,
To the great love I bear you.—
    GONERIL. Pray you, content. What, Oswald, ho!

[*To the* FOOL.] You, sir, more knave than fool, after your master.

FOOL. Nuncle Lear, nuncle Lear! tarry, and take the fool with
thee.

> A fox, when one has caught her,
> And such a daughter,
> Should sure to the slaughter,
> If my cap would buy a halter;
> So the fool follows after.

GONERIL. This man hath had good counsel. A hundred
  knights!
'Tis politic and safe to let him keep
At point a hundred knights; yes, that on every dream,
Each buzz, each fancy, each complaint, dislike,
He may enguard his dotage with their powers,
And hold our lives in mercy. Oswald, I say!

ALBANY. Well, you may fear too far.

GONERIL.   Safer than trust too far.
Let me still take away the harms I fear,
Not fear still to be taken: I know his heart.
What he hath utter'd I have writ my sister;
If she sustain him and his hundred knights,
When I have show'd the unfitness,—

  Re-enter OSWALD.

                  How now, Oswald!
What! have you writ that letter to my sister?

OSWALD. Ay, madam.

GONERIL. Take you some company, and away to horse:
Inform her full of my particular fear;
And thereto add such reasons of your own
As may compact it more. Get you gone,
And hasten your return. [*Exit* OSWALD.] No, no, my lord,
This milky gentleness and course of yours
Though I condemn not, yet, under pardon,
You are much more attask'd for want of wisdom
Than prais'd for harmful mildness.

ALBANY. How far your eyes may pierce I cannot tell:
Striving to better, oft we mar what's well.

GONERIL. Nay, then—

ALBANY. Well, well; the event.   [*Exeunt.*

Scene V.   *Court before the Same*

Enter LEAR, KENT, *and* FOOL.

LEAR. Go you before to Gloucester with these letters. Acquaint my daughter no further with any thing you know than comes from her demand out of the letter. If your diligence be not speedy I shall be there before you.

KENT. I will not sleep, my lord, till I have delivered your letter.   [*Exit.*

FOOL. If a man's brains were in's heels, were't not in danger of kibes?

LEAR. Ay, boy.

FOOL. Then, I prithee, be merry; thy wit shall not go slipshod.

LEAR. Ha, ha, ha!

FOOL. Shalt see thy other daughter will use thee kindly; for though she's as like this as a crab is like an apple, yet I can tell what I can tell.

LEAR. What canst tell, boy?

FOOL. She will taste as like this as a crab does to a crab. Thou canst tell why one's nose stands i' the middle on's face?

LEAR. No.

FOOL. Why, to keep one's eyes of either side's nose, that what a man cannot smell out, he may spy into.

LEAR. I did her wrong,—

FOOL. Canst tell how an oyster makes his shell?

LEAR. No.

FOOL. Nor I neither; but I can tell why a snail has a house.

LEAR. Why?

FOOL. Why, to put his head in; not to give it away to his daughters, and leave his horns without a case.

LEAR. I will forget my nature. So kind a father! Be my horses ready?

FOOL. Thy asses are gone about 'em. The reason why the seven stars are no more than seven is a pretty reason.

LEAR. Because they are not eight?

FOOL. Yes, indeed: thou wouldst make a good fool.

LEAR. To take it again perforce! Monster ingratitude!

FOOL. If thou wert my fool, nuncle, I'd have thee beaten for being old before thy time.

LEAR. How's that?

FOOL. Thou shouldst not have been old before thou hadst been wise.

LEAR. O! let me not be mad, not mad, sweet heaven; Keep me in temper; I would not be mad!

Enter GENTLEMAN.

How now! Are the horses ready?

GENTLEMAN. Ready, my lord.

LEAR. Come, boy.

FOOL. She that's a maid now, and laughs at my departure, Shall not be a maid long, unless things be cut shorter.   [*Exeunt.*

Act 2

Scene I. *A Court within the Castle of the Earl of Gloucester*

Enter EDMUND *and* CURAN, *meeting.*

EDMUND. Save thee, Curan.

CURAN. And you, sir. I have been with your father, and given him notice that the Duke of Cornwall and Regan his duchess will be here with him to-night.

EDMUND. How comes that?

CURAN. Nay, I know not. You have heard of the news abroad? I mean the whispered ones, for they are yet but ear-kissing arguments?

EDMUND. Not I: pray you, what are they?

CURAN. Have you heard of no likely wars toward, 'twixt the Dukes of Cornwall and Albany?

EDMUND. Not a word.

CURAN. You may do then, in time. Fare you well, sir.   [*Exit.*

EDMUND. The duke be here to-night! The better! best!
This weaves itself perforce into my business.
My father hath set guard to take my brother;
And I have one thing, of a queasy question,
Which I must act. Briefness and fortune, work!
Brother, a word; descend: brother, I say!

    Enter EDGAR.

My father watches: O sir! fly this place;
Intelligence is given where you are hid;
You have now the good advantage of the night.

Have you not spoken 'gainst the Duke of Cornwall?
He's coming hither, now, i' the night, i' the haste,
And Regan with him; have you nothing said
Upon his party 'gainst the Duke of Albany?
Advise yourself.

EDGAR.   I am sure on't, not a word.

EDMUND. I hear my father coming; pardon me;
In cunning I must draw my sword upon you;
Draw; seem to defend yourself; now 'quit you well.
Yield;—come before my father. Light, ho! here!
Fly, brother. Torches! torches! So, farewell.   [*Exit* EDGAR.
Some blood drawn on me would beget opinion

                                  [*Wounds his arm.*

Of my more fierce endeavour: I have seen drunkards
Do more than this in sport. Father! father!
Stop, stop! No help?

    Enter GLOUCESTER, *and* SERVANTS *with torches.*

GLOUCESTER. Now, Edmund, where's the villain?

EDMUND. Here stood he in the dark, his sharp sword out,
Mumbling of wicked charms, conjuring the moon
To stand auspicious mistress.

GLOUCESTER.   But where is he?

EDMUND. Look, sir, I bleed.

GLOUCESTER.   Where is the villain, Edmund?

EDMUND. Fled this way, sir. When by no means he could—

GLOUCESTER. Pursue him, ho! Go after. [*Exeunt some* SERV-
ANTS.] 'By no means' what?

EDMUND. Persuade me to the murder of your lordship;
But that I told him, the revenging gods
'Gainst parricides did all their thunders bend;
Spoke with how manifold and strong a bond
The child was bound to the father; sir, in fine,
Seeing how loathly opposite I stood
To his unnatural purpose, in fell motion,
With his prepared sword he charges home
My unprovided body, lanc'd mine arm:

But when he saw my best alarum'd spirits
Bold in the quarrel's right, rous'd to the encounter,
Or whether gasted by the noise I made,
Full suddenly he fled.

    GLOUCESTER.   Let him fly far:
Not in this land shall he remain uncaught;
And found—dispatch. The noble duke my master,
My worthy arch and patron, comes to-night:
By his authority I will proclaim it,
That he which finds him shall deserve our thanks,
Bringing the murderous coward to the stake;
He that conceals him, death.

   EDMUND. When I dissuaded him from his intent,
And found him pight to do it, with curst speech
I threaten'd to discover him: he replied,
'Thou unpossessing bastard! dost thou think,
If I would stand against thee, would the reposal
Of any trust, virtue, or worth, in thee
Make thy words faith'd? No: what I should deny,—
As this I would; ay, though thou didst produce
My very character,—I'd turn it all
To thy suggestion, plot, and damned practice:
And thou must make a dullard of the world,
If they not thought the profits of my death
Were very pregnant and potential spurs
To make thee seek it.'

    GLOUCESTER.   Strong and fasten'd villain!
Would he deny his letter? I never got him.   [*Tucket within.*
Hark! the duke's trumpets. I know not why he comes.
All ports I'll bar; the villain shall not 'scape;
The duke must grant me that: besides, his picture
I will send far and near, that all the kingdom
May have due note of him; and of my land,
Loyal and natural boy, I'll work the means
To make thee capable.

    Ener CORNWALL, REGAN, *and* ATTENDANTS.

CORNWALL. How now, my noble friend! since I came hither,—
Which I can call but now,—I have heard strange news.

REGAN. If it be true, all vengeance comes too short
Which can pursue the offender. How dost, my lord?

GLOUCESTER. O! madam, my old heart is crack'd, it's crack'd.

REGAN. What! did my father's godson seek your life?
He whom my father nam'd? your Edgar?

GLOUCESTER. O! lady, lady, shame would have it hid.

REGAN. Was he not companion with the riotous knights
That tend upon my father?

GLOUCESTER. I know not, madam; 'tis too bad, too bad.

EDMUND. Yes, madam, he was of that consort.

REGAN. No marvel then though he were ill affected;
'Tis they have put him on the old man's death,
To have the expense and waste of his revenues.
I have this present evening from my sister
Been well-inform'd of them, and with such cautions
That if they come to sojourn at my house,
I'll not be there.

CORNWALL.   Nor I, assure thee, Regan.
Edmund, I hear that you have shown your father
A child-like office.

EDMUND.   'Twas my duty, sir.

GLOUCESTER. He did bewray his practice; and receiv'd
This hurt you see, striving to apprehend him.

CORNWALL. Is he pursu'd?

GLOUCESTER.   Ay, my good lord.

CORNWALL. If he be taken he shall never more
Be fear'd of doing harm; make your own purpose,
How in my strength you please. For you, Edmund,
Whose virtue and obedience doth this instant
So much commend itself, you shall be ours:
Natures of such deep trust we shall much need;
You we first seize on.

EDMUND.   I shall serve you, sir,
Truly, however else.

GLOUCESTER.   For him I thank your Grace.

CORNWALL. You know not why we came to visit you,—
REGAN. Thus out of season, threading dark-ey'd night:
Occasions, noble Gloucester, of some prize,
Wherein we must have use of your advice.
Our father he hath writ, so hath our sister,
Of differences, which I best thought it fit
To answer from our home; the several messengers
From hence attend dispatch. Our good old friend,
Lay comforts to your bosom, and bestow
Your needful counsel to our businesses,
Which craves the instant use.
GLOUCESTER.   I serve you, madam.
Your Graces are right welcome.   [*Exeunt.*

Scene II. *Before Gloucester's Castle*

Enter KENT *and* OSWALD, *severally.*

OSWALD. Good dawning to thee, friend: art of this house?
KENT. Ay.
OSWALD. Where may we set our horses?
KENT. I' the mire.
OSWALD. Prithee, if thou lovest me, tell me.
KENT. I love thee not.
OSWALD. Why, then I care not for thee.
KENT. If I had thee in Lipsbury pinfold, I would make thee
care for me.
OSWALD. Why dost thou use me thus? I know thee not.
KENT. Fellow, I know thee.
OSWALD. What dost thou know me for?
KENT. A knave, a rascal, and eater of broken meats; a base,
proud, shallow, beggarly, three-suited, hundred-pound, filthy,
worsted-stocking knave; a lilly-liver'd, action-taking knave; a
whoreson, glass-gazing, superserviceable, finical rogue; one-
trunk-inheriting slave; one that wouldst be a bawd, in way of
good service, and art nothing but the composition of a knave,
beggar, coward, pandar, and the son and heir of a mongrel bitch:

one whom I will beat into clamorous whining if thou deniest the least syllable of thy addition.

OSWALD. Why, what a monstrous fellow art thou, thus to rail on one that is neither known of thee nor knows thee!

KENT. What a brazen-faced varlet art thou, to deny thou knowest me! Is it two days since I tripped up thy heels and beat thee before the king? Draw, you rogue; for, though it be night, yet the moon shines: I'll make a sop o' the moonshine of you. [*Drawing his sword.*] Draw, you whoreson, cullionly, barber-monger, draw.

OSWALD. Away! I have nothing to do with thee.

KENT. Draw, you rascal; you come with letters against the king, and ake vanity the puppet's part against the royalty of her father. Draw, you rogue, or I'll so carbonado your shanks: draw, you rascal; come your ways.

OSWALD. Help, ho! murder! help!

KENT. Strike, you slave; stand, rogue, stand; you neat slave, strike.   [*Beating him.*

OSWALD. Help, oh! murder! murder!

Enter EDMUND *with his rapier drawn.*

EDMUND. How now! What's the matter?   [*Parting them.*

KENT. With you, goodman boy, if you please: come, I'll flesh ye; come on, young master.

Enter CORNWALL, REGAN, GLOUCESTER, *and* SERVANTS.

GLOUCESTER. Weapons! arms! What's the matter here?

CORNWALL. Keep peace, upon your lives:
He dies that strikes again. What is the matter?

REGAN. The messengers from our sister and the king.

CORNWALL. What is your difference? speak.

OSWALD. I am scarce in breath, my lord.

KENT. No marvel, you have so bestirred your valour. You cowardly rascal, nature disclaims in thee: a tailor made thee.

CORNWALL. Thou art a strange fellow; a tailor make a man?

KENT. Ay, a tailor, sir: a stone-cutter or a painter could not

have made him so ill, though they had been but two hours o'
the trade.

CORNWALL. Speak yet, how grew your quarrel?

OSWALD. This ancient ruffian, sir, whose life I have spar'd at
suit of his grey beard,—

KENT. Thou whoreson zed! thou unnecessary letter! My lord,
if you will give me leave, I will tread this unbolted villain into
mortar, and daub the wall of a jakes with him. Spare my grey
beard, you wagtail?

CORNWALL. Peace, sirrah!
You beastly knave, know you no reverence?

KENT. Yes, sir; but anger hath a privilege.

CORNWALL. Why art thou angry?

KENT. That such a slave as this should wear a sword,
Who wears no honesty. Such smiling rogues as these,
Like rats, oft bite the holy cords a-twain
Which are too intrinse t' unloose; smooth every passion
That in the natures of their lords rebel;
Bring oil to fire, snow to their colder moods;
Renege, affirm, and turn their halcyon beaks
With every gale and vary of their masters,
Knowing nought, like dogs, but following.
A plague upon your epileptic visage!
Smile you my speeches, as I were a fool?
Goose, if I had you upon Sarum plain,
I'd drive ye cackling home to Camelot.

CORNWALL. What! art thou mad, old fellow?

GLOUCESTER. How fell you out? say that.

KENT. No contraries hold more antipathy
Than I and such a knave.

CORNWALL. Why dost thou call him knave? What is his fault?

KENT. His countenance likes me not.

CORNWALL. No more, perchance, does mine, nor his, nor hers.

KENT. Sir, 'tis my occupation to be plain:
I have seen better faces in my time
Than stands on any shoulder that I see
Before me at this instant.

CORNWALL.   This is some fellow,
Who, having been prais'd for bluntness, doth affect
A saucy roughness, and constrains the garb
Quite from his nature: he cannot flatter, he,
An honest mind and plain, he must speak truth:
An they will take it, so; if not, he's plain.
These kind of knaves I know, which in this plainness
Harbour more craft and more corrupter ends
Than twenty silly-ducking observants,
That stretch their duties nicely.

    KENT. Sir, in good sooth, in sincere verity,
Under the allowance of your grand aspect,
Whose influence, like the wreath of radiant fire
On flickering Phœbus' front,—

    CORNWALL.   What mean'st by this?

    KENT. To go out of my dialect, which you discommend so
much. I know, sir, I am no flatterer: he that beguiled you in a
plain accent was a plain knave; which for my part I will not be,
though I should win your displeasure to entreat me to't.

    CORNWALL. What was the offence you gave him?

    OSWALD. I never gave him any:
It pleas'd the king his master very late
To strike at me, upon his misconstruction;
When he, conjunct, and flattering his displeasure,
Tripp'd me behind; being down, insulted, rail'd,
And put upon him such a deal of man,
That worthied him, got praises of the king
For him attempting who was self-subdu'd;
And, in the fleshment of this dread exploit,
Drew on me here again.

    KENT.   None of these rogues and cowards
But Ajax is their fool.

    CORNWALL.   Fetch forth the stocks!
You stubborn ancient knave, you reverend braggart,
We'll teach you.

    KENT.   Sir, I am too old to learn,
Call not your stocks for me; I serve the king,

On whose employment I was sent to you;
You shall do small respect, show too bold malice
Against the grace and person of my master,
Stocking his messenger.

    CORNWALL. Fetch forth the stocks! As I have life and honour,
There shall he sit till noon.

    REGAN. Till noon! Till night, my lord; and all night too.

    KENT. Why, madam, if I were your father's dog,
You should not use me so.

    REGAN.   Sir, being his knave, I will.

    CORNWALL. This is a fellow of the self-same colour
Our sister speaks of. Come, bring away the stocks.

                                      [Stocks brought out.

    GLOUCESTER. Let me beseech your Grace not to do so.
His fault is much, and the good king his master
Will check him for't: your purpos'd low correction
Is such as basest and contemned'st wretches
For pilferings and most common trespasses
Are punish'd with: the king must take it ill,
That he, so slightly valu'd in his messenger,
Should have him thus restrain'd.

    CORNWALL.   I'll answer that.

    REGAN. My sister may receive it much more worse
To have her gentleman abus'd, assaulted,
For following her affairs. Put in his legs.

                        [KENT is put in the stocks.
Come, my good lord, away.

                  [Exeunt all but GLOUCESTER and KENT.

    GLOUCESTER. I am sorry for thee, friend; 'tis the duke's pleasure,
Whose disposition, all the world well knows,
Will not be rubb'd nor stopp'd: I'll entreat for thee.

    KENT. Pray, do not, sir. I have watch'd and travell'd hard;
Some time I shall sleep out, the rest I'll whistle.
A good man's fortune may grow out at heels:
Give you good morrow!

GLOUCESTER. The duke's to blame in this; 'twill be ill taken.

[*Exit.*

KENT. Good king, that must approve the common saw,
Thou out of heaven's benediction com'st
To the warm sun.
Approach, thou beacon to this under globe,
That by thy comfortable beams I may
Peruse this letter. Nothing almost sees miracles
But misery: I know 'tis from Cordelia,
Who hath most fortunately been inform'd
Of my obscured course; and shall find time
From this enormous state, seeking to give
Losses their remedies. All weary and o'er-watch'd,
Take vantage, heavy eyes, not to behold
This shameful lodging.
Fortune, good night, smile once more; turn thy wheel!

[*He sleeps.*

Scene III.   *A Part of the Heath*

Enter EDGAR.

EDGAR. I heard myself proclaim'd;
And by the happy hollow of a tree
Escap'd the hunt. No port is free; no place,
That guard, and most unusual vigilance,
Does not attend my taking. While I may 'scape
I will preserve myself; and am bethought
To take the basest and most poorest shape
That ever penury, in contempt of man,
Brought near to beast; my face I'll grime with filth,
Blanket my loins, elf all my hair in knots,
And with presented nakedness outface
The winds and persecutions of the sky.
The country gives me proof and precedent
Of Bedlam beggars, who with roaring voices,
Strike in their numb'd and mortified bare arms

Pins, wooden pricks, nails, sprigs of rosemary;
And with this horrible object, from low farms,
Poor pelting villages, sheep-cotes, and mills,
Sometime with lunatic bans, sometime with prayers,
Enforce their charity. Poor Turlygood! poor Tom!
That's something yet: Edgar I nothing am.   [*Exit.*

Scene IV.   *Before Gloucester's Castle.*
Kent in the stocks

Enter LEAR, FOOL, *and* GENTLEMAN.

LEAR. 'Tis strange that they should so depart from home,
And not send back my messenger.

GENTLEMAN.   As I learn'd,
The night before there was no purpose in them
Of this remove.

KENT.   Hail to thee, noble master!

LEAR. Ha!
Mak'st thou this shame thy pastime?

KENT.   No, my lord.

FOOL. Ha, ha! he wears cruel garters. Horses are tied by the
head, dogs and bears by the neck, monkeys by the loins, and
men by the legs: when a man is over-lusty at legs, then he wears
wooden nether-stocks.

LEAR. What's he that hath so much thy place mistook
To set thee here?

KENT.   It is both he and she,
Your son and daughter.

LEAR. No.

KENT. Yes.

LEAR. No, I say.

KENT. I say, yea.

LEAR. No, no; they would not.

KENT. Yes, they have.

LEAR. By Jupiter, I swear, no.

KENT. By Juno, I swear, ay.

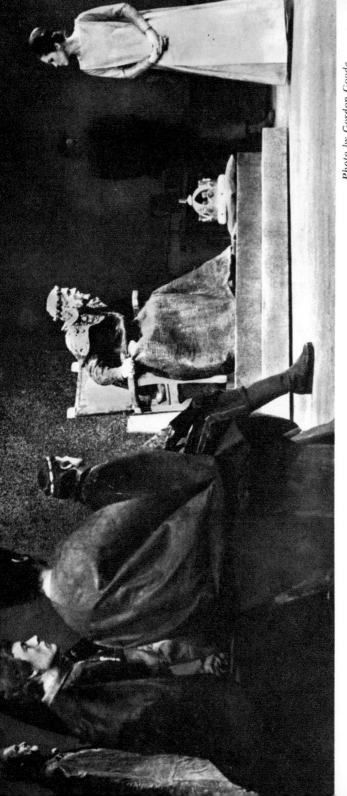

A scene from the Royal Shakespeare Company's production of *King Lear* at Stratford-upon-Avon in 1962, with Paul Scofield as Lear and Diana Rigg as Cordelia.

LEAR.   They durst not do't;
They could not, would not do't; 'tis worse than murder,
To do upon respect such violent outrage.
Resolve me, with all modest haste, which way
Thou mightst deserve, or they impose, this usage,
Coming from us.

    KENT.   My lord, when at their home
I did commend your highness' letters to them,
Ere I was risen from the place that show'd
My duty kneeling, there came a reeking post,
Stew'd in his haste, half breathless, panting forth
From Goneril his mistress salutations;
Deliver'd letters, spite of intermission,
Which presently they read: on whose contents
They summon'd up their meiny, straight took horse;
Commanded me to follow, and attend
The leisure of their answer; gave me cold looks:
And meeting here the other messenger,
Whose welcome, I perceiv'd, had poison'd mine,—
Being the very fellow which of late
Display'd so saucily against your highness,—
Having more man than wit about me,—drew:
He rais'd the house with loud and coward cries.
Your son and daughter found this trespass worth
The shame which here it suffers.

    FOOL. Winter's not gone yet, if the wild geese fly that way.

> Fathers that wear rags
>   Do make their children blind,
> But fathers that bear bags
>   Shall see their children kind.
> Fortune, that arrant whore,
> Ne'er turns the key to the poor.

But for all this thou shalt have as many dolours for thy daughters as thou canst tell in a year.

    LEAR. O! how this mother swells up toward my heart;
Hystericapassio! down, thou climbing sorrow!

Thy element's below. Where is this daughter?

KENT. With the earl, sir: here within.

LEAR. Follow me not; stay here. [*Exit.*

GENTLEMAN. Made you no more offence than what you speak of?

KENT. None.

How chance the king comes with so small a number?

FOOL. An thou hadst been set i' the stocks for that question, thou hadst well deserved it.

KENT. Why, fool?

FOOL. We'll set thee to school to an ant, to teach thee there's no labouring i' the winter. All that follow their noses are led by their eyes but blind men; and there's not a nose among twenty but can smell him that's stinking. Let go thy hold when a great wheel runs down a hill, lest it break thy neck with following it; but the great one that goes up the hill, let him draw thee after. When a wise man gives thee better counsel, give me mine again: I would have none but knaves follow it, since a fool gives it.

>That sir which serves and seeks for gain,
>   And follows but for form,
>Will pack when it begins to rain,
>   And leave thee in the storm.
>But I will tarry; the fool will stay,
>   And let the wise man fly:
>The knave turns fool that runs away;
>   The fool no knave, perdy.

KENT. Where learn'd you this, fool?

FOOL. Not i' the stocks, fool.

Re-enter LEAR, *with* GLOUCESTER.

LEAR. Deny to speak with me! They are sick! they are weary,
They have travell'd hard to-night! Mere fetches,
The images of revolt and flying off.
Fetch me a better answer.

GLOUCESTER.   My dear lord,
You know the fiery quality of the duke;

How unremovable and fix'd he is
In his own course.
    LEAR. Vengeance! plague! death! confusion!
Fiery! what quality? Why, Gloucester, Gloucester,
I'd speak with the Duke of Cornwall and his wife.
    GLOUCESTER. Well, my good lord, I have inform'd them so.
    LEAR. Inform'd them! Dost thou understand me, man?
    GLOUCESTER. Ay, my good lord.
    LEAR. The king would speak with Cornwall; the dear father
Would with his daughter speak, commands her service:
Are they inform'd of this? My breath and blood!
Fiery! the fiery duke! Tell the hot duke that—
No, but not yet; may be he is not well:
Infirmity doth still neglect all office
Whereto our health is bound; we are not ourselves
When nature, being oppress'd, commands the mind
To suffer with the body. I'll forbear;
And am fall'n out with my more headier will,
To take the indispos'd and sickly fit
For the sound man. Death on my state! [*Looking on* KENT.]
Wherefore
Should he sit here? This act persuades me
That this remotion of the duke and her
Is practice only. Give me my servant forth.
Go, tell the duke and's wife I'd speak with them
Now, presently: bid them come forth and hear me,
Or at their chamber-door I'll beat the drum
Till it cry sleep to death.
    GLOUCESTER. I would have all well betwixt you.   [*Exit.*
    LEAR. O, me! my heart, my rising heart! but, down!
    FOOL. Cry to it, nuncle, as the cockney did to the eels when
she put 'em i' the paste alive; she knapped 'em o' the coxcombs
with a stick, and cried, 'Down, wantons, down!' 'Twas her
brother that, in pure kindness to his horse, buttered his hay.

    Enter CORNWALL, REGAN, GLOUCESTER, *and* SERVANTS.

    LEAR. Good morrow to you both.

CORNWALL.   Hail to your Grace!

[KENT *is set at liberty.*

REGAN. I am glad to see your highness.

LEAR. Regan, I think you are; I know what reason
I have to think so: if thou shouldst not be glad,
I would divorce me from thy mother's tomb,
Sepulchring an adult'ress.—[*To* KENT.] O! are you free?
Some other time for that. Beloved Regan,
Thy sister's naught: O Regan! she hath tied
Sharp-tooth'd unkindness, like a vulture, here:

[*Points to his heart.*

I can scarce speak to thee; thou'lt not believe
With how deprav'd a quality—O Regan!

REGAN. I pray you, sir, take patience. I have hope
You less know how to value her desert
Than she to scant her duty.

LEAR.   Say, how is that?

REGAN. I cannot think my sister in the least
Would fail her obligation: if, sir, perchance
She have restrain'd the riots of your followers,
'Tis on such ground, and to such wholesome end,
As clears her from all blame.

LEAR. My curses on her!

REGAN.   O, sir! you are old;
Nature in you stands on the very verge
Of her confine: you should be rul'd and led
By some discretion that discerns your state
Better than you yourself. Therefore I pray you
That to our sister you do make return;
Say, you have wrong'd her, sir.

LEAR.   Ask her forgiveness?
Do you but mark how this becomes the house:
'Dear daughter, I confess that I am old;
Age is unnecessary: on my knees I beg   [*Kneeling.*
That you'll vouchsafe me raiment, bed, and food.'

REGAN. Good sir, no more; these are unsightly tricks:
Return you to my sister.

LEAR. [*Rising.*] Never, Regan.
She hath abated me of half my train;
Look'd black upon me; struck me with her tongue,
Most serpent-like, upon the very heart.
All the stor'd vengeances of heaven fall
On her ingrateful top! Strike her young bones,
You taking airs, with lameness!

CORNWALL. Fie, sir, fie!

LEAR. You nimble lightnings, dart your blinding flames
Into her scornful eyes! Infect her beauty,
You fen-suck'd fogs, drawn by the powerful sun,
To fall and blast her pride!

REGAN. O the blest gods! So will you wish on me,
When the rash mood is on.

LEAR. No, Regan, thou shalt never have my curse:
Thy tender-hefted nature shall not give
Thee o'er to harshness: her eyes are fierce, but thine
Do comfort and not burn. 'Tis not in thee
To grudge my pleasures, to cut off my train,
To bandy hasty words, to scant my sizes,
And, in conclusion, to oppose the bolt
Against my coming in: thou better know'st
The offices of nature, bond of childhood,
Effects of courtesy, dues of gratitude;
Thy half o' the kingdom has thou not forgot,
Wherein I thee endow'd.

REGAN. Good sir, to the purpose.

LEAR. Who put my man i' the stocks?   [*Tucket within.*

CORNWALL. What trumpet's that?

REGAN. I know't, my sister's; this approves her letter,
That she would soon be here. Is your lady come?

Enter OSWALD.

LEAR. This is a slave, whose easy-borrow'd pride
Dwells in the fickle grace of her he follows.
Out, varlet, from my sight!

CORNWALL. What means your Grace?

LEAR. Who stock'd my servant? Regan, I have good hope
Thou didst not know on't. Who comes here? O heavens,

Enter GONERIL.

If you do love old men, if your sweet sway
Allow obedience, if yourselves are old,
Make it your cause; send down and take my part!
[*To* GONERIL.] Art not asham'd to look upon this beard?
O Regan, wilt thou take her by the hand?
    GONERIL. Why not by the hand, sir? How have I offended?
All's not offence that indiscretion finds
And dotage terms so.
    LEAR.   O sides! you are too tough;
Will you yet hold? How came my man i' the stocks?
    CORNWALL. I set him there, sir: but his own disorders
Deserv'd such less advancement.
    LEAR.   You! did you?
    REGAN. I pray you, father, being weak, seem so.
If, till the expiration of your month,
You will return and sojourn with my sister,
Dismissing half your train, come then to me:
I am now from home, and out of that provision
Which shall be needful for your entertainment.
    LEAR. Return to her? and fifty men dismiss'd!
No, rather I abjure all roofs, and choose
To wage against the enmity o' the air;
To be a comrade with the wolf and owl,
Necessity's sharp pinch! Return with her!
Why, the hot-blooded France, that dowerless took
Our youngest born, I could as well be brought
To knee his throne, and squire-like, pension beg
To keep base life afoot. Return with her!
Persuade me rather to be slave and sumpter
To this detested groom.   [*Pointing at* OSWALD.
    GONERIL.   At your choice, sir.
    LEAR. I prithee, daughter, do not make me mad:
I will not trouble thee, my child; farewell.

We'll no more meet, no more see one another;
But yet thou art my flesh, my blood, my daughter;
Or rather a disease that's in my flesh,
Which I must needs call mine: thou art a boil,
A plague-sore, an embossed carbuncle,
In my corrupted blood. But I'll not chide thee;
Let shame come when it will, I do not call it:
I do not bid the thunder-bearer shoot,
Nor tell tales of thee to high-judging Jove.
Mend when thou canst; be better at thy leisure:
I can be patient; I can stay with Regan,
I and my hundred knights.

REGAN.   Not altogether so:
I look'd not for you yet, nor am provided
For your fit welcome. Give ear, sir, to my sister;
For those that mingle reason with your passion
Must be content to think you old, and so—
But she knows what she does.

LEAR.   Is this well spoken?

REGAN. I dare avouch it, sir: what! fifty followers?
Is it not well? What should you need of more?
Yea, or so many, sith that both charge and danger
Speak 'gainst so great a number? How, in one house,
Should many people, under two commands,
Hold amity? 'Tis hard; almost impossible.

GONERIL. Why might not you, my lord, receive attendance
From those that she calls servants, or from mine?

REGAN. Why not, my lord? If then they chanc'd to slack you
We could control them. If you will come to me,—
For now I spy a danger,—I entreat you
To bring but five-and-twenty; to no more
Will I give place or notice.

LEAR. I gave you all—

REGAN.   And in good time you gave it.

LEAR. Made you my guardians, my depositaries,
But kept a reservation to be follow'd
With such a number. What! must I come to you

With five-and-twenty? Regan, said you so?

REGAN. And speak't again, my lord; no more with me.

LEAR. Those wicked creatures yet do look well-favour'd,
When others are more wicked; not being the worst
Stands in some rank of praise. [*To* GONERIL.] I'll go with thee:
Thy fifty yet doth double five-and-twenty,
And thou art twice her love.

GONERIL.   Hear me, my lord.
What need you five-and-twenty, ten, or five,
To follow in a house, where twice so many
Have a command to tend you?

REGAN.   What need one?

LEAR. O! reason not the need; our basest beggars
Are in the poorest thing superfluous:
Allow not nature more than nature needs,
Man's life is cheap as beast's. Thou art a lady;
If only to go warm were gorgeous,
Why, nature needs not what thou gorgeous wear'st,
Which scarcely keeps thee warm. But, for true need,—
You heavens, give me that patience, patience I need!
You see me here, you gods, a poor old man,
As full of grief as age; wretched in both!
If it be you that stir these daughters' hearts
Against their father, fool me not so much
To bear it tamely; touch me with noble anger,
And let not women's weapons, water-drops,
Stain my man's cheeks! No, you unnatural hags,
I will have such revenges on you both
That all the world shall—I will do such things,—
What they are yet I know not,—but they shall be
The terrors of the earth. You think I'll weep;
No, I'll not weep:
I have full cause of weeping, but this heart
Shall break into a hundred thousand flaws
Or ere I'll weep. O fool! I shall go mad.

                    [*Exeunt* LEAR, GLOUCESTER, KENT, *and* FOOL.

An engraving of David Garrick (*center*), a great British actor of the mid-eighteenth century, as King Lear, Act 3, Scene II: "I am more sinn'd against than sinning."

CORNWALL. Let us withdraw; 'twill be a storm.

[*Storm heard at a distance.*

REGAN. This house is little: the old man and his people
Cannot be well bestow'd.

GONERIL. 'Tis his own blame; hath put himself from rest,
And must needs taste his folly.

REGAN. For his particular, I'll receive him gladly,
But not one follower.

GONERIL.   So am I purpos'd.
Where is my Lord of Gloucester?

CORNWALL. Follow'd the old man forth. He is return'd.

Re-enter GLOUCESTER.

GLOUCESTER. The king is in high rage.

CORNWALL.   Whither is he going?

GLOUCESTER. He calls to horse; but will I know not whither.

CORNWALL. 'Tis best to give him way; he leads himself.

GONERIL. My lord, entreat him by no means to stay.

GLOUCESTER. Alack! the night comes on, and the bleak winds
Do sorely ruffle; for many miles about
There's scarce a bush.

REGAN.   O! sir, to wilful men,
The injuries that they themselves procure
Must be their schoolmasters. Shut up your doors;
He is attended with a desperate train,
And what they may incense him to, being apt
To have his ear abus'd, wisdom bids fear.

CORNWALL. Shut up your doors, my lord; 'tis a wild night:
My Regan counsels well: come out o' the storm.   [*Exeunt.*

Act 3

Scene I. A Heath

A storm, with thunder and lightning. Enter KENT *and a* GENTLEMAN, *meeting.*

KENT. Who's here, beside foul weather?

GENTLEMAN. One minded like the weather, most unquietly.

KENT. I know you. Where's the king?

GENTLEMAN. Contending with the fretful elements;
Bids the wind blow the earth into the sea,
Or swell the curled waters 'bove the main,
That things might change or cease; tears his white hair,
Which the impetuous blasts, with eyeless rage,
Catch in their fury, and make nothing of;
Strives in his little world of man to out-scorn
The to-and-fro-conflicting wind and rain.
This night, wherein the cub-drawn bear would couch,
The lion and the belly-pinched wolf
Keep their fur dry, unbonneted he runs,
And bids what will take all.

KENT.   But who is with him?

GENTLEMAN. None but the fool, who labours to out-jest
His heart-struck injuries.

KENT.   Sir, I do know you;
And dare, upon the warrant of my note,
Commend a dear thing to you. There is division,
Although as yet the face of it be cover'd
With mutual cunning, 'twixt Albany and Cornwall;
Who have—as who have not, that their great stars

268

Thron'd and set high—servants, who seem no less,
Which are to France the spies and speculations
Intelligent of our state; what hath been seen,
Either in snuffs and packings of the dukes,
Or the hard rein which both of them have borne
Against the old kind king; or something deeper,
Whereof perchance these are but furnishings;
But, true it is, from France there comes a power
Into this scatter'd kingdom; who already,
Wise in our negligence, have secret feet
In some of our best ports, and are at point
To show their open banner. Now to you:
If on my credit you dare build so far
To make your speed to Dover, you shall find
Some that will thank you, making just report
Of how unnatural and bemadding sorrow
The king hath cause to plain.
I am a gentleman of blood and breeding,
And from some knowledge and assurance offer
This office to you.
    GENTLEMAN. I will talk further with you.
    KENT.   No, do not.
For confirmation that I am much more
Than my out-wall, open this purse, and take
What it contains. If you shall see Cordelia,—
As doubt not but you shall,—show her this ring,
And she will tell you who your fellow is
That yet you do not know. Fie on this storm!
I will go seek the king.
    GENTLEMAN. Give me your hand. Have you no more to say?
    KENT. Few words, but, to effect, more than all yet;
That, when we have found the king,—in which your pain
That way, I'll this,—he that first lights on him
Holla the other.   [*Exeunt severally.*

Scene II. Another Part of the Heath. Storm still

    Enter LEAR *and* FOOL.

LEAR. Blow, winds, and crack your cheeks! rage! blow!
You cataracts and hurricanoes, spout
Till you have drench'd our steeples, drown'd the cocks!
You sulphurous and thought-executing fires,
Vaunt-couriers to oak-cleaving thunderbolts,
Singe my white head! And thou, all-shaking thunder,
Strike flat the thick rotundity o' the world!
Crack nature's moulds, all germens spill at once
That make ingrateful man!

    FOOL. O nuncle, court holy-water in a dry house is better than
this rain-water out o' door. Good nuncle, in, and ask thy daughters' blessing; here's a night pities neither wise man nor fool.

    LEAR. Rumble thy bellyful! Spit, fire! spout, rain!
Nor rain, wind, thunder, fire, are my daughters:
I tax not you, you elements, with unkindness;
I never gave you kingdom, call'd you children,
You owe me no subscription: then, let fall
Your horrible pleasure; here I stand, your slave,
A poor, infirm, weak, and despis'd old man.
But yet I call you servile ministers,
That have with two pernicious daughters join'd
Your high-engender'd battles 'gainst a head
So old and white as this. O! O! 'tis foul.

    FOOL. He that has a house to put his head in has a good head-
piece.

            The cod-piece that will house
               Before the head has any,
            The head and he shall louse;
               So beggars marry many.
            The man that makes his toe
               What he his heart should make,
            Shall of a corn cry woe,
               And turn his sleep to wake.

For there was never yet fair woman but she made mouths in a glass.

Enter KENT.

LEAR. No, I will be the pattern of all patience;
I will say nothing.

KENT. Who's there?

FOOL. Marry, here's grace and a cod-piece; that's a wise man and a fool.

KENT. Alas; sir, are you here? things that love night
Love not such nights as these; the wrathful skies
Gallow the very wanderers of the dark,
And make them keep their caves. Since I was man
Such sheets of fire, such bursts of horrid thunder,
Such groans of roaring wind and rain, I never
Remember to have heard; man's nature cannot carry
The affliction nor the fear.

LEAR.   Let the great gods,
That keep this dreadful pother o'er our heads,
Find out their enemies now. Tremble, thou wretch,
That hast within thee undivulged crimes,
Unwhipp'd of justice; hide thee, thou bloody hand;
Thou perjur'd, and thou simular of virtue
That art incestuous; caitiff, to pieces shake,
That under covert and convenient seeming
Hast practis'd on man's life; close pent-up guilts,
Rive your concealing continents, and cry
These dreadful summoners grace. I am a man
More sinn'd against than sinning.

KENT.   Alack! bare-headed!
Gracious my lord, hard by here is a hovel;
Some friendship will it lend you 'gainst the tempest;
Repose you there while I to this hard house,—
More harder than the stone whereof 'tis rais'd,—
Which even but now, demanding after you,
Denied me to come in, return and force
Their scanted courtesy.

LEAR.   My wits begin to turn.
Come on, my boy. How dost, my boy? Art cold?
I am cold myself. Where is this straw, my fellow?
The art of our necessities is strange,
That can make vile things precious. Come, your hovel.
Poor fool and knave, I have one part in my heart
That's sorry yet for thee.

FOOL.

> He that has a little tiny wit,
>   With hey, ho, the wind and the rain,
> Must make content with his fortunes fit,
>   Though the rain it raineth every day.

LEAR. True, my good boy. Come, bring us to this hovel.

                              [*Exeunt* LEAR *and* KENT.

FOOL. This is a brave night to cool a courtezan. I'll speak a
prophecy ere I go:

> When priests are more in word than matter;
> When brewers mar their malt with water;
> When nobles are their tailors' tutors;
> No heretics burn'd, but wenches' suitors;
> When every case in law is right;
> No squire in debt, nor no poor knight;
> When slanders do not live in tongues;
> Nor cutpurses come not to throngs;
> When usurers tell their gold i' the field;
> And bawds and whores do churches build;
> Then shall the realm of Albion
> Come to great confusion:
> Then comes the time, who lives to see't,
> That going shall be us'd with feet.

This prophecy Merlin shall make; for I live before his time.

                                             [*Exit.*

Scene III. *A Room in Gloucester's Castle*

Enter GLOUCESTER *and* EDMUND.

GLOUCESTER. Alack, alack! Edmund, I like not this unnatural dealing. When I desired their leave that I might pity him, they took from me the use of mine own house; charged me, on pain of their perpetual displeasure, neither to speak of him, entreat for him, nor any way sustain him.

EDMUND. Most savage, and unnatural!

GLOUCESTER. Go to; say you nothing. There is division between the dukes, and a worse matter than that. I have received a letter this night; 'tis dangerous to be spoken; I have locked the letter in my closet. These injuries the king now bears will be revenged home; there's part of a power already footed; we must incline to the king. I will seek him and privily relieve him; go you and maintain talk with the duke, that my charity be not of him perceived. If he ask for me, I am ill and gone to bed. If I die for it, as no less is threatened me, the king, my old master, must be relieved. There is some strange thing toward, Edmund; pray you, be careful. *[Exit.*

EDMUND. This courtesy, forbid thee, shall the duke
Instantly know; and of that letter too:
This seems a fair deserving, and must draw me
That which my father loses; no less than all:
The younger rises when the old doth fall. *[Exit,*

Scene IV. *The Heath. Before a Hovel*

Enter LEAR, KENT, *and* FOOL.

KENT. Here is the place, my lord; good my lord, enter:
The tyranny of the open night's too rough
For nature to endure. *[Storm still,*

LEAR.   Let me alone.

KENT. Good my lord, enter here.

LEAR.   Wilt break my heart?

KENT. I'd rather break mine own. Good my lord, enter.

LEAR. Thou think'st 'tis much that this contentious storm
Invades us to the skin: so 'tis to thee;
But where the greater malady is fix'd,
The lesser is scarce felt. Thou'dst shun a bear;
But if thy flight lay toward the roaring sea,
Thou'dst meet the bear i' the mouth. When the mind's free
The body's delicate; the tempest in my mind
Doth from my senses take all feeling else
Save what beats there. Filial ingratitude!
Is it not as this mouth should tear this hand
For lifting food to't? But I will punish home:
No, I will weep no more. In such a night
To shut me out! Pour on; I will endure.
In such a night as this! O Regan, Goneril!
Your old kind father, whose frank heart gave all,—
O! that way madness lies; let me shun that;
No more of that.

KENT.   Good my lord, enter here.

LEAR. Prithee, go in thyself; seek thine own ease:
This tempest will not give me leave to ponder
On things would hurt me more. But I'll go in.
[*To the* FOOL.] In, boy; go first. You houseless poverty,—
Nay, get thee in. I'll pray, and then I'll sleep.   [FOOL *goes in.*
Poor naked wretches, wheresoe'er you are,
That bide the pelting of this pitiless storm,
How shall your houseless heads and unfed sides,
Your loop'd and window'd raggedness, defend you
From seasons such as these? O! I have ta'en
Too little care of this. Take physic, pomp;
Expose thyself to feel what wretches feel,
That thou mayst shake the superflux to them,
And show the heavens more just.

EDGAR. [*Within.*] Fathom and half, fathom and half! Poor
Tom!   [*The* FOOL *runs out from the hovel.*

FOOL. Come not in here, nuncle; here's a spirit.
Help me! help me!

KENT. Give me thy hand. Who's there?

FOOL. A spirit, a spirit: he says his name's poor Tom.

KENT. What art thou that dost grumble there i' the straw?
Come forth.

Enter EDGAR *disguised as a madman.*

EDGAR. Away! the foul fiend follows me!
Through the sharp hawthorn blow the winds.
Hum! go to thy cold bed and warm thee.

LEAR. Didst thou give all to thy two daughters?
And art thou come to this?

EDGAR. Who gives anything to poor Tom? whom the foul
fiend hath led through fire and through flame, through ford and
whirlpool, o'er bod and quagmire; that hath laid knives under
his pillow, and halters in his pew; set ratsbane by his porridge;
made him proud of heart, to ride on a bay trotting-horse over
four-inched bridges, to course his own shadow for a traitor. Bless
thy five wits! Tom's a-cold. O! do de, do de, do de. Bless thee
from whirlwinds, star-blasting, and taking! Do poor Tom some
charity, whom the foul fiend vexes. There could I have him now,
and there, and there again, and there.   [*Storm still.*

LEAR. What! have his daughters brought him to this pass?
Couldst thou save nothing? Didst thou give them all?

FOOL. Nay, he reserved a blanket, else we had been all
shamed.

LEAR. Now all the plagues that in the pendulous air
Hang fated o'er men's faults light on thy daughters!

KENT. He hath no daughters, sir.

LEAR. Death, traitor! nothing could have subdu'd nature
To such a lowness, but his unkind daughters.
Is it the fashion that discarded fathers
Should have thus little mercy on their flesh?
Judicious punishment! 'twas this flesh begot
Those pelican daughters.

EDGAR. Pillicock sat on Pillicock-hill:
Halloo, halloo, loo, loo!

FOOL. This cold night will turn us all to fools and madmen.

EDGAR. Take heed o' the foul fiend. Obey thy parents; keep thy word justly; swear not; commit not with man's sworn spouse; set not thy sweet heart on proud array. Tom's a-cold.

LEAR. What hast thou been?

EDGAR. A servingman, proud in heart and mind; that curled my hair, wore gloves in my cap, served the lust of my mistress's heart, and did the act of darkness with her; swore as many oaths as I spake words, and broke them in the sweet face of heaven; one that slept in the contriving of lust, and waked to do it. Wine loved I deeply, dice dearly, and in woman out-paramoured the Turk: false of heart, light of ear, bloody of hand; hog in sloth, fox in stealth, wolf in greediness, dog in madness, lion in prey. Let not the creaking of shoes nor the rustling of silks betray thy poor heart to woman: keep thy foot out of brothels, thy hand out of plackets, thy pen from lenders' books, and defy the foul fiend. Still through the hawthorn blows the cold wind; says suum, mun ha no nonny. Dolphin my boy, my boy; sessa! let him trot by. *[Storm still.*

LEAR. Why, thou wert better in thy grave than to answer with thy uncovered body this extremity of the skies. Is man no more than this? Consider him well. Thou owest the worm no silk, the beasts no hide, the sheep no wool, the cat no perfume. Ha! here's three on's are sophisticated; thou art the thing itself; unaccommodated man is no more but such a poor, bare, forked animal as thou art. Off, off, you lendings! Come; unbutton here.

[Tearing off his clothes.

FOOL. Prithee, nuncle, be contented; 'tis a naughty night to swim in. Now a little fire in a wide field were like an old lecher's heart; a small spark, all the rest on's body cold. Look! here comes a walking fire.

Enter GLOUCESTER *with a torch.*

EDGAR. This is the foul fiend Flibbertigibbet: he begins at curfew, and walks till the first cock; he gives the web and the pin, squints the eye, and makes the harelip; mildews the white wheat, and hurts the poor creature of earth.

Swithold footed thrice the old;
He met the night-mare, and her nine-fold;
Bid her alight,
And her troth plight,
And aroint thee, witch, aroint thee!

KENT. How fares your Grace?

LEAR. What's he?

KENT. Who's there? What is't you seek?

GLOUCESTER. What are you there? Your names?

EDGAR. Poor Tom; that eats the swimming frog; the toad, the tadpole, the wall-newt, and the water; that in the fury of his heart, when the foul fiend rages, eats cow-dung for sallets; swallows the old rat and the ditch-dog; drinks the green mantle of the standing pool; who is whipped from tithing to tithing, and stock-punished, and imprisoned; who hath had three suits to his back, six shirts to his body, horse to ride, and weapon to wear;

But mice and rats and such small deer
Have been Tom's food for seven long year.

Beware my follower. Peace, Smulkin! peace, thou fiend.

GLOUCESTER. What! hath your Grace no better company?

EDGAR. The prince of darkness is a gentleman; Modo he's call'd, and Mahu.

GLOUCESTER. Our flesh and blood, my lord, is grown so vile, That it doth hate what gets it.

EDGAR. Poor Tom's a-cold.

GLOUCESTER. Go in with me. My duty cannot suffer
To obey in all your daughters' hard commands:
Though their injunction be to bar my doors,
And let this tyrannous night take hold upon you,
Yet have I ventur'd to come seek you out
And bring you where both fire and food is ready.

LEAR. First let me talk with this philosopher.
What is the cause of thunder?

KENT. Good my lord, take his offer; go into the house.

LEAR. I'll talk a word with this same learned Theban.

What is your study?

 EDGAR. How to prevent the fiend, and to kill vermin.

 LEAR. Let me ask you one word in private.

 KENT. Importune him once more to go, my lord;
His wits begin to unsettle.

 GLOUCESTER.   Canst thou blame him? [*Storm still.*
His daughters seek his death. Ah! that good Kent;
He said it would be thus, poor banish'd man!
Thou sayst the king grows mad; I'll tell thee, friend,
I am almost mad myself. I had a son,
Now outlaw'd from my blood; he sought my life,
But lately, very late; I lov'd him, friend,
No father his son dearer; true to tell thee, [*Storm continues.*
The grief hath craz'd my wits. What a night's this!
I do beseech your Grace,—

 LEAR.   O! cry you mercy, sir.
Noble philosopher, your company.

 EDGAR. Tom's a-cold.

 GLOUCESTER. In, fellow, there, into the hovel: keep thee warm.

 LEAR. Come, let's in all.

 KENT.   This way, my lord.

 LEAR.   With him;
I will keep still with my philosopher.

 KENT. Good my lord, soothe him; let him take the fellow.

 GLOUCESTER. Take him you on.

 KENT. Sirrah, come on; go along with us.

 LEAR. Come, good Athenian.

 GLOUCESTER.   No words, no words: hush.

 EDGAR. Child Rowland to the dark tower came,
   His word was still, Fie, foh, and fum,
   I smell the blood of a British man. [*Exeunt.*

Scene V. *A Room in Gloucester's Castle*

Enter CORNWALL *and* EDMUND.

CORNWALL. I will have my revenge ere I depart his house.

EDMUND. How, my lord, I may be censured, that nature thus gives way to loyalty, something fears me to think of.

CORNWALL. I now perceive it was not altogether your brother's evil disposition made him seek his death; but a provoking merit, set a-work by a reproveable badness in himself.

EDMUND. How malicious is my fortune, that I must repent to be just! This is the letter he spoke of, which approves him an intelligent party to the advantages of France. O heavens! that this treason were not, or not I the detector!

CORNWALL. Go with me to the duchess.

EDMUND. If the matter of this paper be certain, you have mighty business in hand.

CORNWALL. True, or false, it hath made thee Earl of Gloucester. Seek out where thy father is, that he may be ready for our apprehension.

EDMUND. [*Aside.*] If I find him comforting the king, it will stuff his suspicion more fully. I will persever in my course of loyalty, though the conflict be sore between that and my blood.

CORNWALL. I will lay trust upon thee; and thou shalt find a dearer father in my love.   [*Exeunt.*

Scene VI. *A Chamber in a Farmhouse adjoining the Castle*

Enter GLOUCESTER, LEAR, KENT, FOOL, *and* EDGAR.

GLOUCESTER. Here is better than the open air; take it thankfully. I will piece out the comfort with what addition I can: I will not be long from you.

KENT. All the power of his wits has given way to his impatience. The gods reward your kindness!   [*Exit* GLOUCESTER.

EDGAR. Frateretto calls me, and tells me Nero is an angler in the lake of darkness. Pray, innocent, and beware the foul fiend.

FOOL. Prithee, nuncle, tell me whether a madman be a gentle-man or a yeoman!

LEAR. A king, a king!

FOOL. No; he's a yeoman that has a gentleman to his son; for he's a mad yeoman that sees his son a gentleman before him.

LEAR. To have a thousand with red burning spits
Come hizzing in upon 'em,—

EDGAR. The foul fiend bites my back.

FOOL. He's mad that trusts in the tameness of a wolf, a horse's health, a boy's love, or a whore's oath.

LEAR. It shall be done; I will arraign them straight.
[*To* EDGAR.] Come, sit thou here, most learned justicer;
[*To the* FOOL.] Thou, sapient sir, sit here. Now, you she foxes!

EDGAR. Look, where he stands and glares! wantest thou eyes at trial, madam?

    Come o'er the bourn, Bessy, to me,—

FOOL. Her boat hath a leak,
    And she must not speak
  Why she dares not come over to thee.

EDGAR. The foul fiend haunts poor Tom in the voice of a nightingale. Hopdance cries in Tom's belly for two white her-ring. Croak not, black angel; I have no food for thee.

KENT. How do you, sir? Stand you not so amaz'd:
Will you lie down and rest upon the cushions?

LEAR. I'll see their trial first. Bring in their evidence.
[*To* EDGAR.] Thou robed man of justice, take thy place;
[*To the* FOOL.] And thou, his yoke-fellow of equity,
Bench by his side. [*To* KENT.] You are o' the commission,
Sit you too.

EDGAR. Let us deal justly.

    Sleepest or wakest thou, jolly shepherd?
        Thy sheep be in the corn;
    And for one blast of thy minikin mouth,
        Thy sheep shall take no harm.

Purr! the cat is grey.

LEAR. Arraign her first; 'tis Goneril. I here take my oath before this honourable assembly, she kicked the poor king her
father.

FOOL. Come hither, mistress. Is your name Goneril?

LEAR. She cannot deny it.

FOOL. Cry you mercy, I took you for a joint-stool.

LEAR. And here's another, whose warp'd looks proclaim
What store her heart is made on. Stop her there!
Arms, arms, sword, fire! Corruption in the place!
False justicer, why hast thou let her 'scape?

EDGAR. Bless thy five wits!

KENT. O pity! Sir, where is the patience now
That you so oft have boasted to retain?

EDGAR. [*Aside.*] My tears begin to take his part so much,
They'll mar my counterfeiting.

LEAR. The little dogs and all,
Tray, Blanch, and Sweet-heart, see, they bark at me.

EDGAR. Tom will throw his head at them. Avaunt, you curs!
　Be thy mouth or black or white,
　Tooth that poisons if it bite;
　Mastiff, greyhound, mongrel grim,
　Hound or spaniel, brach or lym;
　Or bobtail tike or trundle-tail;
　Tom will make them weep and wail:
　For, with throwing thus my head,
　Dogs leap the hatch, and all are fled.
Do de, de, de. Sessa! Come, march to wakes and fairs and market-
towns. Poor Tom, thy horn is dry.

LEAR. Then let them anatomize Regan, see what breeds about
her heart. Is there any cause in nature that makes these hard
hearts? [*To* EDGAR.] You, sir, I entertain you for one of my hundred; only I do not like the fashion of your garments: you will
say, they are Persian attire; but let them be changed.

KENT. Now, good my lord, lie here and rest awhile.

LEAR. Make no noise, make no noise; draw the curtains: so, so,
so. We'll go to supper i' the morning: so, so, so.

FOOL. And I'll go to bed at noon.

Re-enter GLOUCESTER.

GLOUCESTER. Come hither, friend: where is the king my master?

KENT. Here, sir; but trouble him not, his wits are gone.

GLOUCESTER. Good friend, I prithee, take him in thy arms;
I have o'erheard a plot of death upon him.
There is a litter ready; lay him in't,
And drive toward Dover, friend, where thou shalt meet
Both welcome and protection. Take up thy master:
If thou shouldst dally half an hour, his life,
With thine, and all that offer to defend him,
Stand in assured loss. Take up, take up;
And follow me, that will to some provision
Give thee quick conduct.

KENT.   Oppress'd nature sleeps:
This rest might yet have balm'd thy broken sinews,
Which, if convenience will not allow,
Stand in hard cure.—[*To the* FOOL.] Come, help to bear thy master;
Thou must not stay behind.

GLOUCESTER.   Come, come, away.

[*Exeunt* KENT, GLOUCESTER, *and the* FOOL,
bearing away LEAR.

EDGAR. When we our betters see bearing our woes,
We scarcely think our miseries our foes.
Who alone suffers suffers most i' the mind,
Leaving free things and happy shows behind;
But then the mind much sufferance doth o'er-skip,
When grief hath mates, and bearing fellowship.
How light and portable my pain seems now,
When that which makes me bend makes the king bow;
He childed as I father'd! Tom, away!
Mark the high noises, and thyself bewray
When false opinion, whose wrong thought defiles thee,
In thy just proof repeals and reconciles thee.

What will hap more to-night, safe 'scape the king!
Lurk, lurk.   [*Exit.*

Scene VII. *A Room in Gloucester's Castle*

Enter CORNWALL, REGAN, GONERIL, EDMUND, *and* SERVANTS

CORNWALL. Post speedily to my lord your husband; show him
this letter: the army of France is landed. Seek out the traitor
Gloucester.   [*Exeunt some of the* SERVANTS.
REGAN. Hang him instantly.
GONERIL. Pluck out his eyes.
CORNWALL. Leave him to my displeasure. Edmund, keep you
our sister company: the revenges we are bound to take upon
your traitorous father are not fit for your beholding. Advise the
duke, where you are going, to a most festinate preparation: we
are bound to the like. Our posts shall be swift and intelligent
betwixt us. Farewell, dear sister: farewell, my Lord of Gloucester.

    Enter OSWALD.

How now? Where's the king?
OSWALD. My Lord of Gloucester hath convey'd him hence:
Some five or six and thirty of his knights,
Hot questrists after him, met him at gate;
Who, with some other of the lord's dependants,
Are gone with him toward Dover, where they boast
To have well-armed friends.
CORNWALL.   Get horses for your mistress.
GONERIL. Farewell, sweet lord, and sister.
CORNWALL. Edmund, farewell.
                  [*Exeunt* GONERIL, EDMUND, *and* OSWALD.
                  Go seek the traitor Gloucester,
Pinion him like a thief, bring him before us.
                    [*Exeunt other* SERVANTS.
Though well we may not pass upon his life
Without the form of justice, yet our power

Shall do a courtesy to our wrath, which men
May blame but not control. Who's there? The traitor?

Re-enter SERVANTS, *with* GLOUCESTER.

REGAN. Ingrateful fox! 'tis he.
CORNWALL. Bind fast his corky arms.
GLOUCESTER. What mean your Graces? Good my friends, con-
sider
You are my guests: do me no foul play, friends.
CORNWALL. Bind him, I say. [SERVANTS *bind him.*
REGAN. Hard, hard. O filthy traitor!
GLOUCESTER. Unmerciful lady as you are, I'm none.
CORNWALL. To this chair bind him. Villain, thou shalt find—
[REGAN *plucks his beard.*
GLOUCESTER. By the kind gods, 'tis most ignobly done
To pluck me by the beard.
REGAN. So white, and such a traitor!
GLOUCESTER. Naughty lady,
These hairs, which thou dost ravish from my chin,
Will quicken, and accuse thee: I am your host:
With robbers' hands my hospitable favours
You should not ruffle thus. What will you do?
CORNWALL. Come, sir, what letters had you late from France?
REGAN. Be simple-answer'd, for we know the truth.
CORNWALL. And what confederacy have you with the traitors
Late footed in the kingdom?
REGAN. To whose hands have you sent the lunatic king?
Speak.
GLOUCESTER. I have a letter guessingly set down,
Which came from one that's of a neutral heart,
And not from one oppos'd.
CORNWALL. Cunning.
REGAN. And false.
CORNWALL. Where hast thou sent the king?
GLOUCESTER. To Dover.
REGAN. Wherefore to Dover? Wast thou not charg'd at peril—
CORNWALL. Wherefore to Dover? Let him answer that.

GLOUCESTER. I am tied to the stake, and I must stand the
  course.

REGAN. Wherefore to Dover?

GLOUCESTER. Because I would not see thy cruel nails
Pluck out his poor old eyes; nor thy fierce sister
In his anointed flesh stick boarish fangs.
The sea, with such a storm as his bare head
In hell-black night endur'd, would have buoy'd up,
And quench'd the stelled fires;
Yet, poor old heart, he holp the heavens to rain.
If wolves had at thy gate howl'd that dern time,
Thou shouldst have said, 'Good porter, turn the key,'
All cruels else subscrib'd: but I shall see
The winged vengeance overtake such children.

CORNWALL. See't shalt thou never. Fellows, hold the chair.
Upon these eyes of thine I'll set my foot.

GLOUCESTER. He that will think to live till he be old,
Give me some help! O cruel! O ye gods!

                     [GLOUCESTER's *eye put out.*

REGAN. One side will mock another; the other too.

CORNWALL. If you see vengeance—

FIRST SERVANT.   Hold your hand, my lord:
I have serv'd you ever since I was a child,
But better service have I never done you
Than now to bid you hold.

REGAN.   How now, you dog!

FIRST SERVANT. If you did wear a beard upon your chin,
I'd shake it on this quarrel. What do you mean?

CORNWALL. My villain!   [*Draws.*

FIRST SERVANT. Nay then, come on, and take the chance of
  anger.   [*Draws. They fight.* CORNWALL *is wounded.*

REGAN. Give me thy sword. A peasant stand up thus!

            [*Takes a sword and runs at him behind.*

FIRST SERVANT. O! I am slain. My lord, you have one eye left
To see some mischief on him. O!   [*Dies.*

CORNWALL. Lest it see more, prevent it. Out, vile jelly!
Where is thy lustre now?

GLOUCESTER. All dark and comfortless. Where's my son Ed-
        mund?
Edmund, enkindle all the sparks of nature
To quit this horrid act.
        REGAN.   Out, treacherous villain!
Thou call'st on him that hates thee; it was he
That made the overture of thy treasons to us,
Who is too good to pity thee.
        GLOUCESTER. O my follies! Then Edgar was abus'd.
Kind gods, forgive me that, and prosper him!
        REGAN. Go thrust him out at gates, and let him smell
His way to Dover. [*Exit one with* GLOUCESTER.]
                                How is't, my lord? How look you?
        CORNWALL. I have receiv'd a hurt. Follow me, lady.
Turn out that eyeless villain; throw this slave
Upon the dunghill. Regan, I bleed apace:
Untimely comes this hurt. Give me your arm.
                                        [*Exit* CORNWALL *led by* REGAN.
        SECOND SERVANT. I'll never care what wickedness I do
If this man come to good.
        THIRD SERVANT.   If she live long,
And, in the end, meet the old course of death,
Women will all turn monsters.
        SECOND SERVANT. Let's follow the old earl, and get the Bedlam
To lead him where he would: his roguish madness
Allows itself to any thing.
        THIRD SERVANT. Go thou; I'll fetch some flax, and whites of
        eggs,
To apply to his bleeding face. Now, heaven help him!
                                                [*Exeunt severally.*

Act 4

Scene I. The Heath

Enter EDGAR.

EDGAR. Yet better thus, and known to be contemn'd,
Than still contemn'd and flatter'd. To be worst,
The lowest and most dejected thing of fortune,
Stands still in esperance, lives not in fear:
The lamentable change is from the best;
The worst returns to laughter. Welcome, then,
Thou unsubstantial air that I embrace:
The wretch that thou hast blown unto the worst
Owes nothing to thy blasts. But who comes here?

ENTER GLOUCESTER, *led by an* OLD MAN.

My father, poorly led? World, world, O world!
But that thy strange mutations make us hate thee,
Life would not yield to age.

OLD MAN.   O my good lord!
I have been your tenant, and your father's tenant,
These fourscore years.

GLOUCESTER. Away, get thee away; good friend, be gone;
Thy comforts can do me no good at all;
Thee they may hurt.

OLD MAN.   You cannot see your way.

GLOUCESTER. I have no way, and therefore want no eyes;
I stumbled when I saw. Full oft 'tis seen,
Our means secure us, and our mere defects
Prove our commodities. Ah! dear son Edgar,

287

The food of thy abused father's wrath;
Might I but live to see thee in my touch,
I'd say I had eyes again.

OLD MAN.   How now! Who's there?

EDGAR. [*Aside.*] O gods! Who is't can say, 'I am at the worst?'
I am worse than e'er I was.

OLD MAN.   'Tis poor mad Tom.

EDGAR. [*Aside.*] And worse I may be yet; the worst is not,
So long as we can say, 'This is the worst.'

OLD MAN. Fellow, where goest?

GLOUCESTER.   Is it a beggar-man?

OLD MAN. Madman and beggar too.

GLOUCESTER. He has some reason, else he could not beg.
I' the last night's storm I such a fellow saw,
Which made me think a man a worm: my son
Came then into my mind; and yet my mind
Was then scarce friends with him: I have heard more since.
As flies to wanton boys, are we to the gods;
They kill us for their sport.

EDGAR.   [*Aside.*] How should this be?
Bad is the trade that must play fool to sorrow,
Angering itself and others.—[*To* GLOUCESTER.] Bless thee, master!

GLOUCESTER. Is that the naked fellow?

OLD MAN.   Ay, my lord.

GLOUCESTER. Then, prithee, get thee gone. If, for my sake,
Thou wilt o'ertake us, hence a mile or twain,
I' the way toward Dover, do it for ancient love;
And bring some covering for this naked soul
Who I'll entreat to lead me.

OLD MAN.   Alack, sir! he is mad.

GLOUCESTER. 'Tis the times' plague, when madmen lead the
 blind.
Do as I bid thee, or rather do thy pleasure;
Above the rest, be gone.

OLD MAN. I'll bring him the best 'parel that I have,
Come on't what will.   [*Exit.*

GLOUCESTER. Sirrah, naked fellow,—

EDGAR. Poor Tom's a-cold. [*Aside.*] I cannot daub it further.

GLOUCESTER. Come hither, fellow.

EDGAR. [*Aside.*] And yet I must. Bless thy sweet eyes, they bleed.

GLOUCESTER. Know'st thou the way to Dover?

EDGAR. Both stile and gate, horse-way and footpath. Poor Tom hath been scared out of his good wits: bless thee, good man's son, from the foul fiend! Five fiends have been in poor Tom at once; of lust, as Obidicut; Hobbididance, prince of dumbness; Mahu, of stealing; Modo, of murder; and Flibbertigibbet, of mopping and mowing; who since possesses chambermaids and waiting-women. So, bless thee, master!

GLOUCESTER. Here, take this purse, thou whom the heavens' plagues
Have humbled to all strokes: that I am wretched
Makes thee the happier: heavens, deal so still!
Let the superfluous and lust-dieted man,
That slaves your ordinance, that will not see
Because he doth not feel, feel your power quickly;
So distribution should undo excess,
And each man have enough. Dost thou know Dover?

EDGAR. Ay, master.

GLOUCESTER. There is a cliff, whose high and bending head
Looks fearfully in the confined deep;
Bring me but to the very brim of it,
And I'll repair the misery thou dost bear
With something rich about me; from that place
I shall no leading need.

EDGAR.   Give me thy arm:
Poor Tom shall lead thee.   [*Exeunt.*

Scene II. *Before the Duke of Albany's Palace*

Enter GONERIL *and* EDMUND.

GONERIL. Welcome, my lord; I marvel our mild husband
Not met us on the way. [*Enter* OSWALD.] Now, where's your
    master?

OSWALD. Madam, within; but never man so chang'd.
I told him of the army that was landed;
He smil'd at it: I told him you were coming;
His answer was, 'The worse:' of Gloucester's treachery,
And of the loyal service of his son,
When I inform'd him, then he call'd me sot,
And told me I had turn'd the wrong side out:
What most he should dislike seems pleasant to him;
What like, offensive.

GONERIL. [*To* EDMUND.] Then, shall you go no further.
It is the cowish terror of his spirit
That dares not undertake; he'll not feel wrongs
Which tie him to an answer. Our wishes on the way
May prove effects. Back, Edmund, to my brother;
Hasten his musters and conduct his powers:
I must change arms at home, and give the distaff
Into my husband's hands. This trusty servant
Shall pass between us; ere long you are like to hear,
If you dare venture in your own behalf,
A mistress's command. Wear this; spare speech;
                          [*Giving a favour.*
Decline your head: this kiss, if it durst speak,
Would stretch thy spirits up into the air.
Conceive, and fare thee well.

EDMUND. Yours in the ranks of death.

GONERIL.   My most dear Gloucester!
                          [*Exit* EDMUND.
O! the difference of man and man!
To thee a woman's services are due:
My fool usurps my bed.

OSWALD. Madam, here comes my lord.   [*Exit.*

Enter ALBANY.

GONERIL. I have been worth the whistle.
ALBANY.   O Goneril!
You are not worth the dust which the rude wind
Blows in your face. I fear your disposition:
That nature, which contemns its origin,
Cannot be border'd certain in itself;
She that herself will sliver and disbranch
From her material sap, perforce must wither
And come to deadly use.
GONERIL. No more; the text is foolish.
ALBANY. Wisdom and goodness to the vile seem vile;
Filths savour but themselves. What have you done?
Tigers, not daughters, what have you perform'd?
A father, and a gracious aged man,
Whose reverence the head-lugg'd bear would lick,
Most barbarous, most degenerate! have you madded.
Could my good brother suffer you to do it?
A man, a prince, by him so benefited!
If that the heavens do not their visible spirits
Send quickly down to tame these vile offences,
It will come,
Humanity must perforce prey on itself,
Like monsters of the deep.
GONERIL.   Milk-liver'd man!
That bear'st a cheek for blows, a head for wrongs;
Who hast not in thy brows an eye discerning
Thine honour from thy suffering; that not know'st
Fools do those villains pity who are punish'd
Ere they have done their mischief. Where's thy drum?
France spreads his banners in our noiseless land,
With plumed helm thy slayer begins threats,
Whilst thou, a moral fool, sitt'st still, and criest
'Alack! why does he so?'
ALBANY.   See thyself, devil!

Proper deformity seems not in the fiend
So horrid as in woman.

GONERIL.　　　　　　O vain fool!

ALBANY. Thou changed and self-cover'd thing, for shame,
Be-monster not thy feature. Were't my fitness
To let these hands obey my blood,
They are apt enough to dislocate and tear
Thy flesh and bones; howe'er thou art a fiend,
A woman's shape doth shield thee.

GONERIL. Marry, your manhood.—Mew!

Enter a MESSENGER.

ALBANY. What news?

MESSENGER. O! my good lord, the Duke of Cornwall's dead;
Slain by his servant, going to put out
The other eye of Gloucester.

ALBANY.　　　　　　Gloucester's eyes!

MESSENGER. A servant that he bred, thrill'd with remorse,
Oppos'd against the act, bending his sword
To his great master; who, thereat enrag'd,
Flew on him, and amongst them fell'd him dead;
But not without that harmful stroke, which since
Hath pluck'd him after.

ALBANY.　　　　　　This shows you are above,
You justicers, that these our nether crimes
So speedily can venge! But, O poor Gloucester!
Lost he his other eye?

MESSENGER.　　　　Both, both, my lord.
This letter, madam, craves a speedy answer;
'Tis from your sister.

GONERIL. [*Aside.*] One way I like this well;
But being widow, and my Gloucester with her,
May all the building in my fancy pluck
Upon my hateful life: another way,
This news is not so tart. [*To* MESSENGER.] I'll read and answer.

　　　　　　　　　　　　　　　　　　　[*Exit.*

ALBANY. Where was his son when they did take his eyes?

MESSENGER. Come with my lady hither.

ALBANY.   He is not here.

MESSENGER. No, my good lord; I met him back again.

ALBANY. Knows he the wickedness?

MESSENGER. Ay, my good lord; 'twas he inform'd against him,
And quit the house on purpose that their punishment
Might have the freer course.

ALBANY.   Gloucester, I live
To thank thee for the love thou show'dst the king,
And to revenge thine eyes. Come hither, friend:
Tell me what more thou knowest.   [*Exeunt.*

Scene III. *The French Camp, near Dover*

Enter KENT *and a* GENTLEMAN.

KENT. Why the King of France is so suddenly gone back know
you the reason?

GENTLEMAN. Something he left imperfect in the state, which
since his coming forth is thought of; which imports to the kingdom so much fear and danger, that his personal return was most
required and necessary.

KENT. Who hath he left behind him general?

GENTLEMAN. The Marshal of France, Monsieur la Far.

KENT. Did your letters pierce the queen to any demonstration
of grief?

GENTLEMAN. Ay, sir; she took them, read them in my pres-
ence;
And now and then an ample tear trill'd down
Her delicate cheek; it seem'd she was a queen
Over her passion; who, most rebel-like,
Sought to be king o'er her.

KENT.   O! then it mov'd her.

GENTLEMAN. Not to a rage; patience and sorrow strove
Who should express her goodliest. You have seen
Sunshine and rain at once; her smiles and tears
Were like a better way; those happy smilets

That play'd on her ripe lip seem'd not to know
What guests were in her eyes: which parted thence,
As pearls from diamonds dropp'd. In brief,
Sorrow would be a rarity most belov'd,
If all could so become it.

    KENT.   Made she no verbal question?

    GENTLEMAN. Faith, once or twice she heav'd the name of
    'father'
Pantingly forth, as if it press'd her heart;
Cried, 'Sisters! sisters! Shame of ladies! sisters!
Kent! father! sisters! What, i' the storm? i' the night?
Let pity not be believed!' There she shook
The holy water from her heavenly eyes,
And clamour-moisten'd, then away she started
To deal with grief alone.

    KENT.   It is the stars,
The stars above us, govern our conditions;
Else one self mate and make could not beget
Such different issues. You spoke not with her since?

    GENTLEMAN. No.

    KENT. Was this before the king return'd?

    GENTLEMAN.   No, since.

    KENT. Well, sir, the poor distress'd Lear's i' the town,
Who sometime, in his better tune, remembers
What we are come about, and by no means
Will yield to see his daughter.

    GENTLEMAN.   Why, good sir?

    KENT. A sovereign shame so elbows him: his own unkindness,
That stripp'd her from his benediction, turn'd her
To foreign casualties, gave her dear rights
To his dog-hearted daughters,—these things sting
His mind so venomously that burning shame
Detains him from Cordelia.

    GENTLEMAN.   Alack! poor gentleman.

    KENT. Of Albany's and Cornwall's powers you heard not?

    GENTLEMAN. 'Tis so, they are afoot.

    KENT. Well, sir, I'll bring you to our master Lear,

And leave you to attend him. Some dear cause
Will in concealment wrap me up awhile;
When I am known aright, you shall not grieve
Lending me this acquaintance. I pray you, go
Along with me.   [*Exeunt.*

Scene IV.   The Same. A Tent

Enter with drum and colours, CORDELIA, DOCTOR, *and* SOL-
DIERS.

CORDELIA. Alack! 'tis he: why, he was met even now
As mad as the vex'd sea; singing aloud;
Crown'd with rank fumiter and furrow weeds,
With burdocks, hemlock, nettles, cuckoo-flowers,
Darnel, and all the idle weeds that grow
In our sustaining corn. A century send forth;
Search every acre in the high-grown field,
And bring him to our eye.   [*Exit an* OFFICER.
                    What can man's wisdom
In the restoring his bereaved sense?
He that helps him take all my outward worth.
   DOCTOR. There is means, madam;
Our foster-nurse of nature is repose,
The which he lacks; that to provoke in him,
Are many simples operative, whose power
Will close the eye of anguish.
   CORDELIA.   All bless'd secrets,
All you unpublish'd virtues of the earth,
Spring with my tears! be aidant and remediate
In the good man's distress! Seek, seek for him,
Lest his ungovern'd rage dissolve the life
That wants the means to lead it.

   Enter a MESSENGER.

MESSENGER.   News, madam;
The British powers are marching hitherward.

CORDELIA. 'Tis known before; our preparation stands
In expectation of them. O dear father!
It is thy business that I go about;
Therefore great France
My mourning and important tears hath pitied,
No blown ambition doth our arms incite,
But love, dear love, and our ag'd father's right,
Soon may I hear and see him!   [*Exeunt.*

Scene V. *A Room in Gloucester's Castle*

Enter REGAN *and* OSWALD.

REGAN. But are my brother's powers set forth?
OSWALD.   Ay, madam.
REGAN. Himself in person there?
OSWALD.   Madam, with much ado:
Your sister is the better soldier.
     REGAN. Lord Edmund spake not with your lord at home?
OSWALD. No, madam.
     REGAN. What might import my sister's letter to him?
OSWALD. I know not, lady.
     REGAN. Faith, he is posted hence on serious matter.
It was great ignorance, Gloucester's eyes being out,
To let him live; where he arrives he moves
All hearts against us. Edmund, I think, is gone,
In pity of his misery, to dispatch
His nighted life; moreover, to descry
The strength o' the enemy.
     OSWALD. I must needs after him, madam, with my letter.
     REGAN. Our troops set forth to-morrow; stay with us,
The ways are dangerous.
     OSWALD.   I may not, madam;
My lady charg'd my duty in this business.
     REGAN. Why should she write to Edmund? Might not you
Transport her purposes by word? Belike,
Something—I know not what. I'll love thee much,

Let me unseal the letter.

OSWALD.   Madam, I had rather—

REGAN. I know your lady does not love her husband;
I am sure of that: and at her late being here
She gave strange œilliades and most speaking looks
To noble Edmund. I know you are of her bosom.

OSWALD. I, madam!

REGAN. I speak in understanding; you are, I know't:
Therefore I do advise you, take this note:
My lord is dead; Edmund and I have talk'd,
And more convenient is he for my hand
Than for your lady's. You may gather more.
If you do find him, pray you, give him this,
And when your mistress hears thus much from you,
I pray desire her call her wisdom to her:
So, fare you well.
If you do chance to hear of that blind traitor,
Preferment falls on him that cuts him off.

OSWALD. Would I could meet him, madam: I would show
What party I do follow.

REGAN.   Fare thee well.   *[Exeunt.*

Scene VI. The Country near Dover

Enter GLOUCESTER, *and* EDGAR *dressed like a peasant.*

GLOUCESTER. When shall I come to the top of that same hill?

EDGAR. You do climb up it now; look how we labour.

GLOUCESTER. Methinks the ground is even.

EDGAR.   Horrible steep:
Hark! do you hear the sea?

GLOUCESTER.   No, truly.

EDGAR. Why, then your other senses grow imperfect
By your eyes' anguish.

GLOUCESTER.   So may it be, indeed.
Methinks thy voice is alter'd, and thou speak'st
In better phrase and matter than thou didst.

EDGAR. Y'are much deceiv'd; in nothing am I chang'd
But in my garments.

GLOUCESTER.   Methinks you're better spoken.

EDGAR. Come on, sir; here's the place: stand still.
How fearful
And dizzy 'tis to cast one's eyes so low!
The crows and choughs that wing the midway air
Show scarce so gross as beetles; half way down
Hangs one that gathers samphire, dreadful trade!
Methinks he seems no bigger than his head.
The fishermen that walk upon the beach
Appear like mice, and yond tall anchoring bark
Diminish'd to her cock, her cock a buoy
Almost too small for sight. The murmuring surge,
That on the unnumber'd idle pebbles chafes,
Cannot be heard so high. I'll look no more,
Lest my brain turn, and the deficient sight
Topple down headlong.

GLOUCESTER.   Set me where you stand.

EDGAR. Give me your hand; you are now within a foot
Of the extreme verge: for all beneath the moon
Would I not leap upright.

GLOUCESTER.   Let go my hand.
Here, friend, 's another purse; in it a jewel
Well worth a poor man's taking: fairies and gods
Prosper it with thee! Go thou further off;
Bid me farewell, and let me hear thee going.

EDGAR. Now fare you well, good sir.

GLOUCESTER.   With all my heart.

EDGAR. Why I do trifle thus with his despair
Is done to cure it.

GLOUCESTER.   O you mighty gods!
This world I do renounce, and, in your sights,
Shake patiently my great affliction off;
If I could bear it longer, and not fall
To quarrel with your great opposeless wills,
My snuff and loathed part of nature should

Edwin Forrest, a famous nineteenth-century American tragedian, as he appeared in the role of Lear. "They told me I was everything; 'tis a lie, I am not ague-proof." Act 4, Scene VI.

Burn itself out. If Edgar live, O, bless him!
Now fellow, fare thee well.   [*He falls forward.*
  EDGAR.   Gone, sir: farewell.
[*Aside.*] And yet I know not how conceit may rob
The treasury of life when life itself
Yields to the theft; had he been where he thought
By this had thought been past. Alive or dead?
[*To* GLOUCESTER.] Ho, you sir! friend! Hear you, sir? speak!
Thus might he pass indeed; yet he revives.
What are you, sir?
  GLOUCESTER.   Away and let me die.
  EDGAR.   Hadst thou been aught but gossamer, feathers, air,
So many fathom down precipitating,
Thou'dst shiver'd like an egg; but thou dost breathe,
Hast heavy substance, bleed'st not, speak'st, art sound.
Ten masts at each make not the altitude
Which thou hast perpendicularly fell:
Thy life's a miracle. Speak yet again.
  GLOUCESTER. But have I fallen or no?
  EDGAR.   From the dread summit of this chalky bourn.
Look up a-height; the shrill-gorg'd lark so far
Cannot be seen or heard: do but look up.
  GLOUCESTER. Alack! I have no eyes.
Is wretchedness depriv'd that benefit
To end itself by death? 'Twas yet some comfort,
When misery could beguile the tyrant's rage,
And frustrate his proud will.
  EDGAR.   Give me your arm:
Up: so. How is't? Feel you your legs? You stand.
  GLOUCESTER. Too well, too well.
  EDGAR.   This is above all strangeness.
Upon the crown o' the cliff, what thing was that
Which parted from you?
  GLOUCESTER.   A poor unfortunate beggar.
  EDGAR. As I stood here below methought his eyes
Were two full moons; he had a thousand noses,
Horns welk'd and wav'd like the enridged sea:

It was some fiend; therefore, thou happy father,
Think that the clearest gods, who make them honours
Of men's impossibilities, have preserv'd thee.

GLOUCESTER. I do remember now; henceforth I'll bear
Affliction till it do cry out itself
'Enough, enough,' and die. That thing you speak of
I took it for a man; often 'twould say
'The fiend, the fiend:' he led me to that place.

EDGAR. Bear free and patient thoughts. But who comes here?

Enter LEAR, *fantastically dressed with flowers.*

The safer sense will ne'er accommodate
His master thus.

LEAR. No, they cannot touch me for coining; I am the king
himself.

EDGAR. O thou side-piercing sight!

LEAR. Nature's above art in that respect. There's your press-
money. That fellow handles his bow like a crow-keeper: draw
me a clothier's yard. Look, look! a mouse. Peace, peace! this
piece of toasted cheese will do't. There's my gauntlet; I'll prove
it on a giant. Bring up the brown bills. O! well flown, bird; i'
the clout, i' the clout: hewgh! Give the word.

EDGAR. Sweet marjoram.

LEAR. Pass.

GLOUCESTER. I know that voice.

LEAR. Ha! Goneril, with a white beard! They flatter'd me like
a dog, and told me I had white hairs in my beard ere the black
ones were there. To say 'ay' and 'no' to everything I said! 'Ay'
and 'no' too was no good divinity. When the rain came to wet me
once and the wind to make me chatter, when the thunder would
not peace at my bidding, there I found 'em, there I smelt 'em
out. Go to, they are not men o' their words: they told me I was
every thing; 'tis a lie, I am not ague-proof.

GLOUCESTER. The trick of that voice I do well remember:
Is't not the king?

LEAR.   Ay, every inch a king:
When I do stare, see how the subject quakes.

I pardon that man's life. What was thy cause?
Adultery?
Thou shalt not die: die for adultery! No:
The wren goes to't, and the small gilded fly
Does lecher in my sight.
Let copulation thrive; for Gloucester's bastard son
Was kinder to his father than my daughters
Got 'tween the lawful sheets.
To't luxury, pell-mell! for I lack soldiers.
Behold yond simpering dame,
Whose face between her forks presageth snow;
That minces virtue, and does shake the head
To hear of pleasure's name;
The fitchew nor the soiled horse goes to't
With a more riotous appetite.
Down from the waist they are Centaurs,
Though women all above:
But to the girdle do the gods inherit,
Beneath is all the fiends':
There's hell, there's darkness, there is the sulphurous pit,
Burning, scalding, stench, consumption; fie, fie, fie! pah! Give
me an ounce of civet, good apothecary, to sweeten my imagina-
tion: there's money for thee.

GLOUCESTER. O! let me kiss that hand!

LEAR. Let me wipe it first; it smells of mortality.

GLOUCESTER. O ruin'd piece of nature! This great world
Shall so wear out to nought. Dost thou know me?

LEAR. I remember thine eyes well enough. Dost thou squiny
at me? No, do thy worst, blind Cupid; I'll not love. Read thou
this challenge; mark but the penning of it.

GLOUCESTER. Were all the letters suns, I could not see.

EDGAR. [*Aside.*] I would not take this from report; it is,
And my heart breaks at it.

LEAR. Read.

GLOUCESTER. What! with the case of eyes?

LEAR. O, ho! are you there with me? No eyes in your head,

nor no money in your purse? Your eyes are in a heavy case, your
purse in a light: yet you see how this world goes.

GLOUCESTER. I see it feelingly.

LEAR. What! art mad? A man may see how this world goes
with no eyes. Look with thine ears: see how yond justice rails
upon yon simple thief. Hark, in thine ear: change places; and,
handy-dandy, which is the justice, which is the thief? Thou hast
seen a farmer's dog bark at a beggar?

GLOUCESTER. Ay, sir.

LEAR. And the creature run from the cur? There thou mightst
behold the great image of authority; a dog's obey'd in office.
Thou rascal beadle, hold thy bloody hand!
Why dost thou lash that whore? Strip thine own back;
Thou hotly lust'st to use her in that kind
For which thou whipp'st her. The usurer hangs the cozener.
Through tatter'd clothes small vices do appear;
Robes and furr'd gowns hide all. Plate sin with gold,
And the strong lance of justice hurtless breaks;
Arm it in rags, a pigmy's straw doth pierce it.
None does offend, none, I say none; I'll able 'em:
Take that of me, my friend, who have the power
To seal the accuser's lips. Get thee glass eyes;
And, like a scurvy politician, seem
To see the things thou dost not. Now, now, now, now;
Pull off my boots; harder, harder; so.

EDGAR. [Aside.] O! matter and impertinency mix'd;
Reason in madness!

LEAR. If thou wilt weep my fortunes, take my eyes;
I know thee well enough; thy name is Gloucester:
Thou must be patient; we came crying hither:
Thou know'st the first time that we smell the air
We waul and cry. I will preach to thee: mark.

GLOUCESTER. Alack! alack the day!

LEAR. When we are born, we cry that we are come
To this great stage of fools. This' a good block!
It were a delicate stratagem to shoe
A troop of horse with felt; I'll put it in proof,

And when I have stol'n upon these sons-in-law,
Then, kill, kill, kill, kill, kill, kill!

    Enter GENTLEMAN, *with* ATTENDANTS.

    GENTLEMAN. O! here he is; lay hand upon him. Sir,
Your most dear daughter—
    LEAR. No rescue? What! a prisoner? I am even
The natural fool of fortune. Use me well;
You shall have ransom. Let me have surgeons;
I am cut to the brains.
    GENTLEMAN.   You shall have any thing.
    LEAR. No seconds? All myself?
Why this would make a man a man of salt,
To use his eyes for garden water-pots,
Ay, and laying autumn's dust.
    GENTLEMAN.   Good sir,—
    LEAR. I will die bravely as a bridegroom. What!
I will be jovial: come, come; I am a king,
My masters, know you that?
    GENTLEMAN. You are a royal one, and we obey you.
    LEAR. Then there's life in it. Nay, an you get it, you shall get
it by running. Sa, sa, sa, sa.   [*Exit.* ATTENDANTS *follow.*
    GENTLEMAN. A sight most pitiful in the meanest wretch,
Past speaking of in a king! Thou hast one daughter,
Who redeems nature from the general curse
Which twain have brought her to.
    EDGAR. Hail, gentle sir!
    GENTLEMAN.   Sir, speed you: what's your will?
    EDGAR. Do you hear aught, sir, of a battle toward?
    GENTLEMAN. Most sure and vulgar; every one hears that,
Which can distinguish sound.
    EDGAR.   But, by your favour,
How near's the other army?
    GENTLEMAN. Near, and on speed foot; the main descry
Stands on the hourly thought.
    EDGAR.   I thank you, sir: that's all.

GENTLEMAN. Though that the queen on special cause is here,
Her army is mov'd on.

EDGAR.   I thank you, sir.   [*Exit* GENTLEMAN.

GLOUCESTER. You ever-gentle gods, take my breath from me:
Let not my worser spirit tempt me again
To die before you please!

EDGAR.   Well pray you, father.

GLOUCESTER. Now, good sir, what are you?

EDGAR. A most poor man, made tame to fortune's blows;
Who, by the art of known and feeling sorrows,
Am pregnant to good pity. Give me your hand
I'll lead you to some biding.

GLOUCESTER.   Hearty thanks:
The bounty and the benison of heaven
To boot, and boot!

        Enter OSWALD.

OSWALD.   A proclaim'd prize! Most happy!
That eyeless head of thine was first fram'd flesh
To raise my fortunes. Thou old unhappy traitor,
Briefly thyself remember: the sword is out
That must destroy thee.

GLOUCESTER.   Now let thy friendly hand
Put strength enough to't.   [EDGAR *interposes.*

OSWALD.   Wherefore, bold peasant,
Dar'st thou support a publish'd traitor? Hence;
Lest that infection of his fortune take
Like hold on thee. Let go his arm.

EDGAR. Chill not let go, zur, without vurther 'casion.

OSWALD. Let go, slave, or thou diest.

EDGAR. Good gentleman, go your gait, and let poor volk pass.
An chud ha' bin zwaggered out of my life, 'twould not ha' bin
zo long as 'tis by a vortnight. Nay, come not near th' old man;
keep out, che vor ye, or ise try whether your costard or my
ballow be the harder. Chill be plain with you.

OSWALD. Out, dunghill!

EDGAR. Chill pick your teeth, zur. Come; no matter vor your
foins.   [*They fight and* EDGAR *knocks him down.*

OSWALD. Slave, thou hast slain me. Villain, take my purse.
If ever thou wilt thrive, bury my body;
And give the letters which thou find'st about me
To Edmund Earl of Gloucester; seek him out
Upon the English party: O! untimely death.   [*Dies.*

EDGAR. I know thee well: a serviceable villain;
As duteous to the vices of thy mistress
As badness would desire.

GLOUCESTER.   What! is he dead?

EDGAR. Sit you down, father; rest you.
Let's see his pockets: these letters that he speaks of
May be my friends. He's dead; I am only sorry
He had no other deaths-man. Let us see:
Leave, gentle wax; and, manners, blame us not:
To know our enemies' minds, we'd rip their hearts;
Their papers, is more lawful.

Let our reciprocal vows be remembered. You have many op-
portunities to cut him off; if your will want not, time and place
will be fruitfully offered. There is nothing done if he return the
conqueror; then am I the prisoner, and his bed my goal; from
the loathed warmth whereof deliver me, and supply the place
for your labour.

> *Your—wife, so I would say—*
> *Affectionate servant,*
>
>   GONERIL.

O undistinguish'd space of woman's will!
A plot upon her virtuous husband's life,
And the exchange my brother! Here, in the sands,
Thee I'll rake up, the post unsanctified
Of murderous lechers; and in the mature time
With this ungracious paper strike the sight
Of the death-practis'd duke. For him 'tis well
That of thy death and business I can tell.

GLOUCESTER. The king is mad: how stiff is my vile sense,

That I stand up, and have ingenious feeling
Of my huge sorrows! Better I were distract:
So should my thoughts be sever'd from my griefs,
And woes by wrong imaginations lose
The knowledge of themselves.   *[Drums afar off.*

EDGAR.   Give me your hand:
Far off, methinks, I hear the beaten drum.
Come, father, I'll bestow you with a friend.   *[Exeunt.*

Scene VII. *A Tent in the French Camp*

Enter CORDELIA, KENT, DOCTOR, *and* GENTLEMAN.

CORDELIA. O thou good Kent! how shall I live and work
To match thy goodness? My life will be too short,
And every measure fail me.

KENT. To be acknowledg'd, madam, is o'erpaid.
All my reports go with the modest truth,
Nor more nor clipp'd, but so.

CORDELIA.   Be better suited:
These weeds are memories of those worser hours:
I prithee, put them off.

KENT.   Pardon me, dear madam;
Yet to be known shortens my made intent:
My boon I make it that you know me not
Till time and I think meet.

CORDELIA. Then be't so, my good lord.—[*To the* DOCTOR.]
   How does the king?

DOCTOR. Madam, sleeps still.

CORDELIA. O you kind gods,
Cure this great breach in his abused nature!
The untun'd and jarring senses, O! wind up
Of this child-changed father!

DOCTOR.   So please your majesty
That we may wake the king? he hath slept long.

CORDELIA. Be govern'd by your knowledge, and proceed
I' the sway of your own will. Is he array'd?

Enter LEAR *in his chair, carried by* SERVANTS.

GENTLEMAN. Ay, madam; in the heaviness of sleep,
We put fresh garments on him.
    DOCTOR. Be by, good madam, when we do awake him;
I doubt not of his temperance.
    CORDELIA.   Very well.   [*Music.*
    DOCTOR. Please you, draw near. Louder the music there.
    CORDELIA. O my dear father! Restoration, hang
Thy medicine on my lips, and let this kiss
Repair those violent harms that my two sisters
Have in thy reverence made!
    KENT.   Kind and dear princess!
    CORDELIA. Had you not been their father, these white flakes
Had challeng'd pity of them. Was this a face
To be expos'd against the warring winds?
To stand against the deep dread-bolted thunder?
In the most terrible and nimble stroke
Of quick cross lightning? to watch—poor perdu!—
With this thin helm? Mine enemy's dog,
Though he had bit me, should have stood that night
Against my fire. And wast thou fain, poor father,
To hovel thee with swine and rogues forlorn,
In short and musty straw? Alack, alack!
'Tis wonder that thy life and wits at once
Had not concluded all. He wakes; speak to him.
    DOCTOR. Madam, do you; 'tis fittest.
    CORDELIA. How does my royal lord? How fares your majesty?
    LEAR. You do me wrong to take me out o' the grave;
Thou art a soul in bliss; but I am bound
Upon a wheel of fire, that mine own tears
Do scald like molten lead.
    CORDELIA.   Sir, do you know me?
    LEAR. You are a spirit, I know; when did you die?
    CORDELIA. Still, still, far wide.
    DOCTOR. He's scarce awake; let him alone awhile.
    LEAR. Where have I been? Where am I? Fair day-light?

I am mightily abus'd. I should even die with pity
To see another thus. I know not what to say.
I will not swear these are my hands: let's see;
I feel this pin prick. Would I were assur'd
Of my condition!

    CORDELIA.   O! look upon me, sir,
And hold your hands in benediction o'er me.
No, sir, you must not kneel.

    LEAR.   Pray, do not mock me:
I am a very foolish fond old man,
Fourscore and upward, not an hour more or less;
And, to deal plainly,
I fear I am not in my perfect mind.
Methinks I should know you and know this man;
Yet I am doubtful: for I am mainly ignorant
What place this is, and all the skill I have
Remembers not these garments; nor I know not
Where I did lodge last night. Do not laugh at me;
For, as I am a man, I think this lady
To be my child Cordelia.

    CORDELIA.   And so I am, I am.

    LEAR. Be your tears wet? Yes, faith. I pray, weep not:
If you have poison for me, I will drink it.
I know you do not love me; for your sisters
Have, as I do remember, done me wrong:
You have some cause, they have not.

    CORDELIA.   No cause, no cause.

    LEAR. Am I in France?

    KENT.   In your own kingdom, sir.

    LEAR. Do not abuse me.

    DOCTOR. Be comforted, good madam; the great rage,
You see, is kill'd in him; and yet it is danger
To make him even o'er the time he has lost.
Desire him to go in; trouble him no more
Till further settling.

    CORDELIA. Will't please your highness walk?

LEAR.   You must bear with me.
Pray you now, forget and forgive: I am old and foolish.

        [Exeunt LEAR, CORDELIA, DOCTOR, *and* ATTENDANTS.

GENTLEMAN. Holds it true, sir, that the Duke of Cornwall was
so slain?

KENT. Most certain, sir.

GENTLEMAN. Who is conductor of his people?

KENT. As 'tis said, the bastard son of Gloucester.

GENTLEMAN. They say Edgar, his banished son, is with the
Earl of Kent in Germany.

KENT. Report is changeable. 'Tis time to look about; the
powers of the kingdom approach apace.

GENTLEMAN. The arbitrement is like to be bloody. Fare you
well, sir.   *[Exit.*

KENT. My point and period will be throughly wrought,
Or well or ill, as this day's battle's fought.   *[Exit.*

Act 5

Scene I. *The British Camp near Dover*

Enter, with drum and colours, EDMUND, REGAN, OFFICERS,
SOLDIERS, *and Others.*

EDMUND. Know of the duke if his last purpose hold,
Or whether since he is advis'd by aught
To change the course; he's full of alteration
And self-reproving; bring his constant pleasure.

                         [To an OFFICER, *who goes out.*

REGAN. Our sister's man is certainly miscarried.

EDMUND. 'Tis to be doubted, madam.

REGAN.   Now, sweet lord,
You know the goodness I intend upon you:
Tell me, but truly, but then speak the truth,
Do you not love my sister?

EDMUND.   In honour'd love.

REGAN. But have you never found my brother's way
To the forefended place?

EDMUND.   That thought abuses you.

REGAN. I am doubtful that you have been conjunct
And bosom'd with her, as far as we call hers.

EDMUND. No, by mine honour, madam.

REGAN. I never shall endure her: dear my lord,
Be not familiar with her.

EDMUND.   Fear me not.
She and the duke her husband!

Enter with drums and colours, ALBANY, GONERIL, *and* SOL-
DIERS.

GONERIL. [*Aside.*] I had rather lose the battle than that sister
Should loosen him and me.

ALBANY. Our very loving sister, well be-met.
Sir, this I heard, the king is come to his daughter,
With others; whom the rigour of our state
Forc'd to cry out. Where I could not be honest
I never yet was valiant: for this business,
It toucheth us, as France invades our land,
Not bolds the king, with others, whom, I fear,
Most just and heavy causes make oppose.

EDMUND. Sir, you speak nobly.

REGAN.   Why is this reason'd?

GONERIL. Combine together 'gainst the enemy;
For these domestic and particular broils
Are not the question here.

ALBANY.   Let's then determine
With the ancient of war on our proceeding.

EDMUND. I shall attend you presently at your tent.

REGAN. Sister, you'll go with us?

GONERIL. No.

REGAN. 'Tis most convenient; pray you, go with us.

GONERIL. [*Aside.*] O, ho! I know the riddle. [*Aloud.*] I will go.

Enter EDGAR, *disguised.*

EDGAR. If e'er your Grace had speech with man so poor,
Hear me one word.

ALBANY.   I'll overtake you. Speak.

[*Exeunt* EDMUND, REGAN, GONERIL, OFFICERS, SOLDIERS,
and ATTENDANTS.

EDGAR. Before you fight the battle, ope this letter.
If you have victory, let the trumpet sound
For him that brought it: wretched though I seem,
I can produce a champion that will prove
What is avouched there. If you miscarry,
Your business of the world hath so an end,
And machination ceases. Fortune love you!

ALBANY. Stay till I have read the letter.

EDGAR.   I was forbid it.
When time shall serve, let but the herald cry,
And I'll appear again.

    ALBANY. Why, fare thee well: I will o'erlook thy paper.
                                             [*Exit* EDGAR.

    Re-enter EDMUND.

    EDMUND. The enemy's in view; draw up your powers.
Here is the guess of their true strength and forces
By diligent discovery; but your haste
Is now urg'd on you.

    ALBANY.   We will greet the time.   [*Exit.*
    EDMUND. To both these sisters have I sworn my love;
Each jealous of the other, as the stung
Are of the adder. Which of them shall I take?
Both? one? or neither? Neither can be enjoy'd
If both remain alive: to take the widow
Exasperates, makes mad her sister Goneril;
And hardly shall I carry out my side,
Her husband being alive. Now then, we'll use
His countenance for the battle; which being done
Let her who would be rid of him devise
His speedy taking off. As for the mercy
Which he intends to Lear, and to Cordelia,
The battle done, and they within our power,
Shall never see his pardon; for my state
Stands on me to defend, not to debate.   [*Exit.*

Scene II. *A Field between the two Camps*

    Alarum within. Enter, with drum and colours, LEAR, COR-
DELIA, *and their Forces; and exeunt. Enter* EDGAR *and*
GLOUCESTER.

    EDGAR. Here, father, take the shadow of this tree
For your good host; pray that the right may thrive.
If ever I return to you again,
I'll bring you comfort.

GLOUCESTER.   Grace go with you, sir!   [*Exit* EDGAR.

Alarum; afterwards a retreat. Re-enter EDGAR.

EDGAR. Away, old man! give me thy hand: away!
King Lear hath lost, he and his daughter ta'en.
Give me thy hand; come on.

   GLOUCESTER. No further, sir; a man may rot even here.

   EDGAR. What! in ill thoughts again? Men must endure
Their going hence, even as their coming hither:
Ripeness is all. Come on.

   GLOUCESTER.   And that's true too.   [*Exeunt.*

Scene III.   *The British Camp, near Dover*

Enter, in conquest, with drum and colours, EDMUND; LEAR
and CORDELIA, *prisoners;* OFFICERS, SOLDIERS, &c.

EDMUND. Some officers take them away: good guard,
Until their greater pleasures first be known
That are to censure them.

   CORDELIA.   We are not the first
Who, with best meaning, have incurr'd the worst.
For thee, oppressed king, am I cast down;
Myself could else out-frown false Fortune's frown.
Shall we not see these daughters and these sisters?

   LEAR. No, no, no, no! Come, let's away to prison;
We two alone will sing like birds i' the cage:
When thou dost ask me blessing, I'll kneel down,
And ask of thee forgiveness: so we'll live,
And pray, and sing, and tell old tales, and laugh
At gilded butterflies, and hear poor rogues
Talk of court news; and we'll talk with them too,
Who loses and who wins; who's in, who's out;
And take upon's the mystery of things,
As if we were God's spies: and we'll wear out,
In a wall'd prison, packs and sets of great ones
That ebb and flow by the moon.

   EDMUND.   Take them away.

LEAR. Upon such sacrifices, my Cordelia,
The gods themselves throw incense. Have I caught thee?
He that parts us shall bring a brand from heaven,
And fire us hence like foxes. Wipe thine eyes;
The goujeres shall devour them, flesh and fell,
Ere they shall make us weep: we'll see 'em starve first.
Come.   [*Exeunt* LEAR *and* CORDELIA, *guarded.*
EDMUND. Come hither, captain; hark,
Take thou this note; [*Giving a paper.*] go follow them to prison:
One step I have advance'd thee; if thou dost
As this instructs thee, thou dost make thy way
To noble fortunes; know thou this, that men
Are as the time is; to be tender-minded
Does not become a sword; thy great employment
Will not bear question; either say thou'lt do't,
Or thrive by other means.
OFFICER.   I'll do't, my lord.
EDMUND. About it; and write happy when thou hast done.
Mark,—I say, instantly, and carry it so
As I have set it down.
OFFICER. I cannot draw a cart nor eat dried oats;
If it be man's work I will do it.   [*Exit.*

Flourish. Enter ALBANY, GONERIL, REGAN, OFFICERS, *and* AT-
TENDANTS.

ALBANY. Sir, you have show'd to-day your valiant strain,
And fortune led you well; you have the captives
Who were the opposites of this day's strife;
We do require them of you, so to use them
As we shall find their merits and our safety
May equally determine.
EDMUND.   Sir, I thought it fit
To send the old and miserable king
To some retention, and appointed guard;
Whose age has charms in it, whose title more,
To pluck the common bosom on his side,
And turn our impress'd lances in our eyes

Which do command them. With him I sent the queen;
My reason all the same; and they are ready
To-morrow, or at further space, to appear
Where you shall hold your session. At this time
We sweat and bleed; the friend hath lost his friend,
And the best quarrels, in the heat, are curs'd
By those that feel their sharpness;
The question of Cordelia and her father
Requires a fitter place.

ALBANY.   Sir, by your patience,
I hold you but a subject of this war,
Not as a brother.

REGAN.   That's as we list to grace him:
Methinks our pleasure might have been demanded,
Ere you had spoke so far. He led our powers,
Bore the commission of my place and person;
The which immediacy may well stand up,
And call itself your brother.

GONERIL.   Not so hot;
In his own grace he doth exalt himself
More than in your addition.

REGAN.   In my rights,
By me invested, he compeers the best.

GONERIL. That were the most, if he should husband you.

REGAN. Jesters do oft prove prophets.

GONERIL.   Holla, holla!
That eye that told you so look'd but a-squint.

REGAN. Lady, I am not well; else I should answer
From a full-flowing stomach. General,
Take thou my soldiers, prisoners, patrimony;
Dispose of them, of me; the walls are thine;
Witness the world, that I create thee here
My lord and master.

GONERIL.   Mean you to enjoy him?

ALBANY. The let-alone lies not in your good will.

EDMUND. Nor in thine, lord.

ALBANY.   Half-blooded fellow, yes.

REGAN. [*To* EDMUND.] Let the drum strike, and prove my title
    thine.

ALBANY. Stay yet; hear reason. Edmund, I arrest thee
On capital treason; and, in thy arrest,
This gilded serpent. [*Pointing to* GONERIL.] For your claim, fair
    sister,
I bar it in the interest of my wife;
'Tis she is sub-contracted to this lord,
And I, her husband, contradict your bans.
If you will marry, make your love to me,
My lady is bespoke.

GONERIL.   An interlude!

ALBANY. Thou art arm'd, Gloucester; let the trumpet sound:
If none appear to prove upon thy person
Thy heinous, manifest, and many treasons,
There is my pledge; [*Throws down a glove.*] I'll prove it on thy
    heart,
Ere I taste bread, thou art in nothing less
Than I have here proclaim'd thee.

REGAN.   Sick! O sick!

GONERIL. [*Aside.*] If not, I'll ne'er trust medicine.

EDMUND. There's my exchange: [*Throws down a glove.*] what
    in the world he is
That names me traitor, villain-like he lies.
Call by thy trumpet: he that dares approach,
On him, on you, who not? I will maintain
My truth and honour firmly.

ALBANY. A herald, ho!

EDMUND.   A herald, ho! a herald!

ALBANY. Trust to thy single virtue; for thy soldiers,
All levied in my name, have in my name
Took their discharge.

REGAN.   My sickness grows upon me.

ALBANY. She is not well; convey her to my tent.

                        [*Exit* REGAN, *led.*

Come hither, herald,

Enter a HERALD.

                    Let the trumpet sound,—
And read out this.

    OFFICER. Sound, trumpet!   [*A trumpet sounds.*

    HERALD. *If any man of quality or degree within the lists of the army will maintain upon Edmund, supposed Earl of Gloucester, that he is a manifold traitor, let him appear at the third sound of the trumpet. He is bold in his defence.*

    EDMUND. Sound!   [*First Trumpet.*

    HERALD. Again!   [*Second Trumpet.*

    HERALD. Again!   [*Third Trumpet.*

                         [*Trumpet answers within.*

Enter EDGAR, *armed, with a Trumpet before him.*

    ALBANY. Ask him his purpose, why he appears
Upon this call o' the trumpet.

    HERALD.   What are you?
Your name? your quality? and why you answer
This present summons?

    EDGAR.   Know, my name is lost;
By treason's tooth bare-gnawn and canker-bit:
Yet am I noble as the adversary
I come to cope.

    ALBANY.   Which is that adversary?

    EDGAR. What's he that speaks for Edmund Earl of Gloucester?

    EDMUND. Himself: what sayst thou to him?

    EDGAR.   Draw thy sword,
That, if my speech offend a noble heart,
Thy arm may do thee justice; here is mine:
Behold, it is the privilege of mine honours,
My oath, and my profession: I protest,
Maugre thy strength, youth, place, and eminence,
Despite thy victor sword and fire-new fortune,
Thy valour and thy heart, thou art a traitor,
False to thy gods, thy brother, and thy father,

Conspirant 'gainst this high illustrious prince,
And, from the extremest upward of thy head
To the descent and dust below thy foot,
A most toad-spotted traitor. Say thou 'No,'
This sword, this arm, and my best spirits are bent
To prove upon thy heart, whereto I speak,
Thou liest.

EDMUND. In wisdom I should ask thy name;
But since thy outside looks so fair and war-like,
And that thy tongue some say of breeding breathes,
What safe and nicely I might well delay
By rule of knighthood, I disdain and spurn;
Back do I toss these treasons to thy head,
With the hell-hated lie o'erwhelm thy heart,
Which, for they yet glance by and scarcely bruise,
This sword of mine shall give them instant way,
Where they shall rest for ever. Trumpets, speak!

[*Alarums. They fight.* EDMUND *falls.*

ALBANY. Save him, save him!

GONERIL.   This is practice, Gloucester:
By the law of arms thou wast not bound to answer
An unknown opposite; thou art not vanquish'd,
But cozen'd and beguil'd.

ALBANY.   Shut your mouth, dame,
Or with this paper shall I stop it. Hold, sir;
Thou worse than any name, read thine own evil:
No tearing, lady; I perceive you know it.

[*Gives the letter to* EDMUND.

GONERIL. Say, if I do, the laws are mine, not thine:
Who can arraign me for't?   [*Exit.*

ALBANY.   Most monstrous!
Know'st thou this paper?

EDMUND.   Ask me not what I know.

ALBANY. Go after her: she's desperate; govern her.

[*Exit an* OFFICER.

EDMUND. What you have charg'd me with, that have I done,
And more, much more; the time will bring it out:

'Tis past, and so am I. But what art thou
That hast this fortune on me? If thou'rt noble,
I do forgive thee.

  EDGAR.   Let's exchange charity.
I am no less in blood than thou art, Edmund;
If more, the more thou hast wrong'd me.
My name is Edgar, and thy father's son.
The gods are just, and of our pleasant vices
Make instruments to plague us:
The dark and vicious place where thee he got
Cost him his eyes.

  EDMUND.   Thou hast spoken right, 'tis true;
The wheel is come full circle; I am here.

  ALBANY. Methought thy very gait did prophesy
A royal nobleness: I must embrace thee:
Let sorrow split my heart, if ever I
Did hate thee or thy father.

  EDGAR.   Worthy prince, I know't.

  ALBANY. Where have you hid yourself?
How have you known the miseries of your father?

  EDGAR. By nursing them, my lord. List a brief tale;
And, when 'tis told, O! that my heart would burst,
The bloody proclamation to escape
That follow'd me so near,—O! our lives' sweetness,
That we the pain of death would hourly die
Rather than die at once!—taught me to shift
Into a madman's rags, to assume a semblance
That very dogs disdain'd: and in this habit
Met I my father with his bleeding rings,
Their precious stones new lost; became his guide,
Led him, begg'd for him, sav'd him from despair;
Never,—O fault!—reveal'd myself unto him,
Until some half hour past, when I was arm'd;
Not sure, though hoping, of this good success,
I ask'd his blessing, and from first to last
Told him my pilgrimage: but his flaw'd heart,—
Alack! too weak the conflict to support;

'Twixt two extremes of passion, joy and grief,
Burst smilingly.

    EDMUND. This speech of yours hath mov'd me,
And shall perchance do good; but speak you on;
You look as you had something more to say.

    ALBANY. If there be more, more woeful, hold it in;
For I am almost ready to dissolve,
Hearing of this.

    EDGAR.   This would have seem'd a period
To such as love not sorrow; but another,
To amplify too much, would make much more,
And top extremity.
Whilst I was big in clamour came there a man,
Who, having seen me in my worst estate,
Shunn'd my abhorr'd society; but then, finding
Who 'twas that so endur'd, with his strong arms
He fasten'd on my neck, and bellow'd out
As he'd burst heaven; threw him on my father;
Told the most piteous tale of Lear and him
That ever ear receiv'd; which in recounting
His grief grew puissant, and the strings of life
Began to crack: twice then the trumpet sounded,
And there I left him tranc'd.

    ALBANY.   But who was this?

    EDGAR. Kent, sir, the banish'd Kent; who in disguise
Follow'd his enemy king, and did him service
Improper for a slave.

    Enter a GENTLEMAN, *with a bloody knife.*

    GENTLEMAN. Help, help! O help!

    EDGAR.   What kind of help?

    ALBANY.   Speak, man.

    EDGAR. What means that bloody knife?

    GENTLEMAN.   'Tis hot, it smokes;
It came even from the heart of—O! she's dead.

    ALBANY. Who dead? speak, man.

    GENTLEMAN. Your lady, sir, your lady: and her sister

By her is poison'd; she confesses it.

EDMUND. I was contracted to them both: all three
Now marry in an instant.

EDGAR.   Here comes Kent.

ALBANY. Produce the bodies, be they alive or dead:
This judgment of the heavens, that makes us tremble,
Touches us not with pity.   [*Exit* GENTLEMAN.

    Enter KENT.

                    O! is this he?
The time will not allow the compliment
Which very manners urges.

KENT.   I am come
To bid my king and master aye good-night;
Is he not here?

ALBANY.   Great thing of us forgot!
Speak, Edmund, where's the king? and where's Cordelia?
Seest thou this object, Kent?

        [*The bodies of* GONERIL *and* REGAN *are brought in.*

KENT. Alack! why thus?

EDMUND.   Yet Edmund was belov'd:
The one the other poison'd for my sake,
And after slew herself.

ALBANY. Even so. Cover their faces.

EDMUND. I pant for life: some good I mean to do
Despite of mine own nature. Quickly send,
Be brief in it, to the castle; for my writ
Is on the life of Lear and on Cordelia.
Nay, send in time.

ALBANY.   Run, run! O run!

EDGAR. To whom, my lord? Who has the office? send
Thy token of reprieve.

EDMUND. Well thought on: take my sword,
Give it the captain.

ALBANY.   Haste thee, for thy life.   [*Exit* EDGAR.

EDMUND. He hath commission from thy wife and me
To hang Cordelia in the prison, and

To lay the blame upon her own despair,
That she forbid herself.

ALBANY. The gods defend her! Bear him hence awhile.

[EDMUND *is borne off.*

Enter LEAR, *with* CORDELIA *dead in his arms:* EDGAR, OFFICER, *and Others.*

LEAR. Howl, howl, howl, howl! O! you are men of stones:
Had I your tongues and eyes, I'd use them so
That heaven's vaults should crack. She's gone for ever.
I know when one is dead, and when one lives;
She's dead as earth. Lend me a looking-glass;
If that her breath will mist or stain the stone,
Why, then she lives.

KENT.   Is this the promis'd end?

EDGAR. Or image of that horror?

ALBANY.   Fall and cease?

LEAR. This feather stirs; she lives! if it be so,
It is a chance which does redeem all sorrows
That ever I have felt.

KENT. [*Kneeling.*] O, my good master!

LEAR. Prithee, away.

EDGAR.   'Tis noble Kent, your friend.

LEAR. A plague upon you, murderers, traitors all!
I might have sav'd her; now, she's gone for ever!
Cordelia, Cordelia; stay a little. Ha!
What is't thou sayst? Her voice was ever soft,
Gentle and low, an excellent thing in woman.
I kill'd the slave that was a hanging thee.

OFFICER. 'Tis true, my lord, he did.

LEAR.   Did I not, fellow?
I have seen the day, with my good biting falchion
I would have made them skip: I am old now,
And these same crosses spoil me. Who are you?
Mine eyes are not o' the best: I'll tell you straight.

KENT. If fortune brag of two she lov'd and hated,
One of them we behold.

LEAR. This is a dull sight. Are you not Kent?
KENT.   The same,
Your servant Kent. Where is your servant Caius?
LEAR. He's a good fellow, I can tell you that;
He'll strike, and quickly too. He's dead and rotten.
KENT. No, my good lord; I am the very man—
LEAR. I'll see that straight.
KENT. That, from your first of difference and decay,
Have follow'd your sad steps.
LEAR.   You are welcome hither.
KENT. Nor no man else; all 's cheerless, dark, and deadly:
Your eldest daughters have fordone themselves,
And desperately are dead.
LEAR.   Ay, so I think.
ALBANY. He knows not what he says, and vain it is
That we present us to him.
EDGAR.   Very bootless.

Enter an OFFICER.

OFFICER. Edmund is dead, my lord.
ALBANY.   That's but a trifle here.
You lords and noble friends, know our intent;
What comfort to this great decay may come
Shall be applied: for us, we will resign,
During the life of this old majesty,
To him our absolute power:—[*To* EDGAR *and* KENT.] You, to
    your rights;
With boot and such addition as your honours
Have more than merited. All friends shall taste
The wages of their virtue, and all foes
The cup of their deservings. O! see, see!
LEAR. And my poor fool is hang'd! No, no, no life!
Why should a dog, a horse, a rat, have life,
And thou no breath at all? Thou'lt come no more,
Never, never, never, never, never!
Pray you, undo this button: thank you, sir.
Do you see this? Look on her, look, her lips,

Look there, look there!   *[Dies.*

EDGAR.   He faints!—my lord, my lord!

KENT.   Break, heart; I prithee, break.

EDGAR.   Look up, my lord.

KENT.   Vex not his ghost: O! let him pass; he hates him
That would upon the rack of this tough world
Stretch him out longer.

EDGAR.   He is gone, indeed.

KENT.   The wonder is he hath endur'd so long:
He but usurp'd his life.

ALBANY.   Bear them from hence. Our present business
Is general woe. [*To* KENT *and* EDGAR.] Friends of my soul, you
     twain
Rule in this realm, and the gor'd state sustain.

KENT.   I have a journey, sir, shortly to go;
My master calls me, I must not say no.

ALBANY.   The weight of this sad time we must obey;
Speak what we feel, not what we ought to say.
The oldest hath borne most: we that are young,
Shall never see so much, nor live so long.

                         [Exeunt, with a dead march.

A GLOSSARY OF WORDS AND PHRASES

The following abbreviations are used in the Glossary: R & J for *Romeo and Juliet;* O for *Othello;* KL for *King Lear.* References are listed by play, act, and scene; e.g. R & J 1, III for *Romeo and Juliet,* Act 1, Scene III.

A HALL, clear the hall R & J 1, V
ABUS'D, naughty KL 1, III
ACHIEVED, won O 2, I
ACKNOWN ON'T, knowledgeable about O 3, III
ADDITION, honor or title O 3, IV; KL 2, II
ADMIRATION, pretense of astonishment KL 1, IV
AFFECTED, had affection for KL 1, I
AFFIN'D, tied by affection O 1, I
AFFINITY, kindred O 3, I
AFTER FLEET, following fleet O 1, III
AJAX, a Greek braggart KL 2, II
ALBION, England KL 3, II
ALLA STOCCATA, a thrust R & J 3, I
ALMAIN, German O 2, III
AMERCE, punish R & J 3, I
ANCIENT, ensign or third officer O 1, I
ANTHROPOPHAGI, cannibals O 1, III
ANTRES, caves O 1, III
APOLOGY, formal introduction for a group of maskers, usually read by someone sent ahead. The practice was already out of date. R & J 1, IV
APPROV'D ALLOWANCE, proved skill O 2, I
ARCH, chief support KL 2, I
ASPIC, asp O 3, III
AT POINT, fully armed KL 1, IV
ATOMIES, tiny creatures R & J 1, IV
ATTASK'D, blamed KL 1, IV

AURICULAR ASSURANCE, proof heard with your own ears KL
1, II

BALLOW, cudgel KL 4, VI
BANS, curses KL 2, III
BARBARY, Moorish O 1, I
BATING, fluttering R & J 3, II
BEAR BAGS, have money KL 2, IV
BECOMED, suitable R & J 4, II
BEHOVEFUL, fit R & J 4, III
BELLS, i.e. ever changing O 2, I
BENISON, blessing KL 1, I
BESHREW, blame R & J 5, II
BESHREW, confound R & J 2, V
BESHREW ME, plague on me O 3, IV
BESORT, attendants O 1, III
BESORT, be suitable for KL 1, IV
BEWRAY, reveal KL 2, I
BILLS, long-handled weapons with small blades R & J 1, I
BLANK, aim KL 1, I
BLAZE, proclaim R & J 3, III
BLIND BOW-BOY, Cupid R & J 2, IV
BLOCK, hat KL 4, VI
BOBBED, cheated O 5, I
BOLSTER, sleep together O 3, III
BOMBAST CIRCUMSTANCE, bombastic words O 1, I
BOOTLESS, vain O 1, III
BOSOM'S LORD, heart R & J 5, I
BRAZED, become brazen KL 1, I
BROKEN MEATS, remains of food sent down from the high table
KL 2, II
BURNING BEAR, the Great Bear constellation O 2, I
BUTCHER OF A SILK BUTTON, an expert fencer who follows
the rules of touching his opponent's button R & J 2, IV
BUTT, aim O 5, II
BUTT-SHAFT, arrow R & J 2, IV

CADENT, falling KL 1, IV
CAITIFF, miserable R & J 5, I
CAITIFF, wretch O 4, I

CALLET, moll O 4, II

CANDLE-HOLDER, onlooker R & J 1, IV

CAPABLE, legitimate KL 2, I

CARRACK, largest Spanish merchant ship O 1, II

CARRY NO CROTCHETS, endure no whims R & J 4, V

CARRY'T, bring off the marriage O 1, I

CASE, mask R & J 1, IV

CAST, dismiss O 1, I

CATLING, catgut fiddle string R & J 4, V

CERTES, assuredly O 1, I

CHAMBERERS, playboys O 3, III

CHAMPAIGNS, fertile fields KL 1, I

CHAPLESS, without jaws R & J 4, I

CHARACTER, handwriting KL 2, I

CHECKS, discipline, scolding KL 1, III

CHINKS, money R & J 1, V

CHOP-LOGIC, arguer R & J 3, V

CHOUGHS, jackdaws KL 4, VI

CIRCUMSTANCE, details R & J 2, V

CIRCUMSTANCE, noteworthiness O 3, III

CIRCUMSTANCED, put off O 3, IV

CLYSTER-PIPES, enema syringe O 2, I

COCK, cockboat, a ship's boat or dinghy KL 4, VI

COGGING, deceiving O 4, II

COIL, fuss R & J 2, V

COLLIED, darkened O 2, III

COLOQUINTIDA, a purgative O 1, III

COMMAND, find supporters O 1, I

COMPACT, make more convincing KL 1, IV

COMPLIMENTS, etiquette R & J 2, IV

COMPOSITION, agreement O 1, III

COMPT, account, i.e. Judgement O 5, II

CONCEIT, idea, conception R & J 4, III; O 3, III

CONJUNCT, joining the king KL 2, II

CONTINENT FORBEARANCE, self-control KL 1, II

CONTINUATE, uninterrupted O 3, IV

COP'ST WITH, encounters R & J 4, I

CORDIAL, reviving drug R & J 5, I

CORSE, corpse R & J 3, II

COSTARD, head KL 4, VI

COTQUEAN, man who meddles in women's work R & J 4, IV
COUNTER-CASTER, calculator or arithmetician O 1, I
COUNTRY FORMS, appearance of her countrymen O 3, III
COUNTY STAYS, County Paris awaits you R & J 1, III
COURT-CUPBOARD, sideboard R & J 1, V
COVER, limit, i.e. a wife R & J 1, III
COVERT, hiding place R & J 1, I
CRAB, crab apple KL 1, V
CRAFTILY QUALIFIED, carefully mixed O 2, III
CROSS, perverse R & J 4, III
CROSSES, troubles KL 5, III
CROW, crowbar R & J 5, III
CULLIONLY, base KL 2, II
CUPID: a typical personage to introduce maskers. See APOLOGY.
  R & J 1, IV
CYNTHIA, the moon R & J 3, V

DAFFEST, put aside O 4, II
DARKER, secret KL 1, I
DAWS, jackdaws, i.e. fools O 1, I
DEBOSHED, debauched KL 1, IV
DEFEAT THY FAVOR, disguise your face O 1, III
DESARTS IDLE, worthless deserts O 1, III
DESMESNES, domains R & J 2, I
DESPISED TIME, rest of a miserable life O 1, I
DEVESTING, undressing O 2, III
DIABLO, the Devil O 2, III
DIAN, Diana, goddess of chastity O 3, III
DIFFUSE, disguise KL 1, IV
DILATE, relate in full O 1, III
DISPUTED ON, argued in court O 1, II
DO NOT USE, am not accustomed R & J 3, V
DRAWER, waiter R & J 3, I
DRIFT, purpose R & J 4, I
DRY-BEAT, bruise R & J 3, I
DUMP, doleful tune R & J 4, V
DWELL IN FORM, behave conventionally R & J 2, II

EAR-KISSING, whispered KL 2, I
EAT NO FISH, i.e. not a Catholic KL 1, IV

ELF-LOCKS, snarls in horses' manes and human hair, attributed
to fairies R & J 1, IV
EPITHETS OF WAR, military terms O 1, I
ESPERANCE, hope KL 4, I
EXHIBITION, allowance O 1, III
EXTEND MY MANNERS, salute your wife O 2, I
EXTERN, external O 1, I

FALCHION, curved sword KL 5, III
FASTEN'D, confirmed KL 2, I
FAY, faith R & J 1, V
FESTINATE, hasty KL 3, VII
FETTLE, make ready R & J 3, V
FILM, spider's thread R & J 1, IV
FINELESS, limitless O 3, III
FITCHEW, polecat O 4, I
FLEER, sneer R & J 1, V; O 4, I
FLESH YOU, give you your first fight KL 2, II
FLESHMENT, excitement KL 2, II
FLIRT-GILLS, light women R & J 2, IV
FOINS, thrusts KL 4, VI
FOND, foolish O 1, III
FORBID, destroyed KL 5, III
FOREFENDED, forbidden KL 5, I
FORKED PLAGUE, i.e. being made a cuckold O 3, III
FRAUGHT, freight O 3, III
FRONTLET, frown KL 1, IV
FULL HARD FORBEAR, have difficulty allowing O 1, II
FULL-FLOWING STOMACH, full wrath KL 5, III
FULSOME, disgusting O 4, I
FUSTIAN, nonsense O 2, III

GAD, prick of a goad, i.e. spur of the moment KL 1, II
GALLOW, terrify KL 3, II
GASTED, terrified KL 2, I
GASTNESS, ghastly look O 5, I
GENNETS, Moorish ponies O 1, I
GERMANS, kinsmen O 1, I
GERMENS, seeds of life KL 3, II
GIVE YOU THE MINSTREL, i.e. beat you R & J 4, V

GLEEK, mock R & J 4, V
GO BY WATER, be said with tears O 4, II
GOSSAMER, spider's web R & J 2, VI
GOSSIP, friend R & J 2, I
GOUJERES, good years, but implying evil KL 5, III
GRANGE, lonely farm O 1, I
GRAVE BESEEMING ORNAMENTS, the ornaments of peace,
    suitable to sober citizens R & J 1, I
GRIPE, grip O 3, III
GRIZE, degree O 1, III
GROSS IN SENSE, obvious O 1, II
GUTTER'D, channeled O 2, I
GYVES, shackles R & J 2, II; O 2, I

Hag, nightmare R & J 1, IV
HAGGARD, a wild hawk O 3, III
HALCYON, kingfisher KL 2, II
HALES, hauls O 4, I
HALIDOM, holy relic, on which an oath was sworn R & J 1, III
HARLOTRY, hussy R & J 4, II
HAY, home thrust R & J 2, IV
HEAD-LUGG'D BEAR, a bear with its head torn by dogs KL 4, II
HEALTHS, toasts R & J 1, IV
HEARTED, heartfelt O 1, III
HECATE, goddess of witchcraft KL 1, I
HILDING, good-for-nothing R & J 3, V
HIS HOUSE, its sheath R & J 5, III
HIS PARTICULAR, himself personally KL 2, IV
HOLD THE MORTISE, stay fast joined O 2, I
HUMOR, moisture R & J 4, I

ICE BROOK'S TEMPER, tempered in ice water O 5, II
ILL AFFECTED, i.e. had traitorous thoughts KL 2, I
INCONTINENT, immediately O 4, III
INCORPORATE, bodily O 2, I
INCREASE, childbearing KL 1, IV
INDIGN, unworthy O 1, III
INDISTINCT REGARD, incapable of being distinguished O 2, I
INDUES, endows O 3, IV
INGENER, inventor O 2, I

INHIBITED AND OUT OF WARRANT, forbidden and illegal
O 1, II
INJOINTED, joined O 1, III
INTERESS'D, share KL 1, I
INVENTION, literary effort O 2, I
IRON CROW, crowbar R & J 5, II

JANUS, two-faced god of the Romans O 1, II
JAUNCE, jaunt R & J 2, V
JESSES, straps attached to a hawk's legs O 3, III
JOINT RING, two-piece ring, a lover's gift O 4, III
JOINT-STOOLS, stools made by a joiner R & J 1, V
JOINTURE, dowry R & J 5, III

KEEP UP, sheathe O 1, II
KIBES, chilblains KL 1, V
KING COPHETUA, hero of a popular ballad who married a beggar R & J 2, I
KITE, bird of prey that eats offal KL 1, IV

LADY-BIRD, literally lady bug; a pretty little thing. Also has a bad meaning; tart. R & J 1, III
LAMMAS-TIDE, August 1 R & J 1, III
LANTHORN, lantern, i.e. a dome set in a roof to give more light R & J 5, III
LAW DAYS, days when courts sit O 3, III
LAY, bet O 2, III
LEET, court held by the lord of the manor O 3, III
LETTER AND AFFECTION, private recommendation and favoritism O 1, I
LIBERAL, gross O 2, I
LIP, kiss O 4, I
LIST, desire O 2, I
LOOPED AND WINDOW'D, full of holes and gaps KL 3, IV
LOWN, lout O 2, III

MAGNIFICO, title of chief men of Venice O 1, II
MAMMERING, hesitating O 3, III
MAMMET, puppet R & J 3, V
MAN OF WAX, a model in wax, i.e. perfect R & J 1, III

MARCHPANE, marzipan R & J 1, V

MARGENT, margin R & J 1, III

MARRY, Mary, by the Virgin Mary R & J 1, I

MASKS, Elizabethan ladies wore masks to protect their faces from the sun R & J 1, I

MASS, by the Mass R & J 4, IV

MAUGRE, in spite of KL 5, III

MAZZARD, slang for "head" O 2, III

MEASURES OF LAWN, "sheer nylon" is an equivalent expression O 4, III

MEAT, serving of supper O 4, II

MEINY, followers KL 2, IV

MERE PERDITION, absolute destruction O 2, II

MESSES, small pieces O 4, I

MEWED UP TO, enclosed with R & J 3, IV

MICKLE, mighty R & J 2, III

MINIKIN, dainty KL 3, VI

MINIM, short R & J 2, IV

MINION, darling O 5, I

MISTRESS MINION, saucy miss R & J 3, V

MODERN, ordinary R & J 3, II

MOE, more O 4, III

MOIETY, share KL 1, I

MONSTERS, make it a monster KL 1, I

MORTAL ENGINES, cannon O 3, III

MOTION, sense O 1, II

MOUSE-HUNT, a woman chaser, in today's terms a wolf R & J 4, IV

MUMMY, mixture made from Egyptian mummies O 3, IV

NICE, trivial, trifling R & J 3, 1

NONSUITS, rejects the request of O 1, I

NUMBERS, verses R & J 2, IV

ODD-EVEN, about midnight O 1, I

ŒILLIADES, loving looks KL 4, V

OFF-CAPP'D, stood cap in hand O 1, I

OLD GRADATION, seniority O 1, I

ORBS, stars KL 1, I

ORISONS, prayers R & J 4, III

OSIER CAGE, wicker basket R & J 2, III
OTTOMITES, Turks O 1, III
OUTSPORT DISCRETION, carry the fun too far O 2, III
OWE, own O 1, I
OU'DST, owned O 3, III

PALMER, pilgrim carrying a palm leaf R & J 1, V
PARLOUS, perilous R & J 1, III
PARTIALLY AFFIN'D, influenced by partiality O 2, III
PASSADO, forward thrust R & J 2, IV
PASTRY, bakehouse R & J 4, IV
PAY THAT DOCTRINE, convince you that you are wrong R & J 1, I
PELTING, paltry KL 2, III
PERDU, sentry KL 4, VII
PHÆTHON, sun god's sun R & J 3, II
PHOEBUS, the sun, drawn across the sky in his chariot R & J 3, II; KL 2, II
PIGHT, determined KL 2, I
PIN, cataract KL 3, IV
PINFOLD, a small enclosure KL 2, II
PLAIN, complain KL 3, I
PLIANT, suitable O 1, III
PLUME UP, glorify O 1, III
POOR JOHN, dried salt hake, a cheap food R & J 1, I
PORTANCE, bearing O 1, III
POTTLE-DEEP, "bottoms up" O 2, III
PRATTLE OUT OF FASHION, talk idly O 2, I
PRICK-SONG, music, carefully noted down R & J 2, IV
PRINCOX, conceited boy R & J 1, V
PROBAL, probable O 2, III
PROBATION, proof O 3, III
PROPINQUITY, relationship KL, 1, I
PROROGUED, postponed R & J 2, II
PROVERB'D WITH A GRANDSIRE PHRASE, provided with an old proverb R & J 1, IV

QUALITIES, different kinds O 3, III
QUALITY, profession O 1, III
QUAT, pimple O 5, I

QUEEN MAB, the fairy queen R & J 1, IV
QUESTRISTS, seekers KL 3, VII
QUICKEN, stir in mother's womb O 3, III
QUILLETS, wisecracks O 3, I
QUOTE, note R & J 1, IV

RANK GARB, gross manner O 2, I
RAZ'D, changed KL 1, IV
REBECK, three-stringed fiddle R & J 4, V
RECREANT, traitor KL 1, I
RELUME, relight O 5, II
REMOTION, removal KL 2, IV
RETORTS IT, turns it back R & J 3, I
RIVE, split open KL 3, II
ROPERY, roguery R & J 2, IV
ROUSE, deep drink O 2, III
RUBBED, turned aside KL 2, II
RUNAGATE, runaway R & J 3, V

SAINTS, images of saints R & J 1, V
SALLETS, salads KL 3, IV
SALT, lecherous O 2, I
SAMPHIRE, a plant that grows on the cliffs KL 4, VI
SAPIENT, wise KL 3, VI
SAVE THEE, God save thee KL 2, I
SECTARY ASTRONOMICAL, one of the sect of astronomers KL
     1, II
SECURE ME, feel secure O 1, III
SEEL, blind O 3, III
SELF-BOUNTY, natural goodness O 3, III
SELF-COVERED, hiding her true self KL 4, II
SENNET, trumpet call KL 1, I
SE'NNIGHT, week O 2, I
SENSE, raw O 5, I
SENTENCE, proverbial saying O 1, III
SEQUESTER, separation O 3, IV
SET, gamble KL 1, IV
SET COCK-A-HOOP, make trouble R & J 1, V
SET DOWN THE PEGS, make you sing in a different key O 2, I
SHAMBLES, slaughterhouse O 4, II

SHEALED PEASCOD, shelled peapod KL 1, IV
SHIELD, forbid R & J 4, I
SHORE, cut O 5, II
SHRIFT, confession, absolution, or place of confession R & J 1, I; O 3, III
SILLY-DUCKING, always bowing KL 2, II
SIMPLES, herbs R & J 5, I
SIMULAR, pretender KL 3, II
SIZES, allowances KL 2, IV
SLIPPER, slippery O 2, I
SLUBBER, tarnish O 1, III
SMATTER, chatter R & J 3, V
SNUFFS AND PACKINGS, resentment and plotting KL 3, I
SOME OF YOUR FUNCTION, get to your business O 4, II
SPECULATIVE AND OFFIC'D INSTRUMENTS, powers of sight and action O 1, III
SPED, done for R & J 3, I
SPINNERS, spiders R & J 1, IV
SPITE, outrage R & J 2, I
STAND IN ACT, are about to begin O 1, I
STANDS IN HOLD CURE, has every hope of cure O 2, I
STAR-BLASTING, evil caused by planets KL 3, IV
STAR-CROSS'D, thwarted by fate R & J 1, Prologue
STEADS, benefits R & J 2, III
STEEP-DOWN GULFS, whirlpools O 5, II
STINTED, stopped R & J 1, III
STONES, lightning bolts O 5, II
SUBSCRIPTION, submission KL 3, II
SUFFERANCE, damage O 2, I
SUIT, meaning both fine clothes and a petition for favor R & J 1, IV
SWASHING, smashing R & J 1, I

TACKLED STAIR, rope ladder R & J 2, IV
TAKE THE WALL, go on inside of sidewalk where there was less mud, i.e. be superior R & J 1, I
TAKING, bad influence of fairies KL 3, IV
TASSEL-GENTLE, male peregime falcon R & J 2, II
TEEN, sorrow R & J 1, III
TELL, count KL 2, IV
TETCHY, peevish R & J 1, III

THE EVENT, we'll see what happens KL 1, IV
THIS HOLY SHRINE, Juliet's hand R & J 1, V
THRICE-DRIVEN, refined three times O 1, III
THROWEST, can afford to lose KL 1, IV
THWART DISNATURED, perverse and unnatural KL 1, IV
TITAN, sun god R & J 2, III
TITHE-PIG, a pig used in paying a parson R & J 1, IV
TITHING, district KL 3, IV
TOGED, wearing togas O 1, I
TOM O' BEDLAM, a lunatic discharged from Bethlehem Hospital
   for lunatics (Bedlam) KL 1, II
TRAVERSE, quickstep O 1, III
TWIGGERS, wicker-covered O 2, III

UNCONSTANT TOY, fickle fancy R & J 4, I
UNFURNISHED, unready R & J 4, II
UNHANDSOME, clumsy O 3, IV
UNHOUSED, unmarried O 1, II
UNSTATE MYSELF, lose my earldom KL 1, II
UNTENTED WOUNDINGS, raw wounds KL 1, IV
UTTERS, sells R & J 5, I

VANITY, emptiness R & J 2, VI
VANTAGE, extra measure O 4, III
VAUNT-COURIERS, forerunners KL 3, II
VIRTUE, power O 1, III
VISOR, a mask and an ugly face R & J 1, IV
VOUCH, good report O 2, I

WAGE, risk O 1, III
WARRANT OF MY NOTE, my observation of you KL 3, I
WEB, eye diseases KL 3, IV
WHIPSTER, whippersnapper O 5, II
WILLOW, emblem of the rejected lover O 4, III
WIND, worm KL 1, II
WITHOUT HIS ROE, half there R & J 2, IV
WORK TA'EN OUT, pattern copied O 3, III

YERK'D, jabbed O 1, II

GREAT ILLUSTRATED CLASSICS

Adam Bede—*Eliot*
The Arabian Nights
Around the World in 80 Days—*Verne*
Autobiography of Benjamin Franklin
Ben-Hur—*Wallace*
The Black Arrow—*Stevenson*
Black Beauty—*Sewell*
The Call of the Wild—*London*
Captains Courageous—*Kipling*
Christmas Tales—*Dickens*
The Cloister and the Hearth—*Reade*
A Connecticut Yankee in King Arthur's Court—*Clemens*
The Cruise of the Cachalot—*Bullen*
David Copperfield—*Dickens*
The Deerslayer—*Cooper*
Dr. Jekyll and Mr. Hyde—*Stevenson*
Emma—*Austen*
Famous Tales of Sherlock Holmes—*Doyle*
From the Earth to the Moon—*Verne*
Great Expectations—*Dickens*
Green Mansions—*Hudson*
Gulliver's Travels—*Swift*
Hawthorne's Short Stories—*Hawthorne*
Henry Esmond—*Thackeray*
The House of the 7 Gables—*Hawthorne*
Huckleberry Finn—*Clemens*
The Hunchback of Notre-Dame—*Hugo*
Ivanhoe—*Scott*
Jane Eyre—*Brontë*
A Journey to the Centre of the Earth—*Verne*
Kenilworth—*Scott*
Kidnapped—*Stevenson*
Kim—*Kipling*
King Arthur—*Malory*
Last Days of Pompeii—*Bulwer-Lytton*
The Last of the Mohicans—*Cooper*
Lord Jim—*Conrad*
Lorna Doone—*Blackmore*
The Luck of Roaring Camp—*Harte*
The Man in the Iron Mask—*Dumas*
The Mill on the Floss—*Eliot*
The Moonstone—*Collins*
The Mysterious Island—*Verne*
The Odyssey—*Homer*
The Old Curiosity Shop—*Dickens*

Oliver Twist—*Dickens*
The Oregon Trail—*Parkman*
The Pathfinder—*Cooper*
Père Goriot—*Balzac*
Pickwick Papers—*Dickens*
The Pilot—*Cooper*
The Pioneers—*Cooper*
The Prairie—*Cooper*
Pride and Prejudice—*Austen*
The Prince and the Pauper—*Clemens*
Quentin Durward—*Scott*
Quo Vadis—*Sienkiewicz*
The Red Badge of Courage—*Crane*
The Return of the Native—*Hardy*
The Rise of Silas Lapham—*Howells*
Robinson Crusoe—*Defoe*
The Scarlet Letter—*Hawthorne*
The Scarlet Pimpernel—*Orczy*
Sense and Sensibility—*Austen*
Silas Marner—*Eliot*
The Sketch Book—*Irving*
The Spy—*Cooper*
A Tale of Two Cities—*Dickens*
Tales—*Poe*
The Talisman—*Scott*
Tess of the D'Urbervilles—*Hardy*
The Three Musketeers—*Dumas*
Three Comedies: A Midsummer Night's Dream, The Merchant of Venice, As You Like It—*Shakespeare*
Three Histories: Henry IV, Part I; Henry IV, Part II; Henry V—*Shakespeare*
Three Tragedies: Julius Caesar, Hamlet, Macbeth—*Shakespeare*
Tom Sawyer—*Clemens*
Treasure Island—*Stevenson*
20,000 Leagues Under the Sea—*Verne*
Two Years Before the Mast—*Dana*
Typhoon—*Conrad*
Uncle Tom's Cabin—*Stowe*
Up From Slavery—*Washington*
Vanity Fair—*Thackeray*
Walden—*Thoreau*
The Way of All Flesh—*Butler*
The White Company—*Doyle*
White Fang and Other Stories—*London*
The Wreck of the Grosvenor—*Russell*
Wuthering Heights—*Brontë*

GREAT ILLUSTRATED CLASSICS—TITANS

Afloat and Ashore—*Cooper*
Anna Karenina—*Tolstoy*
Autobiography of Benvenuto Cellini
Barnaby Rudge—*Dickens*
Bleak House—*Dickens*
Crime and Punishment—*Dostoevsky*
Dombey & Son—*Dickens*
Don Quixote—*Cervantes*

Everybody's Plutarch
Little Dorrit—*Dickens*
Martin Chuzzlewit—*Dickens*
Nicholas Nickleby—*Dickens*
Our Mutual Friend—*Dickens*
Short Novels of Henry James—*James*
Twenty Years After—*Dumas*
Westward Ho!—*Kingsley*